Deep Management

Deep Management

Game and Software Development

John Bible

Cover image: Rubin's Vase by Martin Janecek

Copyright © 2019 John Bible
All Rights Reserved.
ISBN-13: 9781096320715

Table of Contents

Table of Contents	v
Dedication	vii
Introduction	1
PART ONE	7
1 Identity and Meaning	9
2 Principles	21
3 Seeking Customer Value	41
4 Seeking Alignment	57
5 The Decision Making Loop	69
PART TWO	75
6 Game and Decision Theory	77
7 Consider the Hideout	109
8 Twisted Reflections	127
9 The Specific Dangers of KPIs	139

10 The Hero Complex	147
11 Creativity	153
PART THREE	167
12 Why Some Engineers Are Amazing	169
13 Never Tolerate Waste	179
14 Historical Foundations	197
15 Common Tools for Modern Software	233
PART FOUR	241
16 Dealing with People	243
17 Cutting Our Projects	255
18 Conway's Law	263
19 Review of the Process	269
Closing Remarks	305
About the Author	313
End Notes	315

Dedication

*For all my colleagues over the years,
through both literal and figurative fires and floods,
without whose passion this book would never have been possible.*

IF YOU CAN TRAVEL ON THE SWORD'S EDGE,
YOU WILL BE FREE IN ALL WAYS.

Yuanwu Keqin

Introduction

In game and software development, we possess a singular goal: deliver customer value. This is the only foundation for success that endures. Yet we humans were not born for such singular purposes. Neither evolution nor society have fine-tuned us for this. We are prone to self-delusion. Our nature has given us a multi-faceted understanding of value that at times breaks with rational expectations. Even without these complications, the world is uncertain. We possess partial knowledge, often only of the most straightforward aspects of reality. We possess even less knowledge about how our actions will change the state of the world. How we make decisions under these circumstances defines who we are.

As our organization scales, our challenges worsen. Not only can access to the signal of customer value diminish for our developers, but we build hierarchies of management that pursue alternative incentives. For our staff, their focus ceases to be customer value and becomes the pursuit of advancement. If the resolution of these personal goals in aggregate drives our projects forward, this is fine. Frequently, though, this generates waste. In the absence of a corporate immune system, game theory tells us that the equilibrium behaviors for agents wishing to advance in an organization are often at odds with its purpose.[1] As our organization grows, we can lose our focus as a customer-oriented business. Proxies to value begin to dominant actual signals. Image, narrative, and prestige eventually matter more than customer impact. The skills engaged in these false pursuits are not necessarily detrimental — wielded appropriately, they can be the tools that allow us to influence others and seek alignment. Left unchecked, however, these behaviors dull our edge. Politics internal to an organization is waste, even if it is not entirely avoidable.

The pace of innovation has made all this more imperative.

Companies that fail to address these challenges suffer afflictions. Developers become lost, pursuing mirages that don't pay off. Projects fail on launch or collapse into unending reboot cycles. Morale crashes.

In this book, we will critique many ingrained norms in game-industry culture. These taken-for-granted truths distract and undermine us. We've seen many companies receive the same post-mortem results year after year, and yet they fail to escape their condition. Organizational culture entraps us because we do not realize that we are in a game of our own making, and that the rules can be rewritten.

Some critics of our approach maintain that these problems cannot be avoided: miracles and magic epitomize development. The challenges are innate. The games industry is a harsh winner-take-all arena. We rip each victory bloody from fate's jaws – every shipped product is an absurdity. Those who believe this admonish their staff to have faith in the system. Even though our project is clearly diseased, we prefer to just endure – everything will come together in the end.

This is the argument of a team trapped within a toxic paradigm. As we discuss the status quo, we will encounter many variations of this. Here, the accepted culture of production tells us that game development must be chaos. Out paradigm filters our perceptions. To an external observer, the problems are obvious and resolvable, albeit perhaps with great effort. For those trapped within, however, the issues are in their blind spot. They are axiomatic to reality.

When we cannot perceive the problem, we cannot define it. Thus, we cannot solve it. Last-minute magic and miracles are snake oils we imbibe rather than cope with tangled messes. They do not resolve our afflictions. We are left naked and exposed before our challenges; we suffer more than necessary to push past to possible success. We must face our problems, refuse to accept that they cannot be solved, and seek to their root causes. All too often, we instead substitute stubbornness — the negative face of grit.[2]

The battle against this is not easy to win, as many consider their fortitude a matter of pride. This is a twisted vision of success. From this view, regardless of the project's outcome, we cannot be blamed, as we bled all that anyone could. Suffering validates us. Even if it was unnecessary.

Innovation is hard; it causes us anxiety. Are we worthy? Are we capable? We substitute sacrifice for problem solving because it is straightforward to do. We always know how to work longer hours. And once we have paid the price, we refuse to admit our mistake.

This is a mental illness.

We can cure ourselves by focusing on root causes. We struggle because we cannot see. Our customers have a problem and a set of associated external conditions. To seek out solutions, we must understand our customers' experience. If we fixate on our purpose of solving customer problems, we can isolate why we struggle. Why do we not see? Why do we go astray? If we refuse to believe that success is magic, then no problem is immune to solution.

Uncertainty is frightening. Our ego cannot bear to be wrong. When we create, we must learn to live with that.

It can be less painful. If we recognize the foundations of sound decision-making, we can form principles that encode this understanding. These principles can be the core of a system that bears the burden of our anxiety for us. This becomes our culture. The refinement of our principles and system must never end. We must perpetually test our system's effectiveness and ensure its consistent expression across our organization. Once we have inoculated ourselves with this process, our culture propagates the reward signal provided by our customers throughout our communication networks; preferably, it links developers to consumers. When our developers directly communicate with customers and solve their needs, our developers can become goal-solving owners rather than consumers of task queues. This frees them to offer their full skillfulness towards solving our customers' problems.

Innovation is hard; we do not deny this. This book will not provide an easy solution, although it is a better path. We need to transform ourselves. Our way will be challenging — many will find that their place in the company changes. Once dominant figures must now serve. If we can engage our humility, however, we can stop patching teetering towers of problems and produce superior solutions. We can resolve root issues. Those who once stood on the pinnacle will now become the foundation, helping to lift everyone up.

We should not expect, however, to discover the golden path. Even if we were perfectly rational agents engaging in optimal processes, in a world with uncertainty we cannot know this path in advance. We can, however, cleave faster to the best path. Of course, we must accept that we are not fully rational either. By understanding how our reasoning tends to fail,[3] we can shield ourselves against our worst errors. In this way, we can seek value as optimally as we can in an unknown world as imperfect agents.

In this book, we will discuss the philosophy and practice of decision-making processes that drive us towards more lean solutions (we mean this both in terms of the general definition of lean and the specific meaning of Lean that we will discuss later in Part III). This is an empirical approach embracing the scientific method. We acknowledge that we do not possess certainty in knowledge. This implies that we embrace data, experimentation, transparency, agility, immediate access to our customers, and analytic skills. We will also need to address the epistemological challenge of unknown unknowns — that we are making decisions about topics where we might not even know what we don't know.

We will cover some modern solutions to these problems: Lean (and the Toyota Way), Theory of Constraints, Agile and its derivatives, and other flavors such as SRE (Site Reliability Engineering) and DevOps. We will discuss normative and descriptive decision-making — for instance, cumulative prospect theory, which empirically establishes ways humans are consistently irrational about choice. Various cognitive fallacies will be addressed. All of this will establish how we ought to operate, and how we can get from our deluded state to one of greater clarity.

We use the AAA games industry for most of our examples, as this is where we've spent most of our careers.[4] Some parts of this book specifically slant to problems unique to AAA game development, but the discussion has relevance for all software developers. Most of our approaches generalize to any innovative industry. Our examples are there primarily to lend concreteness. For companies which are subject to heavyweight regulation, such as those in the nuclear industry or in aircraft embedded-software development, adjustments to our principles might be necessary to make sense for their requirements.[5]

Overview:

This book has been structured into four parts, meant to build upon each other.

In Part I, we consider the root of our philosophy, which is our focus on customer value. Here we consider the foundations of decision-making and the principles that guide our system. This generates our culture.

Part II focuses on the afflictions that divert us from the best path. We begin with a discussion of game and decision theory, covering both rational and realistic agents. We then examine a case of customer value for a game. Next, we define and examine twisted reflections, which produce our greatest challenges.

In Part III, we focus on waste, which prevents us from reaching optimal customer value. This is also where we cover the historical philosophies and methodologies that underpin this book.

In Part IV, we bring everything together, consider some final topics, and then run over a standard AAA gate process, viewed considering our system.

The truth is a difficult thing to touch, hence why we so often prefer not to delve beneath the surface. It is simpler to assume our challenges are endemic to our space and thus unresolvable, rather than arising from our own systemic processes, and thus our own fault. The phantasms of our minds obscure everything we perceive. If we have the courage to be humble, we can see software development not as we have been led to believe it must be, but instead as it could be.

Our goal is not to produce perfect success rates, but to do better than our competitors, who often rely on luck.[6] Innovation is not a matter of miracles or magic; it is managing probabilistic outcomes in a way that gets us faster to better solutions for our customers. We will still fail; we will just fail less often. Over time, even small differentials add up.

PART ONE

Choice and Customer Value

1

Identity and Meaning

Who are we?

Some of our self-definition comes from heritage and environment. Many characterize themselves by nation, family, or ethnicity. Others seek meaning through job, religion, or political stance. Not all these traits are within our control. We distinguish between those aspects that were chosen for us versus the choices we made for ourselves.

Agency defines us. Where we are free to choose, our choices frame our identity.

Regardless of our decisions, however, we do not control their outcomes. The fruits of our actions are akin to our initial conditions in many ways. We make choices, but the outcomes are doubly uncertain, due both to an uncertain world and the probabilistic results of any action.[7] The same choice can lead to fame and fortune or to ruin and ignominy. Perhaps superior choices more likely lead to excellent outcomes, but we all know tragic figures who made the right call, but in the wrong world. Our outcomes can describe who we are, but we prefer that it is the choice we made instead that defines us, not the roll of the dice.

Consider who has the greater grasp of our nature: the person who knows the facts of our history, or the person who understands how we see the world and make decisions?

This is true not only of ourselves as individuals, but of our organizations as well. A company expresses at all levels of scale its quality by its decisions. A company also reveals its dysfunctions when its decisions are inconsistent and inexplicable. The decisions we have made come to define our culture, where our history of choice provides a default channel for our future actions.[8]

Meanwhile, many companies are dysfunctional in ways that healthy individuals are not. Quite a few organizations are composed of members who make decisions idiosyncratically, and sometimes at odds with each other. These companies maintain what consistency they have only so long as the decision-makers remain the same. The successful organizations of this type have established a *de facto* equilibrium, but not a stable one. This is an organization with no identity, except at best a cult of personality. Such companies do not tend to endure long term.

Other organizations solidify their decision-making through the strength of their culture. The primary and best purpose of culture is consistent decision-making.[9] We select our choices based on who we are. Naturally, if our culture is one of chaos, we might not be a dependable organization; nevertheless, we would be consistently undependable. While we cannot control outcomes, we can control our decisions, the quality of which defines the likelihood of our success. Beyond this, our meta decision-making processes allow us to make decisions about how we make decisions, which allows us to grow.

Bear in mind, from where we are today, it is only through our choices that we can shape where we will be tomorrow.

Thus, decision-making must be the core of our personal and organizational culture. We must orchestrate everything around our decision-making system. It is meaningless to have cultural pillars unless those pillars exist to shape all decisions generated by this machine. At many companies, cultural pillars are given short shrift. Leadership and special committees form safe feel-good planks that offend no one and mean nothing. This signals weak organizational decision-making. Our culture is defined by the rules we use to craft our choices. As such, our principles must be sharp. Far from offending no one, our pillars must be precise and strong enough to drive out unaligned staff.

Gut Instinct Versus Algorithms

Even as individuals, adhering to the rules of our decision-making processes generates better results. This is a battle between our gut instincts and an algorithm that forces a gut check.

One of the differences between neophytes and masters is the degree to which they have internalized expertise as instinct — what we might also call fast thinking.[10] From the 1940s, the Dutch psychologist Adrian de Groot pioneered work on expertise by studying the differences between how beginners, masters, and grandmasters played chess.[11] Beginners were found to explore all move options from a board state — an arduous process. They considered many branches and frequently backtracked to reconsider. Everyone regardless of skill does this to some degree. De Groot had believed before commencing his studies that grandmasters did more calculations, so they did the same thing but faster, but what he discovered was quite different. Grandmasters considered fewer options, and while they also backtracked, they did so far less — they culled decision sub-trees and evaluated board states automatically.

Gary Klein and his fellow researchers followed up with a similar idea, evaluating intuitive expertise most famously in the case of firefighters. In an early paper in 1986, they described this case:[12]

> A firefighter led his men into a burning house, found the apparent seat of the fire in the rear of the house, and directed a stream of water on it. The water did not have the effect expected, so he backed off, then hit it again. At the same time, he noticed that it was getting intensely hot and very quiet. He stated that he had no idea what was going on, but he suddenly ordered his crew to evacuate the house. Within a minute after they evacuated, the floor collapsed. It turned out that the real fire had been in the basement. He had never expected this. This was why his stream of water was ineffective, and it was why the house could become hot and quiet at the same time. He attributed his decision to a 'sixth sense.'

Klein and his co-authors disagreed with the firefighter's explanation of his own ESP. This was a case akin to De Groot's with chess. Years of training and experience internalized pattern-recognition skills into the subject's fast-thinking mental processes. Even without being able to articulate why there was a threat, he was able to recognize the pattern and react.

Thus, given these cases, it might seem reasonable to trust the gut instincts of experts, at least within their field. Without question, these skills allow experts to outperform others, and to do so at great speed. Humans, however, are imperfect. We can do better.

Consider this different case, not between an expert and an amateur, but instead between an expert and an algorithmic model built using the expert's knowledge. In 1960, the researcher Paul Hoffman conducted an experiment to determine how experts made decisions. He chose to start with radiologists evaluating stomach cancer by examining imaging of ulcers.[13] As part of the experiment, Hoffman had the radiologists enumerate the rules they used for judgments, which consisted of seven basic indicators. This was made into a model using a linear combination to create a base comparison. The radiologists were then given many images to evaluate, where there were duplicates of cases spaced out in each set. The model then was run over the same set of images given to the radiologists. While it wasn't the original intention of his research, Hoffman was astonished to find that experts often gave opposite diagnoses to ulcers as benign or malignant from each other; moreover, even the same radiologist could make different diagnoses on the same image at different times. Even more critically, the simple model they'd whipped up on the advice of experts outperformed the experts themselves.[14]

The faults of the radiologists were multi-fold. Sometimes, it was random human error — machines don't get tired and if their software is well-written, they produce identical diagnoses from identical inputs.[15] Other times, the errors arose from systemic biases. Paul Hoffman did not at that time supply more concrete explanations for the full phenomenon, but this and similar results inspired later researchers. Over the next decades, we came to understand that humans suffer from deep biases and heuristics that conflict with our previous beliefs about how human cognition works. Even when experts generated the rules used by the models, they and not the model were often blinded by these glitches!

Thus, even though a facet of expertise is fast processing that generates gut calls, reliance on this fast path also exposes us to the filtering errors of our minds.

Later in this book, we will discuss work by Daniel Kahneman and Amos Tversky in particular, which was inspired by early research such as this. This pair of researchers broke apart the assumptions of earlier dogma by enumerating our faults and providing a framework for evaluating them, rather than assuming that we humans average out to rational decision-makers. We focus more on this foundational work in the field of behavior psychology, rather than its latest developments, as this is a book about our decision-making system, not the frontier of research. There exists, however, a rich literature that considers how our perceptions and our internal modeling systemically deviates from reality. In many fields, protecting ourselves against our own faults has been a key advance.[16] As a more recent example, Daniel Kahneman collaborated with Gary Klein to study the boundary conditions that differentiate between intuitive skill and overconfident, biased judgments.[17]

In terms of decision-making, we must embrace these studies of our faults as a warning. Over-reliance on the gut instincts of decision-making experts is a good way not only to get inconsistent results unique to each individual, but also to expose our decisions to cognitive glitches. Moreover, the nastiest aspect of these errors is that we are blind to them.

Adhering to our decision-making system not only leads to more consistent results, but it also triggers metacognition. When appropriate, it forces a pause that slows us down and reminds us to check our gut call. Our expert judgments can be skillful, but we should reflect on their validity before committing.[18]

Consistency in Decisions and History

Before delving into complications, we must start with the basics. An immediate aspect to address is consistency. If we want our decisions to define our identity, then our decisions must be coherent.

Many companies do not record decisions unless the choice is particularly critical. In such organizations, we keep our history in our heads. The companies that do record medium- and small-scale decisions often do not leave a record of the reasoning and evidence that gave rise to their choices. This means two things: we lack insight into our behavior, and we lose the capability to establish why a decision succeeded or not. If the decision-maker moves on to another company, there might be no one left to supply context. Our ability to learn is lost. Subsequent projects succeed or fail erratically as there is no path to follow. This can lead to repeating bad decisions. New team members, after all, often believe they are superior — they were brought in to fix the project, were they not! Without context to determine whether a decision was sound when it was made, however, the same causes that led the previous team to a choice might bring their successors to that same choice as well. They then discover why that decision led to its original failed outcome. While our decisions define us, we have lost the knowledge of what we have done and why. In such a case, our decision history becomes a story we remember, rather than the actual events that occurred. As we'll discuss in later chapters, narrative is both seductive and delusional.

As a case we discuss further in later chapters, Diane Vaughan was only able to reconstruct a revisionist history of the events that led up to the Challenger disaster because NASA kept robust notes and records of decisions, which she then nuanced with personal interviews. This allowed a unique look into the phenomenon she would term "normalization of deviance," which she describes in her book *The Challenger Launch Decision*. We will discuss this later in more detail in our chapter *Never Tolerate Waste*. Without this record, the pre-existing narrative might have prevailed, and taught us nothing. While NASA is a particularly heavyweight case of a decision history, and one we might not wish to fully emulate, the value offered parallels the amount we choose to invest.

Recording our decisions and their context is part of the principles of measurement and transparency that we'll discuss next chapter. We need to record not only the metrics that result from our choices, but the motivations, judgments, and environment that framed the choice. The record should also indicate how the decision was generated by our principles, or if it was an exception. It's also wise to store our estimates of the probabilities of different outcomes[19] — not because we expect those estimates to be valid, but because they offer perspective on our understanding of the problem at the time.

Not all decisions are worth recording. We want to avoid noise, so we need to establish a baseline for when a decision merits tracking. It might be that any decision that impacts architecture needs recording, but not choices about algorithms behind module interfaces; or perhaps for our company, that does in fact require a history. We will have to find our level in terms of the cost of recording and the difficulty of retrieving a historical decision that we are later interested in. Sometimes this involves building tools to facilitate these processes.

When we record decision histories, we should strive to do so as if we were planning for a post-mortem after we ship. From the beginning, we should assume the possibility of failure; thus, we should provide context to enable our inheritors to unpack why we made these choices. We must remember that all post-mortems suffer from hindsight bias, so we should supply our native perspective for the state of the world as we saw it at the time.

Decisions then become a trace that we can evaluate to determine the quality of our decision-making system. We can consider problems and our resulting choices as experiments. Based on what we learn, we can then evaluate the quality of our principles. Remember, however, that these experiments are small sample-set tests. Inferring a strong belief given only a few cases is fallacious.

Another motivation for recording decisions is to inoculate ourselves against conscious and unconscious behaviors that arise in organizations with limited tracking. Humans are storytelling creatures. Given some evidence, it is in our nature to weave this into a narrative that then sticks in our mind and is difficult to root out, even though the evidence is usually far too sparse for sound inference. This happens to us for many reasons — specific details, for example, cause us to forget base probability rates for categories;[20] narratives are inherently compelling to our minds, and so becomes highly available to our memory's recall, which makes us rate them as more certain than they actually are;[21] the uncertainties of a past problem at the time of the decision get lost in the certainty of what actually happened, causing us to perceive specific patterns as significant when they're just noise;[22] and so on. We'll discuss such topics more in Chapter Six and throughout this book.

These problems happen even to our best and most upstanding employees — no malice is necessary for this to occur. Not all our employees are moral, however; eventually all organizations attract toxic staff. These individuals use their storytelling skills to exploit cognitive flaws and rewrite history to their own benefit — almost always at the cost of our organization and thus the customer. When our culture does not root out such behavior, management gradually becomes a gang of gaslighters.[23]

Our decision traces also help stabilize projects when we bring in new leaders to replace the old guard. For example, it is commonly the case that fresh managers flip decisions on arrival to frame themselves as "doers." This relates to the notion that decisiveness signals competency. Oftentimes, though, these snap decisions are flawed — especially those made before the new leader understands the project. This is not surprising when the manager has no access to history. On the other hand, when decisions and conditions are recorded, and it is required to consider them, the new leader will at least see why these choices were made. Then, as part of our culture, we can require that they provide a foundation for the direction change they advocate. While they still might wish to make a big splash at the start, they at least must do so in a considered fashion.

As such, decisions should be stored in a secure and immutable way in a data store or version-control system.[24] It should require extreme levels of access to destroy any decision record; typically, such a removal should only be done in the case where privileged information was accidentally inserted into the system (for example, something that might violate SEC restrictions for a publicly traded company in the United States). The histories should be exposed to everyone within the company.[25] Delving through these can be a powerful guide for future choices. Naturally, we should not let the past constrain the possible risks we are willing to undertake. Previous failures do not equate to failure in the future. We should, however, understand why that failure occurred and why we believe the outcome might be different this time. We should never allow ourselves to loop on decisions, where we duplicate mistakes without clear understandings of what change justifies the repetition.

For this to work, we must make sure that our organizational culture allows for error. If our culture punishes mistakes, then people will become afraid of making decisions, and we will create paralysis. Accept mistakes as opportunities to learn and understand that anyone who never makes mistakes isn't taking enough risks. This is not to say that failure is good, just that it is unavoidable in a sufficiently aggressive innovation culture.

If we are recording decisions and their conditions, then we should also have a system for making decisions that explains why the choice was taken. As we discuss next chapter in *Principles*, to make a sound, transparent, and consistent decision-making culture, we need to establish the set of rules that takes inputs and generate actions. This is the mechanical aspect of decision-making that can counter the biases and heuristics that undermine our expert gut calls. These principles are unique to our company and should generate our decisions, and thus who we are. It is critical that we minimize factors such as the mood of the day. It should not be the case that a passing thunderstorm results in a timid call on a new feature, or that a colleague being on vacation results in a radically different path taken (we're sure that we have all known the fear of going on vacation for exactly this reason). If we review a decision later, in the absence of further data, the same outcome should be expected.

This steadiness of decision-making is fundamental to team morale and consistent progress. As we'll discuss later, sometimes our principles will inspire us to take bold leaps because we wish to explore new spaces quickly. If we understand that our system gives rise to this, our teams will enter that work knowing the risk and the reason why we took that choice. For our staff, functioning decision systems give rise to faith and stability. From the perspective of the people funding our project, such systems give rise to trust in the team.

When there is consistency, such a system can work well even in the face of changes in direction! If the team understands why decisions were taken in the past, and that an unexpected event has changed the calculus of our choices, they will accept the change if the new motivations are clear.

We should note another form of dysfunction that benefits from our system. There are leaders who refuse to alter decisions because they do not wish to be wrong. To them, error signals weakness, which ironically they fear.[26] In our system, since the justification for their previous choices is recorded, if we can show that those reasons no longer apply, we can show that the decision is no longer valid. This can still raise hackles, but if the decision-making process was used for the original choice, it doesn't necessarily mean bad decision-making on their part, but bad inputs. It moves blame from the gut to the decision-making machine. This is far easier to take. Innovation is a space we enter knowing little, and then strive to learn swiftly. Necessarily, some decisions will be invalidated as time progresses; assumptions can later be shown to be incorrect or we can discover new factors. This is to be expected on a healthy project.

Who we are — at least at any point in time — is best demonstrated by the decisions we make. This provides the character that defines our culture. Teams with transparent, consistent decision-making are a joy to work with. Staff understands where the team is, and there is a general agreement on where the project is. If people disagree with an assessment, all decisions are transparent, so they can challenge on that basis. Through validation, our choices become sounder.

2

Principles

Sometimes, all parties view specific decisions as objectively superior. Most decisions, however, are at least partially subjective; they are given value by the framing of the decider. For example, consider one narrative about Dong Nguyen's motivations for shutting down his viral hit *Flappy Bird*: according to this version based on his public statements, he chose to take the game off the market because he was concerned that it was "too addictive." He did this at a time when it was making $50,000 USD a day.[27] For a different person, that decision would have been ridiculous — their choice might have been to see if they could extract more money. Dong Nguyen's principles, however — whether explicitly written down or not — led him to make the decision that it was better to shut down *Flappy Bird* and move on to create other games that were not prone to tweaking people's addictive tendencies.[28]

This means that first we must understand what success looks like. For Dong Nguyen, the value of his bank account was not the primary driver for his estimation of his own worth. If we are to have a healthy and coherent relationship with success, we must critically evaluate how we perceive it. Especially for aspects that are not fiscal incentives.

Decisions are only good or bad relative to a set of principles we accept as fundamental. If we have not enumerated our principles and considered what they entail, then different people in our organization will have different opinions about which decisions are correct. Naturally, once we adopt these codes, those who do not agree with them will reject our choices, but if we are clear about our guidelines and stick to them, these individuals will self-select out. Many companies are afraid of losing employees in this way, but in the long term, coherence strengthens us.

Principles form the foundation, but they do not supply the mechanism for decision making. We need to establish shared methods for selecting choices and leaving artifacts for our history. These mechanisms must make sense in terms of the culture we intend to build. There is no perfect solution. The rules we enact should be effective for our particular environment. A system that no one understands or uses is worthless.

As one example, we could use a variant of Bayesian analysis, which we ourselves prefer as it's familiar given our background. We could start by constructing a graph on paper. First, we evaluate the conditions of our environment as we understand them. Then we enumerate our choices. Some options we cull out because they violate our principles upfront. For others, we connect the nodes for environmental conditions to the outcomes of the choices they affect — note, choices can have multiple outcomes. The conditional probability of an outcome is affected by the environment and the choice made, which is why we connect the environment to the outcome, not the choice. We can do this approximately and ball park what impact our conditions will have on outcomes given choices.

We can then apply standard Bayesian analysis to produce estimates of probabilities for outcomes along with corresponding value or loss. We shouldn't take the results too seriously as forecasting is a notoriously problematic art. The key is to engage sufficiently so that our decisions are based on explicit criteria, rather than intuition. Explicit points can be subjected to constructive criticism, but hunches cannot be. As part of the record for the choice, our decision-makers should note what probabilities they assigned to conditions in the environment, and what conditional probabilities they assigned to outcomes given those conditions. We do this to avoid hindsight bias when later we review a choice.

As an artificial and simplified example, consider a product that offers a staycation experience after work for stressed adults. It could resemble Nintendo's Wii Sports Resort, except we make it more realistic and exploit the HDR capabilities of modern TVs, so that the game offers a window into a bright, awe-inspiring therapeutic experience. Perhaps we design it to run as background noise and lighting, rather than have the customer play it as if it were a standard game. As developers, we have limited resources, so we must prioritize the environments to assemble. One possibility is a tropical beach version meant to offset the grim winter weather of our customers. Another is a ski resort in the mountains, offering a break in the summer (we assume our core audience is in the northern hemisphere, which could become a third condition if we chose to open that as an option). We must choose which to build. We will consider two environmental conditioning factors: our estimate of our launch date, and our assumption that a tropical paradise in the winter is more desirable than a ski resort. Our launch date can be framed as a cumulative probability distribution by our staff. This is just a curve that estimates our probability that we ship by various dates, going from 0 to 1, perhaps with a long tail. For example, we might estimate 70% probability to ship by Oct 1. Our second hypothesis about the desirability of tropical beaches in the winter and ski resorts in the summer can be an estimate of how certain we are that this premise is true, given the player testing and research we have already done. If the second hypothesis has high certainty, then the customer will value a tropical paradise in the winter far more than a ski resort, and vice versa for a summer release. Thus, the critical factor for the choice becomes when we ship. If the second hypothesis has low certainty, then the choices cannot be distinguished. It could even be the case that customers prefer ski resorts in winter. This likely tells us that we require more customer interaction, which is another choice. If we can't afford to investigate further, then we're forced to flip a coin, which is hardly sound, but sometimes necessary.

This process uses simpler graphs than allowed in full Bayesian reasoning;[29] some people might desire to employ more complex networks. This would imply adding environmental states conditioned on other environmental states, where only some conditions are known. Or our choices might impact a direct outcome, but there are further outcomes conditioned on that result, over which we want to establish a spread of probabilities. That's fine but dangerous. It can useful for us as a tool of reasoning, but almost always our understanding of the world is uncertain, and we ourselves are subject to many cognitive fallacies. The outputs of this process can appear more valid than they are, thus deceiving us. If we maintain appropriate skepticism, however, this can be a valid approach.

The key is to make us stand outside our gut call, and then consider our choices.

The process should be adjusted by the user to their liking — they should feel free to substitute other methods they are more comfortable with. This is part of the meta-process to improve our decision-making. There might be other techniques the organization finds more effective. All approaches should be tested to see if they make the process more lightweight, consistent, and valuable.

Our set of principles and the process we use for their application forms a system for decision-making.

A key advantage to this system is that its application is independent of specific individuals. We want the algorithm to handle most of our decisions, while we act to tune it and handle the harder cases. It is inevitable that leaders come and go from companies. Many organizations have been associated with iconic figures: Facebook, Apple, Amazon, Microsoft, Oracle, etc. When these leaders have done their job well, the company's culture continues to operate independently after the leader moves on. If achieved, this is the highest level of quality a leader can have — that they institute a culture of greatness that can exist autonomously of them.[30] A great company is a system, not a human personality — a self-correcting system, yes, not one frozen and fragile in an unchangeable state, but one that exists in and of itself. Many companies have lost their leaders and then stumbled or collapsed. This is a sign of organizational weakness.

The principles of our company can then attract like-minded future employees. We as individuals are not all the same, so we should not expect that companies ought to be the same either. We will argue for the adoption of specific core principles, but there are many more that can exist. Those who disagree with our proposed guidelines can still succeed — it is our argument only that success then comes more erratically. Despite many principles being subjective, the framework of principles for a company is a critical factor in decision-making from small to large — governing how we treat overtime to how we make choices about which projects to pursue. Google and its parent company Alphabet are caught up at the time of this book's writing in an internal debate about numerous issues that Googlers feel violate the principles of the company: for example, the Dragonfly censored search-engine project for China, and Google's work on A.I. for the US Department of Defense. Facebook similarly is having internal arguments about the place of their platform in the world and how they handle user data (with impacts ranging from genocidal violence to the rigging of democratic elections, among other concerns[31]).

Our Core Principles

First and foremost, before any other principle in business, customer value reigns supreme. We will discuss value more next chapter, since it can be subtle, but at a basic level we ought to grasp its meaning. We must meet the users' needs as cleanly as we can.

Now, the skeptic will note that this applies fully only when the customer pays us directly for our services. Indirect compensation – advertising, for instance – subverts this contract. In that case, all or some of our funding comes from people who want access to our customers. There are two ways to handle this. One, we outright serve the advertisers and treat them as our customers. We don't recommend this as while this does allow us to serve the advertisers' needs directly, the populace becomes a commodity that will not appreciate their position once they understand it. It is they, not the advertisers, who determine the value of our company. If we lose them, the advertisers will move on. Or second, and our preferred choice, we protect our customers as much as we can, and curate the impact that advertisers have upon them. This is tricky, as we'll discuss in later chapters. Advertising often hampers our capability to meet our customers' needs and can even force us to harm them. This can be a tightrope we must walk for a while, but we should never normalize the fraught position it places us in.

We should note that there are those in business who argue against customer value as primary. Some top managers still view business as a game, where they compete with their colleagues and competitors as if life were a jungle fight for high scores. In large companies, CEOs are often subject more to the board than to the customer. It can be the case that for a greedy, rational agent acting as CEO, short-term revenues matter more than long-term corporate health, and that consolidating the support of specific individuals forming their political coalition overrides value delivered.[32] While we understand these actions given the context, organizations that prevent or penalize such behaviors will reduce waste and deliver stronger customer propositions.

Regardless, articles and books on management began to shift away from this view towards the end of the 1980s. In 1984, as an example of the old way, Goldratt published *The Goal*, which describes Theory of Constraints in a business-novel format.[33] His approach doesn't particularly focus on customer value, but instead frames our challenges as optimization problems against a numeric target of our choice, which is usually assumed to be profit. It's not that these older models disdained the customer, just that customers were secondary.

In the 1980s, however, Japan challenged this viewpoint. Especially after Toyota trounced their American competitors, managers in the United States changed their stance and began to consider the customer as the priority, and leadership as servant-based. In the late 1980s this began with a sense of bewilderment, as managers struggled to understand why they were failing, and then in the 1990s and 2000s came a generation of business philosophers who embraced these ideas whole-heartedly. It remains the case that many management teams' behavior aligns more with older points of view. There is a natural appeal to the older style for competitive individuals. It is just that the philosophy of management for the most resilient companies has moved on.

We aren't saying that customer focus was unheard of before — the phrase "the customer is always right," is an ancient one — although we should be careful to note that seeking customer value is not the same as assuming that the customer is always right. Customers sometimes say one thing and want another. Regardless, customer value is often subordinated to the goal of immediate profits first (or at least the appearance of them). This, ironically, causes companies to fail in the long term.

Jeff Bezos made a remark on this topic concerning Amazon after he was asked about the Sears bankruptcy filing: "Amazon is not too big to fail [...] In fact, I predict one day Amazon will fail. Amazon will go bankrupt. If you look at large companies, their lifespans tend to be thirty-plus years, not a hundred-plus years." His answer to forestall this as long as possible was "[not to] focus on ourselves, and instead focus on our customers.[34]" We exist to provide products and services that our customers prefer over alternative demands on their time and resources. If we forget that, our customers will move on, and we will cease to exist.

Another dangerous path related to excessive focus on profits can be the prioritization of marketing over customer value. Here, companies fall into the trap of moving away from innovation because it is hard, and instead focus on image and framing because they provide easier means to move the needle on our profit meter. This happens when companies have either reached monopolistic positions or are fighting over the scraps left from an established fad. Again, this is a trap. We open ourselves up to attack — or worse disruption — and we lose our edge at delivering value. Many companies never recover from it.

Beyond value, there are several core principles that we assert are also necessary for efficiently addressing the problems of customers. We put forward six additional precepts that are excellent foundations for a modern, innovative company. The first three are foundational moral principles. We considered not listing them as they are implicit in the later cases; however, we decided that they are too significant not to explicitly state. It is important that our team members exhibit these traits, and the more senior the team member, the more critical it is that they are exemplars. If managers fail to demonstrate these characteristics, but we still promote them to top positions, that will signal to the floor that our emphasis on these principles is in name only. This will undermine our culture, perhaps fatally. The final three principles uphold our decision-making system but remain valuable for any innovative culture. The first principle, of course, we have already discussed.

Core Principles:

1) Customer Value
2) Humility
3) Trust
4) Boldness
5) Measurement
6) Transparency
7) Root Cause Analysis

Humility:

To operate in an innovative environment, we must embrace that we never know the exact path forward. Our first step in any project is not mapping out the production schedule or even answering questions but figuring out what the questions even are. To do this effectively, we must allow that we can be wrong, and that the solutions probably do not come from us. If we strive to only hire the best, we should be quite surprised if this were otherwise!

We must recognize that doubt is fertilizer for progress. When we are certain of our actions and our path, we become stuck on a road that might not be headed where we wish to go. While we should not project uncertainty to our teams, it is necessary to acknowledge that the best choices and the exact state of the world are unknowable. We can always improve our position.

Thus, we must place humility as one of our primary principles. Humility allows us to cast off the beliefs that are trapping us, and to embrace the solutions that come from others.

Trust:

We find that for our principles to work, trust must also be a pillar. If we lack trust, we must allocate effort to counter our fellow employees. With trust, we can relax.

If we exist in a culture where everyone struggles against each other, the humble can see their voices drowned out. Without trust, we can lose faith in metrics. The dark side of data can be alleviated when we trust our employees to not exploit the system for their advantage. If we lack trust in transparent cultures, many will censor themselves lest an imperfectly considered remark result in an attack. Moreover, without trust, many will find life in a transparent culture intolerable. Even when we seek root causes of problems, we require trust — after all, what happens if we find out that we ourselves are the root cause of dysfunction! Without trust, we will be afraid to dig deeper. If, however, we believe that we as an organization are working together for a greater end, and that we all look out for each other rather than for ourselves, we will then be able to investigate dark corners and expose what we find. We will become a more resilient culture.

Boldness:

Boldness is also requisite. Like trust, this is a pillar we could view as implicit, but it requires calling out. For root-cause analysis to work, we must be willing to face *any* root-cause problem, even if what we find might be terrifying. It can happen that we have neglected a serious problem that will cost us dearly. Ignoring problems, however, does not make them go away. We must face them.

We might discover that we have constrained our project because of a supposed technical limitation, which has caused us to repeatedly fail when we don't reach customer value. If we are timid, we will keep making small steps and never get out of our local trap. We could spend years in this state. Or we can recognize that we need to make a big move. In the long term, boldness can be less costly than timidity.[35]

Measurement:

Before we can proceed on solving problems, we must have some understanding of the actual world. There is always a model of our environment in our head, but this model doesn't necessarily align with reality — part of humility is recognizing this! We must constantly test our hypotheses against what exists. This is best done through ubiquitous data collection.

Thus, another core principle is that we must answer all questions through measurement, not through feelings. Projects should be operated as loops of questions and answers. These loops are the inner core of our innovation engine. Questions that aren't testable through measurement are meaningless. If we lack the data to support an answer, we are blind. We can't even say that we have an answer unless there is data to support it, since the only valid questions are empirical. Even with the growth of Big Data, there are still many companies where measurement is delayed till the end of the development process or restricted to monitoring customer behavior only. This is a mistake as everything in our project is a question: How long does a build take? How many defects do we detect per week? How often do developers engage particular features?

As we'll discuss later in Part II, however, there can be a dark side to measurement. While we can only properly answer questions that are testable and for which we have data, not everything is efficiently or easily measurable, even though it has impact on final customer value. We must live with partial knowledge only, never total. If we forget that there is hidden state, and moreover attach incentives to manipulating visible state, we can end up producing sub-par results for our customers. This is an example of what we'll later describe as a twisted reflection.

As we argued last chapter, a history of our decisions is also an aspect of measurement. In this case the experiment is some sub-range of the full project, with the world state and our decisions as the measured inputs. To support this, we should make sure that our decisions are stored in an immutable data store. Decisions are point-in-time — reversing a decision is treated as a negative decision, not as an erasure of the original choice. Any artifacts associated with the decision should be stored alongside it — the graph representation, the probability estimates, everything we mentioned previously should be kept. We'll discuss the evolution of principles more later in this chapter, but we should also store the set of principles or a reference to the set that was valid at the point when we made the decision. When we make a choice, we must prepare from the start for the post-mortem that might eventually come.

As part of measurement, we should also store versions of our working software that can be restored later. It is often necessary to record changes to the environment as well, along with the artifacts. If we have a back-end for our game, it must be possible to restore that to its previous state. This might require archiving images for cloud deployments. All aspects of this process should be automated. Work is required to support this, but it is worthwhile so that we can have honest comparisons between our past and current versions. We often distort our memory positively or negatively, depending on where we are at later times. As this work is fundamental to modern service-oriented development, it benefits us for other reasons as well.

Transparency:

Maximal transparency constitutes our next pillar. Since we are striving to answer questions, hiding or obscuring information impedes our search. Decision-makers cannot make their best choices if they do not have access to the best-known state of the world. We've frequently seen technical teams make architectural choices based on one release date, while secretly higher-level management has another release date in mind. This results in numerous forms of waste. Moreover, part of our system is that the floor can challenge decisions and contribute maximally to providing solutions. If our team lacks the information that the specific decision-maker possessed, the team will not see the decision as sound. This leads to distrust. Also, oftentimes someone on the floor has a solution to our problem but fails to recognize that it matches because the details are concealed.

We tend to be anxious about transparency. It exposes us before we feel ready. This is because we fear we will be attacked. If we can build a more constructive culture, however, we can rid ourselves of these anxieties and reap the benefits of distributed problem solving.

In some cases, however, there are limits on transparency. We often wish to preserve the privacy of our employees, and so do not wish to expose personal issues. Legally, we are sometimes forbidden to share information that would violate insider-trading laws. Some trade secrets must be held tightly. We might have NDAs with other companies that restrict access to their technology to subsets of the team — knowledge of Google's Stadia and Microsoft's Project xCloud, or new console hardware from Sony, Nintendo, and Microsoft would all be common examples of this. It can even be that exposure short-circuits the creativity of some of our staff.[36] We need to evaluate what makes sense for our organization, but our inclination should always be towards greater transparency. Opacity always favors individual agents rather than the customer. It is a form of waste.

We try to hire the best candidates, but if we hamstring them by hoarding privileged knowledge, we reduce them to B- or C-level contributors.

Root-Cause Analysis:

We must also adopt the core principle of root-cause analysis. Measurement and transparency exist to support this. It is never enough to mitigate the symptom of the problem only; we must always seek to the cause. In fact, we must do more than that, and dig deeper to the root cause of that cause as well — to the deepest level of causality we can find. It is easy to handle the surface problem only, but in so doing we doom ourselves to repeating our mistake. Once the true root is resolved, we will eliminate swathes of problems, many of which we might have been unaware of. This builds integrity into our products from the ground up. We will discuss the benefits of this more in Part III, especially when we discuss the practice of the Five Whys. Done well, root-cause analysis generates a strong virtuous cycle.

THESE PRINCIPLES are the ones we see as necessary to high-functioning organizations. They aren't the only ones, however; we will discuss many more possibilities throughout the course of this book! Not all principles make sense for every organization. We must determine what suits our needs. For one company, expediency might be paramount, as a slow time-to-market might result in products that are out-of-date and thus useless from the view of customers. For other organizations, correctness might be paramount, especially in safety-critical application spaces. Some principles are unique to what we are doing. A factory manufacturing car parts requires detailed guidelines that would make no sense to a small game-development shop.

Moreover, some principles exist to define our organization's subjective morals, not just to serve customer value. Part of who we are might be that there are ways we do not work. One company might value absolute delivery on time regardless of how much overtime is required. Another company might value steady forty-hour weeks. These principles are just as important as the rest. They will also often be key attracting points for employees and sometimes for organizational partnerships. Even customers might find our products more appealing because of principles that we adhere to.

In all cases, our principles must be actionable. A principle that cannot be understood and executed by our staff is not a principle. Vague imperatives are meaningless. "Do good" is useless. Do good how? By what measure? "Do no evil" is also too abstract — hence Google's current problems with Dragonfly. For some people, engaging in any form of capitalism no matter how cutthroat is morally good, even if it involves selling dangerous products. These people believe that the market corrects itself and that we have the fundamental right to engage in transactions — that the act of doing so freely is itself moral. For others, selling violent video games is immoral regardless of how well they sell. We must be clear on what our principles mean, so that our staff can execute on them. Many leadership teams create principles to give a facade of culture and values — the lists so generated are stereotypical outputs of committees that offend no one and mean nothing. The clearest signal we can find that we have generated a sharp principle is that we know people who would choose to not work at our company because of it. Principles must exclude as well as support.

Most importantly, we must follow through. If we say that our principle is the absolute protection of our users' data, then our decisions must follow from that. This can result in lawsuits and conflicts with legal bodies, so it requires strength. Before we enact a rule, we must ask whether we can stick with it. Knowing that the government will request our user data, how far will we go? In fact, we should embed how far in a statement included in an appendix to our principle list. If our limit is that we will protect data so long as there isn't a proper warrant through public courts, we should state that. Practically, that might be a necessary limit — while some companies have chosen to shut down rather than expose data after receiving search warrants with gag orders,[37] we might be unwilling to go that far. We must be clear. We should strive not to rely too much on our capacity to change our guidelines. While we can do so when a serious conflict arises, if we cannot stick to our code, our staff will view it as meaningless.

Adoption

It might seem that the system I've described is a hard one to enact, but if our principles are honest in terms of our corporate goals, it will be as easy as decision-making ever can be — not simple, but consistent and less chaotic. Alignment wastes less of our energy keeping teams on the proper course, which frees us to focus on propositions that add value elsewhere.

When first generating the decision-making axioms unique to our organization, it is useful to start with the most challenging decisions from our past. We should break them down and try to extract the unstated assumptions that were used to make those choices. An off-site can be a good venue for this. We could begin with a large table of such cases and create simple decision trees: if this, do that. Then we take those specific trees and try to extract the general rules that produced them. We should not overgeneralize. Rules that are generic are hard to apply; eventually they are useless. Overly specific principles, on the other hand, result in hundreds or thousands of cases. This would not be manageable. We must gradually learn the proper balance between specificity and generality.[38]

We should begin this process of principle building transparently. No one should be surprised by our results. We should make it clear that we aren't using these guidelines in the company yet as it is a work in progress, but we should broadcast changes as they occur. In some companies, such meetings are recorded on video for anyone to peruse later, but that might not suit our culture. Sometimes, people when watched are less able to contribute creatively. This is, in fact, a nuance of our system that we will need to consider for ourselves!

We must also be honest in terms of accepting the real world as it is. Feedback should be embraced, but also practical. Some of our staff might complain that our principles aren't moral enough, but we should remember that while we are providing solutions to customer problems, we are doing so for profit. We might find, for example, that some monetization techniques are "evil" in their exploitation of users' addictive tendencies, but we still need some monetization to be a successful business. We must not adopt a rule that will result in actions that run counter to how we expect our business to operate. Such a principle is useless unless our plan is to fail. This is not a feel-good process, and it can be the case that we will be forced to ask hard questions about what we will or will not do. Sometimes we won't feel entirely comfortable. Some people might choose to leave the company if our principles conflict with their own ethics. As we've said, this is not bad! That problem would arise regardless. It is better that it arises early rather than later, after the choice is already on the table.

Principles also usually aren't flat but have hierarchical priorities. We place customer value at the top, but below that we have humility, trust, boldness, transparency, measurement (including decision histories), and root-cause analysis. These are actionable but high level. There might be more specific rules that govern day-to-day behavior — for example, some companies might have a rule that all service tickets must be answered within some time window. For other companies, that might be nice, but not a requirement. Typically, higher-level principles should trump lower-level ones. Some lower-level rules are specific to teams.

The highest-level principles make a smaller set that can be presented to new employees immediately on arrival. These form the foundation of the company. For example, if a specified level of green environmental impact is a cultural pillar, then it should also be reflected as a top-level principle. Typically, the high-level set should be below ten, fewer being better. Seven is nice as it is roughly the size of the set most people can memorize in one shot. Too few can be bad as well. That will generate principles which either fail to cover our situations or are too general to be applied.

Beyond the core top-level set, there could be fifty or sixty principles that apply broadly across the culture to cover specific issues. The number often varies year to year. These are typically produced by our continuing meta-analysis of our decision-making processes. It's also common for some teams to have specific principles related to their problem spaces. It is best that these rules for specific teams be unique to their work, as we don't want culture to divide just because a group of team leads hold values that differ from the company at large. All work groups form sub-cultures within their larger organization, but we should be careful to make sure these variations conform rather than deviate from our norms.[39]

Once we generate a set of principles, we should test them. One of our teams might be selected to enact this list and start evaluating recent and ongoing decisions to see how predictive the principles are. This team should iterate on the list and keep testing until everything settles. Once we are convinced, we can roll them out. Again, we should monitor this to make sure that we are delivering the alignment we expect. We are striving to be sharper and leaner, not more bureaucratic. There will be some impact on our processes because we are trying to correct a weakness in our decision-making, but ultimately the users of the system should feel empowered by it. They can resolve the bulk of their decisions easily and focus on tougher issues.

Our principles are expected to shift and grow — just not too fast. We do not want them to flip daily, but they do need to react to the world. Too fundamental a change will overthrow our culture, so we should be careful to differentiate between adaptations and revolutions. Decisions that change our principles should be tracked according to the regular decision-history rules. In cases of emergency, we reserve the right to change principles on the spot — after all, part of humility is recognizing that our ability to forecast problems is limited. A normal cadence is twice per year.

It can absolutely be that a decision taken in the past is now invalidated by alterations in our principles, and that this might result in the need to reverse the decision. If we understand what changed and why, we can know that we are not repeating a previous experiment

John Bible

3

Seeking Customer Value

Our pole star is customer value. But what is that? What do we mean when we say that a feature delivers customer value, but another does not? Or that one feature delivers more than another? This is a difficult question that often lead us into dangerous waters.

At the highest level, we know that our customers value our product if they purchase it over other options. But why do they?

Let us consider this quote by Clayton Christensen: "People don't want to buy a quarter-inch drill. They want a quarter-inch hole."[40] This is an important distinction to remember. People don't want our product specifically; they want what it enables for them. Our product or service is often the mediator of value, not the thing of value itself.

Imagine that I have a customer who wants to bake things. I'm probably going to sell them an oven, but it depends. Do they only need to warm things up? That suggests a microwave oven instead.

Are they baking bread? Maybe a bread maker would solve their problem instead. Perhaps they want to cook home-bake pizzas – nothing fancy would be required, only a basic oven model. Someone else, though, might need multiple racks in the oven, advanced heating controls – maybe even a smart oven they can control from their phone.

Oftentimes, we as developers fixate on the oven, not on what it enables for our users. We write features without considering how they align with need. Sometimes we pile on ever more shiny features, adding robot arms inside the oven to shuffle pies between racks, chemical sniffers to test the aroma of bread, cameras to get real-time footage of our lasagna's progress, none of which anyone wanted and all of which obscures the core proposition. It can even be that there's a better solution than an oven! Maybe an oven was the only option they'd heard of, but we can provide alternatives. By not seeing actual need, we generate an offering that can only disappoint.

In game development, we face a similar problem. People don't want the software, they want the experience the software enables — it's not more features, it's the right features. Further, they encounter the experience we offer within a specific context. After an intense day writing software, a mom might want to play a slow-paced exploration game after her kids go to sleep. Her children, however, might desire a completely different experience on Saturdays. Each of these customers purchases their product because there is a compelling offering for them.

Sometimes, the danger is that we fail to recognize the full constraints of a user's need — we see only one factor and disregard the rest. Some games render a luscious world, but to keep all the supporting data in memory, they break up the experience with minute-long loading screens that kick the player out of the fantasy every five or ten minutes. Unlike the previous two cases, no niche finds this a desirable trade-off. Even so, developers sometimes fixate on final visual quality, without considering the side effects. Specialists face this risk as they often place exorbitant value on the dimensions

Deep Management

of the product that correspond with their interests. This can also arise with erratic frame rates, or with frame rates that are too low for our genre (below 60 in a twitchy first-person shooter, for example).

In all cases, we must understand who we are serving. Just because a feature is exciting, doesn't mean it meets our customers' needs. Some niches offer unique problems. In other cases, a spicy feature comes with an undesirable aftertaste. In any event, it is an absolute rule that no product should try to serve everyone.

The Value of Features

To explore some complexities of value, imagine that we had a perfect oracle that could tell us the impact a feature would have on our final revenues. One immediate point is that sometimes only clusters of features are valuable, while the individual increments are often neutral or even detrimental. Consider the set of changes necessary to take a single-player game to multi-player with dedicated servers. First, the simulation of the game itself now is no longer entirely local to the players' machines (perhaps nothing is local); this has ramifications for how the game responds to user inputs — we often strive to conceal the impact of this from the user, but all approaches have their limitations.[41] Many features are necessary to enable this transition from single to multiplayer, and oftentimes the short-term result is imprecise shooting and clumsier motion. A perfect oracle might tell us that these incremental changes are harmful. This might continue until we add the capstone feature, at which point there is a sudden reversal (we're assuming our customer wants a server-based multi-player experience). Thus, even if we could know the current value of our product, we must consider the value of some changes in the aggregate only. The features synergize, but only once we've exceeded a bar.

It has become more common in software development to get our final customers into our product as early as possible — thus, we would no longer need an oracle. We have the true source. This is key to Lean and Agile thinking, as we'll discuss in Part III. Instead of conceiving of a product, planning it out, and then delivering it, we instead start with a direct customer need and use concurrent engineering[42] to deliver it as rapidly as possible.

Despite the power of this approach, it remains uncommon in AAA development. We usually only bring in small numbers of play testers early on, and then engage them in ways that limit their ability to express their needs. They often aren't treated as equals; we consume them for comparative feature evaluations or to estimate future review scores. In some cases, the play testers are influencers that we want to promote our product or to seed a future community, and so we present them with slanted views meant to capture their interest. To discover our customers' real needs, we must listen to them deeply. There are business concerns that run against early customer interactions as we will discuss later, but our advice is to work past that and get to real feedback. The value is too great. This is an area where we must overthrow habit.

The gate process for games that we discuss in Part IV is specifically built to keep costs low until we have captured the customers' problems and posed our solutions, although the time to reach that point can be quite long. If we follow this process, we wait until we've authentically grasped the need and then surge in development effort to solve it.

It's become popular in indie game development to use Kickstarter and Early Access to get customers involved in the project before it reaches a final state.[43] While value and money aren't the same, money is often a proxy for how much the customer values the product. Thus, the earlier we can find out how much more they are willing to pay for individual features, the less we will waste.

For some AAA GaaS products, it has also become prevalent to launch in an incomplete state. Of course, the developers never admit this upfront. These releases always come with bad press. Such a strategy could make sense if such launches were perceived as in-progress versions with lower initial sales targets. Marketing would communicate that this version is only for the hardcore who want to influence the game from the start. This would expose us to paying customers earlier. In the current market, however, this violates norms. The marketing campaigns as they stand now promise final not preliminary products. As we'll discuss later, when releasing anything, the perceived category that it belongs to will establish consumer expectations for quality. Until things change, it is better to use non-paying beta testers, although it is worthwhile to give them fake currency to see how they prefer to spend it.

In already live services, A/B testing is another commonplace practice to establish how much value a customer places on a feature. Here, we segment our population into two groups A and B, where A is a null hypothesis where nothing changes, and B is a change. We then consider how player behavior shifts as a result of this. We'll note that oftentimes in games (and elsewhere), these A/B tests use small sample sizes. As such, we can't say results are statistically sound. Nonetheless, there is some information to be had if we don't grant it too much authority. It should also be noted that A/B tests run the risk that we exploit our customers, deliberately or otherwise. These tests often iterate rapidly using proxies to value, which can manipulate addictive tendencies rather than refine customer happiness.

It is also common for developers to use stand-ins rather than direct customers. Product owners would be a common example from the Scrum methodology. These individuals represent the needs of the customer to the development team. It should be obvious that the lack of a connection between a product owner and the customer can be a risk. We must strive as much as possible for our product owners to connect with the customers, so that they can represent their needs. Agile sometimes uses what are called Personas to handle this, where practitioners try to model and empathize as much as they can with archetypal customers they expect to support.

Some product owners are technical proxies, such as those representing the tools needs for art teams. These individuals are less of a moral hazard. We should be careful here as well, however. The ultimate customer value for the tools developers comes from the actual paying customer, not the art team — or the design team, or whichever internal department the tools serve. It is possible to allocate too many resources to internal problems relative to the needs of the end user. The product owner while representing the internal team's demands must also evaluate the impact of features in terms of what the customers' experience will be, which includes the fact that tools development resources could be spent elsewhere — building a better streaming system for loading, for example.

In our chapter *Consider the Hideout*, we will consider how a substantial example feature in a game might be evaluated relative to the many possible customers we could pursue.

The Complexities of Value

Establishing value isn't trivial.

We have discussed value as if it were a score, but in recent decades it has been established that we do not perceive it in this fashion.[44] The origins of numerical utility began with Daniel Bernoulli in the 18th century, who proposed the expected utility hypothesis to explain some behavioral conundrums. This included, for example, the idea that we prefer money in the pocket now, rather than a hypothetical bet with a greater average value later. This was meant to resolve some paradoxes in terms of how people viewed bets over time. Until the 20th century, variants of this utility hypothesis were considered standard, although many commented on its limitations. It used to be the foundation of the economic concept of the rational agent used by economists to justify the optimality of free-market behavior. As we'll discuss more in our chapter *Game and Decision*

Theory, this has been replaced by notions such as prospect theory and its relatives.

The meaning of value becomes even more complicated as our estimations are biased by framing. Prospect theory tells us that rather than absolute utility, we perceive value by gains and losses, but gains and losses relative to what? As we'll discuss later, this can result in the strange situation where adding a feature that a player wants causes the player to view the product as worth less than it was before the feature addition. This can happen if the new feature causes our player to perceive our game as belonging to a different category. Customer value is *perceived value*, not "real" value in any sense.

Games further are entertainments, unlike tax or billing software. Our players engage with our products to solve an emotional need.[45] That could be just boredom. It could also be the desire to experience mind-blowing sci-fi reality inceptions! Or anything else. We should suspect any system that assigns precise numerical values to subjective experience. Here we might have to rely more on our gut. We could use a simple code for the value of each feature — low, medium, high, and must-have, perhaps. It has been noted, however, that if we allow for more specific estimates and then refine our judgments over time, it is likely that our results will be improved, even if they are initially biased. This has been noted as a common attribute in skilled forecasters, who often operate with precise probabilities, even though those probabilities are estimates with large error bars. For this to make sense, the precision of these estimates should arise from analysis of sub-components of the feature and how they synergize, not just off-the-cuff guesses.[46] As always, we must test our gut calls with users.

Because valuation is hard, we often resort to proxies. For example, for games that are live, we might track Daily Active Users (DAU). This is the number of unique players that logged in during a 24-hour period, regardless of duration. The commonly used term engagement is supported partially by this metric. Frequently, this DAU score is used as a proxy for how happy we believe our customers are with the product. The more they log in to play, the happier they must be, right?

As we later discuss in Part II, proxies can be dangerous. If these proxies have incentives, we can create moral hazards for our developers. After all, high DAU rates can also be explained by promoting addiction. People who are addicted to products often grow to hate them. If we exploit our customers' cognitive glitches, we compel them to engage — should they realize we are doing this, trust will be broken. Time-limited rewards that expire can be an example of this. Even though the players don't want to log in, they do so anyway to avoid missing out (FOMO, or fear of missing out).

Thus, when we consider whether a feature has the potential to move the estimator of value or not, we should ask why the feature does so. We should get at the root. If the feature drives the metric because it better meets the customers' needs, then it grows value. If the feature drives the metric because it exploits a cognitive hook, then it detracts value. Our product owners must be relentlessly defensive of our customers.

This is doubly true when we are indirectly compensated for the value we deliver, as is the case when advertising pays our bills. We connect with our customers by solving their problems, which generates customer attachment. This is the commodity we then offer to advertisers. When the customer already desires the product the advertiser offers, this is a serendipitous alignment, but usually the advertisers wish to shape customer demand further. For example, the beauty and cosmetics industry has long supplied the bulk of revenue for many women's magazines. This gave these companies such clout that they could impose editorial demands on content. This resulted in puff pieces that offered hidden advertising for cosmetic surgery and snake-oil skin treatments, among other anti-customer practices.[47]

While this specific situation is better regulated now, the core hazard remains relevant – we need only consider the data generated from social media enterprises as a modern conundrum. Customer backlash and distrust grows more prevalent as evidence mounts for cases of negligence and exploitation of user data. It is a fine line as many of these companies receive no direct revenue from users, while simultaneously enduring pressure from investors to grow at obscene rates.

This is a problem for free-to-play (F2P) games as well (and increasingly buy-to-play games). In these cases, money comes not only from advertising, but also derives from exploitation of addictive cognitive glitches in consumers known as whales and dolphins.

If we wish to develop an enduring company that grows healthily over the long term, we must exercise extreme caution when customer expectations and business conditions force us to engage in these models. Our product owners must be both relentless and empowered to defend our customers from abuse. Especially as it is all too easy for new levels of exploitation to become normalized.

The Razor

From the start of our project, we should construct a deep mapping of the type of player who will engage in our offering — basically, we want the Persona idea of Agile mixed in with an elevator pitch but engineered to burn out any unnecessary work. We need to define a short statement — usually a few sentences at most — which tells us who we are serving and why they are engaging with us. We need to refine the experience that our customer desires. This is the Razor. It is the tool we use to slice out everything that does not serve our customer, while it simultaneously tells us how to reach them. The sharper the Razor, the less waste we will suffer.

Steve Jobs had a relevant point on this: "People think focus means saying yes to the thing you've got to focus on. But that's not what it means at all. It means saying no to the hundred other good ideas that there are [...] I'm actually as proud of the things we haven't done as the things I have done." This quote was made in a broader context than the Razor, but it gets to exactly how we must think.[48]

The Razor needs to be a living artifact of our process stored in our version-control system. It is akin to a principle from the previous chapter, but for a specific project, not the culture at large. The Razor should be an empirical product. While we might construct it initially as a model, we should expose it as soon as possible to actual customers for validation. If we shift to a different target audience, then we must change the Razor. Every team member requires access to the up-to-date version, as they will use it to evaluate whether the work they are doing supports the Razor or not.

To validate the Razor, we need to get a working version of our game as early as possible. This does not mean that this initial version is final code that will be shipped. If we establish that certain elements define the Razor, we might make a 2D version of our game with low realization early on. Sometimes, we can just build a boardgame or a paper RPG version. The key is to prove that users want the experience we offer. General quality is not necessary to validate our design, just quality in the right places. We don't expect to hit the bar the first time out, but rather to iterate until we find the best fit. Where full realization is critical to proving out the experience, we will have to wait until vertical slices of the game's content exist in pre-production before this can be demonstrated. However, a game that relies on realization for product value is missing the opportunity for having an engaging game experience irrespective of visuals. A game that is sound to its roots will be a better game (and I would assert this is true of any product).

It might even be useful to offer this early version at some low price under a side brand, just to test how willing people are to engage with it (this is akin to cross-testing a feature in a separate live offering for another game). Doing so has its risks and is not for all organizations. However, I've seen teams maintain indie-level quality versions of their game throughout production. At times, I've seen products I might have been willing to pay for, albeit at a lower price point. When customers give us money, we receive the most valid form of feedback we're going to get, even if — as we've said —

money doesn't always match value perfectly. Naturally, none of this confirms the value of the AAA realization for our product, which must wait until our product has reached sufficient maturity.

Again, our focus is practical empirical knowledge, not theory. We start with ideas and a framing, but as soon as possible we expose it to users. Then, once we get feedback, we might try to tell stories that explain what we have seen. This in turn might lead to another theory. These theories are not useless. They can be used to shave off branches of the decision hierarchy. We merely must remember that they are potentially wrong hypotheses and always subject them to the reality of customers.

We tell stories because raw data is often useless for our intuitions, but we must be cautious in that a narrative can prevent us from seeing signals that run counter to the story. We must be humble here and attempt to see what is there. As stated by Daniel Kahneman and Amos Tversky in their early work: "The production of a compelling scenario is likely to constrain future thinking. There is much evidence showing that, once an uncertain situation has been perceived or interpreted in a particular fashion, it is quite difficult to view it in any other way.[49]" We will note later in Part III that Diane Vaughan discovered a similar situation at NASA, which she analyzed in her book *The Challenger Launch Decision*.

A sound approach for considering the meaning of customer value is the work of Clayton Christensen, especially his Theory of Jobs.[50] His core thesis is that every service and product should be created to solve a specific job for a customer, which includes the conditions that exist when the customer wants the job solved. For example, the solution for a problem when a customer is tired from a long day of work might differ from the solution they desire on a weekend when they have more time. This could be the difference between a microwave dinner being valuable versus a service that delivers raw farm-fresh cooking ingredients to our door for a home-cooked meal.

A canonical example Clayton uses in his books is the following: that of milkshake consumption at a fast-food restaurant.[51] A company wants to sell more milkshakes, but their customer studies heretofore have not improved results. They had tried various parameters to no measurable effect. Clayton's team then came in and applied their theory to frame what they saw in restaurants. His team observed and interviewed customers; they came to discover that classes of people were buying milkshakes at different times and for different reasons — this was part of why the company's parameter variation had no effect, as it changed the value differently for these groups, and thus averaged out to no impact. In the morning, customers wanted something to make their work commute more interesting — this suggested a thicker milkshake that would take longer to consume, perhaps studded with fruit to make it more surprising. Perhaps a milkshake machine to allow the customers to get in and out faster would be advisable. In the afternoon and evening, milkshake purchases were more often parents buying for their children: from interviews and through applied story-telling, the team posited that parents tired after work wanted a small win to make themselves feel better by giving their children this indulgence. They wanted smaller milkshakes that were less thick, as currently they needed to wait until their child finished before they could return home. The key of Clayton's approach is to analyze the customer in order to see their problems and their context in higher resolution. In the milkshake case, the company observed their customers from afar and blurred them together. By seeing with higher fidelity, Clayton's team was able to construct better stories, which could then be tested (although in this case, the company didn't proceed to enact their suggestions).

We can apply the same logic to our own processes. We need to get to users early, try to understand them directly through stories about their behavior, and then test these stories. Users won't understand feature specifications, so we need to get working software into their hands, even if the product is a prototype that we throw away later. Proxies are sometimes necessary, but they can deceive us. We must go to the source when possible.

Blocking

Suppose that we've invented the most magnificent chocolate experience in bar form — our key innovation is the foamy perfection of the chocolate substrate beneath the caramel. We then permeate our confection with cilantro. Now, it's possible that our innovation here is cilantro-infused chocolate, and if so ... okay. But if the core experience is the chocolate, then we've blocked anyone who dislikes cilantro, even though they might otherwise have been delighted. Whether cilantro chocolate is ever good or not, at least some people experience the taste of cilantro as soap.

The key here is to extract what we are doing that is uniquely valuable. Oftentimes, this core aspect is surrounded by other product attributes that our current customers accept but don't care as much about. New customers might want the core offering but are off-put by these secondary attributes. If we removed or fixed these obstacles, then current customers would remain satisfied, while new customers would be able to enjoy the product. Adding these new customers then is not a hazard.

This is not the same as a generic demand to broaden the pool of customers. Business and marketing teams often push features and changes to appeal to alternative audiences, but that also erode the value of our core proposition. Such additions must be avoided at all costs. We are discussing only the case where an unnecessary or low-value attribute of our product blocks a group of customers from accessing the primary value of our offering.

From Software's *Dark Souls*, *Bloodborne*, and *Sekiro* products all exemplify the situation where broadening the pool seems unwise. These games are specifically famous for being hard, not for being fantasy action RPGs. Because they are renowned, many try to play but get repelled by the difficulty. These players demand an easy mode. Much of the appeal, though, is that they are a sort of club. Players need to "git gud" as the entry fee. Their organic popularity also correlates to how heavily they are streamed on places like

Twitch and YouTube. We know several streamers who specialize in running these games with handicaps self-imposed. The mystique of difficulty is inextricably wound into the game. Mind, we have never managed entry into the club ourselves.

Another interesting case of blocking occurs when developers default to a specific protagonist — where the gender, race, nationality, personality, and name are chosen for us. This isn't bad necessarily — for games that are more akin to film experiences, a specific character can be an interesting narrative choice. Most games make no use of this, however. It never comes up. Many potential customers might not like the protagonist, and so choose to skip the product. For games where exploring that character's experiences provide the value, these lost customers are acceptable. The proposition was in the details. For other games, it's just unnecessary — a clear case of blocking.

This is one reason why character customization has become the norm. Players often want to embody themselves. Many of us find representations of ourselves attractive as avatars. Meanwhile, other customers don't want to be themselves in the game — they want to project as something else, often crossing identity lines. Here, we open the game to more customers with no impact on our core proposition.

If, however, the specificity is significant, then it can be powerful. A product that delivers higher value for a tighter audience can be a reasonable proposition if we accept lower sales figures. Sometimes, such products can even become iconic classics with long burns, as happens with some books and movies.[52]

Imagine our game is a first-person shooter (FPS) set in the United States, where we explore an African-American male's relationship with the police and other social institutions. This could be a psychological study that provides a twist on an otherwise worn genre. In that case, it might be necessary to have this specific character, because the game is about both an individual's mindset and a group's relationship to America. Or imagine instead that the main character is

Deep Management

a woman freshly arrived from Ghana, or that it's a tale about a black British transwoman visiting family — these are each entirely different takes on the emotional experience and value this game might offer, each of which appeals to a distinct niche. Here, the specific experience of a character generates our core value, so we must accept that we will exclude some customers. This is fine. It's just not usually the case.

Further, be careful not to allow personal agendas to leak into these decisions, unless we've established that a specific subjective principle for our culture governs this case. If there is such a principle, be transparent to fans, and respect those who disagree. After all, we've blocked them from enjoying our product. They have good reason to feel disgruntled.

4

Seeking Alignment

It has become received wisdom that the team is more important than the outcome of a specific project. By this logic, fixation on a single release can burn out top-notch employees, stymieing future development. Team growth must be our central pillar. Through our staff, we seek to develop an engine that generates subsequent successes.

This isn't wrong, but it's easy to misunderstand.

Consider the previous story of the oven. This example was meant to clarify customer value and its centrality. The oven itself doesn't matter. We do not strive to realize the platonic ideal of a master oven. We solve the customer's problem — they just want pizzas. In a similar fashion, we can become stuck on the idea of the team. We imagine that if we grew the perfect ensemble of creators, then success would fall naturally out of that. But like the oven, it is not the team itself that matters, but what it produces. The customer must be the focus. For those of us operating at the organizational level, however, the health of our people is paramount. Even for us, though, we must remember that it is not the team that matters, but the succession of their deliveries. We must build ourselves around the characteristics of our many customers and their needs.

This situation resembles the product that tries to do everything. We focus on the most cohesive, flexible team; we go on retreats; we embrace failure. Our teams never get skilled at solving the projects we put before them, because the projects are never the priority. We forget that teams aren't generic — not really. Every team exists to solve a class of problems for a set of customers. Every domain space has unique characteristics that successful teams need to address.

AAA and indie game development each pose distinct challenges. AAA often requires specialization; people can spend entire careers focused within disciplines such as high-end rendering. The AAA developer must exhibit depth and mastery; within their specialty, they must compete at the cutting edge of research. Meanwhile, managers in AAA must be skilled at coordinating hundreds of employees, many in different countries. Indie teams, on the other hand, are small and often co-located. There is no place for the specialist. A typical indie developer must tackle many jobs, some of which they have no previous experience with. Every day, the challenge might be a new one. They succeed or not based on providing an experience that operates outside the box of AAA offerings, which requires a unique brand of creativity. Teams are not fungible. And these two cases arise within the same industry; outside games, there are even more distinctions.

Early on in Facebook's history, Mark Zuckerberg framed the principle that it's better to move fast and break things than to worry about consequences — the justification being that we can fix problems later, but we can't fix being slow. In Facebook's early days, this worked well. However, if we're writing software for a nuclear power plant, that would be a catastrophe in the making. Even for

Facebook, this core value might no longer be valid. When Facebook became more than just a platform for delivering media, expectations of editorial judgment arose. They inherited a social responsibility they had never expected. Ten years ago, who on the staff of Facebook would have imagined that they might bear responsibility one day as a contributing factor to a genocide in Myanmar?[53]

There's a meta-layer to customer value and teams, and it's critical that we separate our view of team development from the needs of specific projects.

For the team, they must focus on the customer above all. They must strive to become great by solving their customer's problem. They might pivot, but again, the team should pivot to better reach customers within their class, even if they are different ones. If the team allows itself to become distracted by hypothetical future customers, they lose track of what is before them.

For those of us managing the studio, however, while we want our teams to solve their projects, we also need teams that deliver value over time. We want them to grow stronger, even if their current project fails. We don't want them to burn out on a single shot at success. Therefore, while the team focuses on solving the customer's problem, we monitor the team to make sure it remains healthy. We intervene as necessary. Rather than give orders, we prefer to give guidance, but if we see the project careening off-course, we direct them back in bounds. If necessary, we can terminate the project, although as we explain in Part IV, it's better when the team recognizes that they need to cut themselves. If we understand that we must reposition ourselves to a new category of customers due to changes in the market or our position within it, then we can change the category our teams are to solve, bearing in mind the challenges this will create.

For our part at the studio level, to achieve the definition of the customer space that our teams will target, we apply techniques akin to those we used in seeking customer value. There are some differences. For every project, we require a sharp understanding of our customer. When shaping teams and our studio, however, we seek to define our business instead — the class of customers and their associated problems that we wish to serve. Here, we strive to determine the characteristics of our teams that produce good outcomes for a class of consumers.

The class of consumers we choose to pursue, though, itself constitutes a foundational choice for our studio, and must not to be taken for granted. We need to also consider this question: what characteristics does our team already possess and for whom would these characteristics provide superior solutions? This might suggest comparative advantages and weaknesses which redirect our business strategy towards better aligned customers. Especially in multinational companies, we should watch out for subsidiaries that copycat other locations, especially those in other countries – learning from experience is wise, but we sometimes carry over the wrong lessons. What works in the North America might not work for us. Moreover, there are always opportunities available to us that aren't available to other locations.

In the end, we must be as precise for our studio as we were with the Razor for the project. We just understand that the object of consideration differs; it is now the sequence of projects that a team might solve over time. When we think this way, we come to the principles we discussed in the chapter *Principles*, and the tools to seek customer value that we discussed in *Seeking Customer Value*. We also discover our unique requirements as an organization.

What Failure Should Mean to Us

It's become a mantra that failure is good, perhaps great! In this view, failure fuels our engine of growth. There are reasons this trend has arisen. Many types of product and service development — especially research-driven innovation — have high failure rates but enormous pay-offs. If failure hits our team morale too hard, we'll wear them out before we hit the big win. Our ability to embrace failure can keep us in the game until we succeed. Beyond that, if we aren't failing at all, we aren't embracing enough challenge. The market pays off inordinately for the right kinds of risk.

Still, we never aim to lose. Failure shouldn't be our purpose. To quote Yoda from the film *The Empire Strikes Back*: "Do. Or do not. There is no try." To try is to accept failure from the beginning. In the movie, Luke Skywalker fails to use the Force to life his X-Wing from the swamp because he believed it was impossible before he even began. "Doing" doesn't always result in success — we can still fail — but we must understand from the start that success is possible, even if it is only one of many possibilities.

The idea that failure is great arose as a reaction to it being a profound stigma. It still can be seen as such, especially in some cultures. In South Korea, for example, it is expected that ministers resign when problems occur under their purview. In Singapore, when problems occurred too often with the SMRT (Singapore Mass Rapid Transit system), there was tremendous public pressure for the minister of transportation to resign. The public expects that a mistake should be met by falling on our sword. When failure is fatal, we avoid it at all costs. This can make us risk-averse. Those who pursue risky and novel ideas get driven out, while the more cautious endure and rise to the highest ranks, thus shaping culture away from the big wins. For modern companies, this is the opposite of the direction they wish to be headed.

When this was realized, many organizations embraced failure. Failure became the route to success! Grit became our personality. Singapore, for example, has actively tried to push back against its risk-penalizing culture by broadcasting messages advising youth to take risks, to fail repeatedly, and thus to grow. As a country that desires to become a hub for innovation, this is a natural step. "You will be an outlier. But every society in its evolutionary process will require such risk-takers," stated Ong Ye Kung, Singapore's Education Minister.[54] They have recognized that to be top-tier, they must foster creativity and entrepreneurship in their youth to face the challenges of a city state in a rough-and-tumble future.

Where there remains a stigma, this view of failure makes a lot of sense. As time passes, however, many have taken this to its opposite extreme.

Failure is not what we want. Strategically, we embrace risk, but we do so because risk allows us to succeed at greater challenges. We kill our failing projects as early as possible to move on to subsequent shots, rather than dragging out their struggle. When we fail, we squeeze every bit of learning we can from it. Leaders shouldn't be punished for their failures if their choices were sound. Right action matters, not outcomes. Leaders who act well should rise, while leaders who behave poorly should be sacked, even if they succeeded. Of course, before sacking them, we should make sure that their behaviors were not the legitimate cause of their success. If their deviance shows us a new path, then we must be humble and embrace what they have taught us.

We don't need to fetishize failure; we just need to have a healthy relationship with it.

Team Formation

Team building is a meta-process of decision-making. Just as the decisions of an individual define their character, so too do the choices of the team illuminate its nature. Despite this, many teams form by luck. We assemble a team out of whomever we happen to have on hand — perhaps employees freshly released from other projects or new hires. Frequently, we are not as careful in shaping team composition as we are with product planning. We want to move forward on the project, after all, and these are the resources available. Without proper consideration, the cultures of our teams can form haphazardly, sometimes even at odds with the organizational culture.[55]

Just as we want our teams focused on solving customers' problems, we need to make sure that there are people whose job it is to build great teams.

Ideally, the people who trigger the creation of the team do so with a cultural philosophy in mind (whether they themselves will ever be part of the group or not — there is a place for managers whose job it is to seed development and adaptation of teams). This cultural philosophy is the recipe for how decisions are made, which must be related to the problems to be solved.

Learning how to clone and instill team philosophy into the formation of a new team that includes outsiders is a critical leadership skill. Many companies have multi-week periods where new joiners attend a small "university.[56]" Other companies are smaller and might only supply documentation to read and schedule meetings to attend. Whenever possible, teams should have enough older employees to ensure continuity. This is especially a problem when we open a new studio, particularly in a different country. Our processes for team formation are part of our system of decision-making; thus, we should record our choices, evaluate their outcomes, and report what worked and did not work when we build these teams and new branches. This will generate a virtuous cycle of self-improvement.

A key factor that we should ingrain into our teams is a radical sense of ownership, which includes ownership of culture. This is non-trivial, as we incorporate most of our staff after many decisions have been made. Nevertheless, if the leadership team alone shapes the culture, then culture will never be deep in the bones of the company.

We do this because we want our employees to engage their expertise for us. Part of why we as leaders must be humble is that we need to be able to hear our staff. It has become accepted that it is fragile for decision-making to be hierarchical. In such a system, leaders become bottlenecks, make decisions about topics they lack expertise on, and often have insufficient mental energy to address questions properly. To solve this, we shift work onto our decision system, and we delegate everything that makes sense downward. We want to be able to spend our energy on the more intransigent problems.

Ownership exists in opposition to task-based employment. In the task-oriented view, employees are giving large backlogs to churn through. This is favored by some leaders as it removes the need to establish collaborative agreement. The employees just grind away. This has been overthrown as the preferred model. It still comes up as it can take a long time for bad habits to be expunged.

Value comes from the floor, not specific leadership geniuses. Task-oriented teams place tremendous pressure on managers and ignore employee solutions, both of which generate waste. As Steve Jobs said, "It doesn't make sense to hire smart people and tell them what to do; we hire smart people so they can tell us what to do.[57]"

We desire instead that our employees be goal-driven. They work for the ultimate customer and thus care about the outcome, not their velocity against a work queue. This is what an owner does. The microservices architecture approach has become prevalent in some software industries to encourage this. In this model, a small team is given total ownership over a microservice from concept to obsolescence. This has allowed companies such as Amazon to grow to massive scale.[58]

We can have a goal-driven mentality regardless of our architectural approach, however. We only need to build into our culture an obsession with results. We need to inspire our employees to feel purpose in what they are doing.

This philosophy is also known as "mission command" and supplies the operating principle for the United States military and the Israeli Defense Forces, among many others. This ideology of ownership has its roots in the philosophy of several Prussian military leaders: Johann David von Scharnhorst, August Graf Neidhardt von Gneisenau, Carl von Clausewitz, and Helmuth Karl Bernhard Graf von Moltke.[59] From Moltke: "No plan of operation extends with certainty beyond the first encounter with the enemy's main strength,[60]" which has been simplified in modern parlance to "no plan survives contact with the enemy.[61]"

This requires high standards for our staff on the ground, who we expect to exercise their judgment to achieve directives in a decentralized fashion. We do not tell them in detail how to achieve their goal, just what we require, and they apply all their expertise and grit to achieve it. Moreover, we expect them to exercise judgment, which at times might cause them to oppose orders that conflict with desired outcomes. This is the opposite of a top-down task-oriented culture.

We also wish to encourage an environment of constant constructive criticism, which corresponds to our culture of ownership. Our employees should challenge weak points in our decisions. At its extreme, this takes the form of red teaming, where we create groups tasked specifically to find weaknesses in our processes and assumptions. If we've built up our decision-making system properly, our employees can test the validity of our past decisions themselves, by reviewing the decision histories we've given them. If they find that a past decision has become invalid, this can be to our advantage — it is an application of their ground-floor knowledge. Sometimes, we might not reach shared agreement either for or against a decision. If the employee understands what led to those choices, however, and we as managers authentically engage with them in discussing it, then the employee's faith in the decision-making system allows them to remain engaged.

To accelerate the on-boarding of new employees, before anything else, we should give them access to our history so they can understand where the project is and how it reached this point. They can exercise their expertise if past decisions were in error. After all, this might be the first time a particular subject-matter expert is on the project! If they know they can do this immediately and resolve problems that make sense to fix, they will be more tied to the outcome. They will feel greater pride in the project's success and thus give greater effort. We should never force our employees to do their best by some proxy such as mandated crunch — we should trust that our employees want to do what is best for the product.

The worst-case scenario is an employee that works for us just because they need a job.

This also means we should not accommodate employees that cannot operate in our environment, even if they are talented. Some people cannot take constructive criticism. These people are toxic to our organization. Some people cannot give constructive criticism — they might be rude, or they might only backstab decision-makers but never address issues to their faces. Some people refuse to address the root causes of why they make poor choices. Some people have difficult relationships with the truth and distort the past to avoid personal responsibility. Some leaders take mistakes out on their staff, which discourages employees from being honest. When these behaviors occur, they hurt our teams, which not only affects our current projects, but can cascade onward to corrupt future ones as well.

We must not tolerate this.

Ideally, we can filter out employees who do not fit before they join our operation. When we fail to do so, we must be hard-nosed on removing them from the company as swiftly as possible. This can be a hard decision for companies that are short of qualified applicants. Managers often cope with problematic employees because they deliver "high value." The truth is that our most toxic employees define the quality bar of our culture.

Because of this, when we interview candidates for our organization, we need to be clear on our values and expectations. Every interview cycle should ensure that these values are discussed in a reinforcing fashion. Our interviewers should not be going into interviews blind but should be trained and have guidelines on how to consistently evaluate talent.[62] Make sure new employees are on-boarded with a clear understanding of our pillars. We prefer to be generous, and so we should give new employees a chance to adapt, but too many chances are disrespectful to the rest of our staff. At the latest by the end of half a year, if an employee hasn't course-corrected, they must be gone.

Nothing in this interview or early employment process should be conveyed as reflecting on the quality of the employee. It is best handled by being transparent that culture is integral to the functioning of the company, and that not all people are proper fits. This can be handled in a way that is respectful. I have friends who can't stand working in large, political environments, and would rather live with less if they are masters of their own fate. I have other friends who would be terrified to do that. Not everyone is meant for every environment, so we thank mismatched employees for their effort and wish them success at their next endeavor!

John Bible

5

The Decision Making Loop

To finish out Part I, we're going to describe the decision loop that is the heart of our process. We constantly make small-scale decisions within the larger decision cycles running constantly throughout our project. From inception, we should practice this pattern, all the way to the final decision to shut down the service. We should engage with this process even when we are alone on the project; when the team is a thousand, we need to exert extra effort to make sure that our processes are executing consistently and generating the requisite artifacts. Habit ingrains our decision-making system into our culture.

Preparation

Early on, to properly operate our system we need to get the foundation in place. We should set up a version-control system or data store (or both) for our living principles, decisions, and Razor. At the start, we could rely on a written record for this, but given how trivial setting up a small database or version-control system is, even with one person on the project it should be in place.

Our artifacts should be available to everyone, but there is value in translating them to more user-friendly access methods such as wikis. If we do this, we should use automated systems that populate these wikis at least daily. It's simple enough to enable triggers that will repopulate on any change, which would be preferable. Oftentimes, our organization already has ready-to-go, easily configurable versions of these software products available on demand.

We should make sure that we store the working software artifacts we are producing as we go. Early on, prototypes might be so hacked together that they cannot be expected to be brought back to life later. As we proceed in the project, however, it is useful for us to be able to retrieve old builds. This includes environmental set-up as our defaults will no doubt have changed, so that previous versions might not run on current configurations.

Obviously, version-control systems for code and content should be set up as soon as required for the rest of the team.

Since our system is founded on empirical measurement, we also need telemetry and logging systems in place as soon as possible (note, telemetry means our automatic data-tracking service for both development and client software, although sometimes companies have two separate services for this). In our earliest days, when we might have only a few people — all doing documentation, customer interviews, and early prototypes — we might not yet need telemetry, but as soon as we scale to a small team, it must be in place (some version of telemetry for clients and developers should be in place no later than the start of dev hell, which we discuss more in Part IV).

For many companies, there are ready-to-go packages to set up telemetry directly into their cloud environments, in which case there's no excuse not to configure and set it up as soon as the project exists on the books. Until we have telemetry, we are blind. Initially, regular logs might be local only, but preferably they get sent to a central repository as soon as possible – several excellent text storage options exist. Data records from telemetry might be sent to Mongo or Cassandra — perhaps we also warehouse the data and generate reports or feed it into our Spark pipelines for further processing. We must be wary that we do not unnecessarily set up multiple data-tracking systems. Sometimes this happens because there are different clients, and so separate groups of developers create solutions independently. The result of this is multiple systems to maintain. The quality of features in our telemetry systems then drops.

Data is useless if we don't expose it. As soon as we can track data, we should surface it in the form of dashboards and reports, available to anyone. Preferably, we should be presenting fresh data, although real-time often isn't necessary — for the current build status, however, rapid feedback is critical. We shouldn't flood our users with useless information. Too many signals will cause our developers to ignore the dashboard altogether. We should establish key indicators and create a clean and readable dashboard, which can be made visible across the floor. More detailed reports can be stored in well-known locations for anyone who wishes to access them. Data that is never consumed is useless. In fact, we should be tracking data accesses as well, and using that to guide our measurement processes.

The Decision Loop

We now have in place the requisite tools to commence our loop of decision-making. This process proceeds by considering our state of uncertainty, selecting tests that improve our understanding, and committing work based on the results. Committing work here is done via set-based development, where we wish to decide as late possible and keep options open. We discuss this more in Part III, but the premise is that we maintain a set of engineer-defined constraints that limit the set of software products we could create, and then commit work as late as possible without violating those constraints. The goal is to avoid work we later cut. Some tasks force us to commit earlier than others, so we should make sure we've reduced our uncertainty about those tasks first. Never use set-based development as an excuse to not make a decision that needs to be made.

1) Consider what we know and what we don't know (by which I mean the questions we know of that we don't know the answers to). These are our knowns and known unknowns.[63] Then consider how much we've tested the space of possible questions — how certain are we of our understanding of the customers' problems and the technologies we plan to solve them with. For instance, have we even spoken to potential players yet? Have we investigated possible technology choices? If no to either, then we are highly uncertain. This establishes what we might be completely unaware of — the unknown unknowns. We will use this as a gauge to establish the "heat" of the questions we should ask.[64]

2) If we are in an early phase with high heat (we are certain of little), prefer options that take great leaps and risks — ask the big questions, not whether particular tweaks of the movement system matter or not.[65] Ask if the world should be huge and continuous — is it procedurally generated at run time or are we using hand-built maps? Ask if it's a console title. Is it a competitive game where we need high integrity of service? In high heat, we search out the rough form of solutions, not how to refine the solution itself. Once we enter a phase with low heat, however, these large experiments would open doors to questions we've already resolved. At that point, unless we can

establish that the basis of previous decisions is wrong now, accept previous outcomes. We should focus on questions of refinement that improve the quality of our discovered solutions. Here we consider details of motion, specifics of interaction with content, and other fine details.

3) Make sure any question posed is testable. Our tests either validate our question or prune many decision-tree branches. Validations can sometimes be questions with biased outcomes (perhaps we expect it to be right, but we want to be sure) and are more typical of "low heat" phases. Pruning questions are often high heat and should have more even probabilities of being right or wrong. A yes/no question, for example, should be set up to be a 50/50 test from an information-theoretic standpoint to maximally advance our knowledge. We must recognize that the branches we cut always seem most desirable by virtue of their unknown promise. We must cleave to our Razor and recognize that greatness comes from focus. Value comes from what we don't do.

4) Determine what metrics we need in order to test the question and ensure that they are in place.

5) Execute the experiment, preferably using real customers — and if we can — real money, even if we must give it to the players first. People exhibit more authentic behaviors when they have a stake.

6) Analyze the result — what did we learn? We must remember to dig deep into the analysis and consider counter-indicating arguments.[66]

7) If analysis allows us to lock down core questions of our technology and design, we can mark that in our data store. If it is time to lock down a decision due to the need to start work, we can remove it from our decision frontier and schedule the work into the backlog, preferably allowing those tasks to commence on the next sprint. We must bear in mind that it is waste to later remove such work from our backlog, although

we retain the capacity to do so if we recognize that circumstances have changed.
8) We then return to step one until eventually we reach the point of a final patch to the product or obsolescence and shutdown of the service.

It is important to note that boldness is a key factor in innovation, but as we discuss further in Part II, boldness unbounded by other factors can lead to bad decisions. We must ask hard questions; we can never ignore the signals that indicate our assumptions are wrong or too limited. At the same time, if we challenge a previous decision, we are invalidating work and generating waste, so it behooves us to justify our challenge by showing that the foundations of the previous choice no longer apply. Avoid looping as a nervous twitch. This is a problem born out of anxiety. In this way, our decision loop will generate a continuing spiral of increasing value.

PART TWO

Distortions of Reality

6

Game and Decision Theory

While the approach of this book arose from real-world experiences, theory also guided and shaped our processes and pillars. Through the application of theory and experiment, we become organizational engineers.[67] To check our gut instincts — even if they are born of expert intuition — we need tools. We will consider two important ones in this chapter: game theory and decision theory. Because this isn't a tome on either topic, our survey will be brief but hopefully enough to guide interested readers to deeper study. We will focus on foundational research. With decision theory, most of our discussion concerns Daniel Kahneman and Amos Tversky's work, with a few exceptions. Nevertheless, new developments in the field provide an ever-expanding landscape; the neuroscience around decision-making has proven particularly interesting, especially that arising from fMRI studies of brain activity.

Game theory studies the strategies of multiple agents seeking optimal solutions, and how those strategies interact. We can use game theory to analyze whether our cultural pillars and environmental conditions align our agents with organizational goals.

Decision theory concerns why and how individual agents make choices. It considers the impact of uncertain worlds, where the outcomes of actions are also probabilistic.

In normative decision theory, we assume the agent is rational. Decision analysis is the practical application of normative decision theory.

Humans do not behave rationally, however. The second part of decision theory is the study of how and why we honestly make decisions, accounting for our biases, heuristics, and other deviations. Because many of these errors are the result of mental shortcuts, we are often blind to them.

In all cases, we must remember that these techniques can lead to false senses of security if we view them as oracular.[68] Excessive faith in tools and automation is itself a cognitive bias after all![69] If we view the use of these tools as supplemental or for exploring alternatives, we can protect ourselves against our flaws and seek value faster. In the end, the actual outcome matters not the prediction.

The application of these ideas can help us understand the afflictions of our organizations. Poorly thought out incentives can cause our employees to undermine customer value. These techniques can identify and remove unnecessary cognitive hooks and expose faulty reasoning. Through greater understanding of human emotion and cognition, they can also help us better empathize with the complications of our very human customers' needs.

All these approaches are interesting subjects for small-scale test games and simulations to explore how changes might improve or hamper our efficiency. Again, skepticism is the rule, as it is unlikely that a simulation will capture the richness of our problems. Nonetheless, it can be an exploratory method to guide us to the root causes of problems. Through understanding we can find resolutions.

Game Theory with Rational Agents

Our primary organizational problem is that we have many independent agents with their own interests, who we wish to align with our global purpose. We can solve part of this problem by culling potential employees that are poor fits when we interview them, but inevitably, conflict remains.

In its original form, game theory covers the strategies of rational agents seeking their own optimal outcomes. This is a good starting point for thought experiments, but we should recognize that practical problems aren't often solved by these pure games. We can establish simple cases that make key points — for example, that the best local agent strategies don't necessarily generate optimal solutions for the organization. From this point, we can have a broader discussion about problems in real-world conditions.

We'll discuss this further later, but many incentive-based distortions that arise from KPIs (Key Performance Indicators) can be analyzed in terms of game theory. If, for example, we reward people for executing a specific kind of task, but we do not reward them for another type of task (perhaps because it is harder to track), then we can show trivially that our employees will overallocate resources to the tracked task. This is equivalent to the Tragedy of the Commons game,[70] where shared resources are overexploited by farmers. In our case, the employees fail to manage a shared responsibility, which in turn builds debt against us because there is an implicit penalization of employees who spend time supporting it. This can help us understand how to prevent these afflictions from arising while still benefiting from measurement.

It is better for the games we create here to be as simple as possible. We engage in them to isolate a minimal case so that we can explore it. Heavyweight examples are counter-productive as they are harder to analyze. When considering rational agents only, no simulation will produce unbiased results, regardless.

As an example, one of the simplest and oldest games would be the well-known prisoner's dilemma. This problem was posed to show that even though there is an outcome that is globally superior, two rational actors will choose strategies that maximize their local benefit instead. The problem is posed as follows: The State wishes to extract confessions from two prisoners, who are not allowed to communicate with each other. The prisoners are each to be charged with two crimes, the lesser of which has already been proved and carries a year of jail time, while the greater crime lacks enough evidence, and so requires one of the prisoners to betray the other. Both prisoners are rational agents, and they know that there will be no repercussions to betraying beyond those mentioned here. They may choose to betray the other prisoner or not. If neither prisoner betrays, they serve the lesser sentence of one year each. If both prisoners betray, they both serve two years. If prisoner A betrays but B does not, then A serves no time, and B serves 3, and vice versa if B betrays A. The strategic logic for the solution is this: if A assumes that B doesn't betray, then A's position is improved by betraying (A serves no time); if A assumes that B betrays, then A's position is still improved by betraying. Thus, A's best strategy is to betray, as is B's. This occurs even though if both did not betray, they would receive the minimal global time of two years in jail combined. Thus, by following their optimal strategy, they end up serving two years each. The structure of the problem and its environment as posed leads to an inferior outcome, which can be the case for our organization as well.

This type of solution is known as a Nash equilibrium, which is a stable outcome for all agents such that altering the strategy causes an inferior result for the agent who made the change. There can be more than one equilibrium. Under some conditions, it is guaranteed that at least one equilibrium exists.[71]

This is the logic that we can apply from a game-theoretic standpoint to understand how our current environment can incline our employees to make non-optimal choices from an organizational standpoint. We can look at a hypothetical employee faced with a choice and consider their options. By analyzing which options benefit our employees and which penalize them, we can understand the evolution of our company (note, for more realistic results, we'll have to consider the agents' view of value as we discuss later, since our employees aren't rational). We can then ask if the preferred choice generates better or worse results for our organizational goals. When there is a mismatch between local and global outcomes, we have identified a flaw in our organizational culture.

We also recommend interested readers seek out the books *The Logic of Political Survival* and *The Dictator's Handbook* by Bruce Bueno de Mesquita, Alastair Smith, Randolph M. Siverson, and James D. Morrow. Or alternatively go directly to their original research. These researchers studied how and why political figures remain in power, including CEOs. We can project these same ideas over to our organizations and evaluate how these structures positively and negatively drive agent behavior.

Game Theory with Real Agents

Game theory has become an umbrella term that includes the analysis of problems with human actors, often to better understand how we behave in groups. Here, the agents are subject to the biases and heuristics we'll discuss at the end of this chapter. Behaviors that we've learned for family, tribal, and village relationships can undermine corporate goals.

These games come in two forms. In one, we take a concept such as fairness, which might be empirically determined through human experiments, and then encode this as a primitive. Then we continue with games using rational actors where fairness is now a quantity that the agent can reason about. In the second case, we work with real agents and what their interactions generate. In research, this is usually done through experiments with human subjects, but we can also do computer simulations with models to observe emergent behavior, where the agents have parameters that control the impacts of their biases.

A well-known example would be the Ultimatum Game. Here, we have two agents, A and B. Agent A is privileged — this is also an example of an asymmetric game. We give Agent A a sum of money X. Agent A is to give some money to agent B, but A can determine the split as they wish. B can then either take the offer or reject it. If B rejects, neither agent gets anything. A's task is to determine what amount of money to give B such that B will accept, but no more.

If A knew that B were perfectly rational, A would give B a single dollar. B's choice is then between a dollar and nothing, so B would choose the dollar. This isn't an interesting game, nor is this how the Ultimatum game plays out.[72] From experiment, humans reject such offers as unfair. We have developed an impulse from our herd behavior that causes us to prefer punishing the other in the case of inequitable deals, even at the price of getting nothing. There are some simulations that suggest this pattern results in better outcomes for the population.[73] A similar reaction occurs with chimpanzees.[74] In real cases of the Ultimatum game, agent A often offers 50/50 splits. When splits are less than 30% to B, B often rejects. This is attributed to the dynamics of long-term group behavior, where we teach each other fairness. Different cultures have different rejection bars for the Ultimatum game, perhaps due to their embedded cultural view of reputation.

When we create games either with real subjects or via computer simulation to model known biases, we allow for more interesting but harder to analyze games. These games can give us guidance for how the predilections of our employees' personalities play out.

An interesting game we might explore, for example, would be how our company evolves with agents that exploit the cognitive faults of others. We might set up a pool of agents with random attributes and strategies, where a strategy is the amount of time dedicated to various activities: prestigious work, mundane work, authentic self-promotion, storytelling, networking, and so on. We then set up rules for our culture (decision recording can limit storytelling, for example). The game runs for several rounds and we watch where the rewards accumulate. In another version, we might allow agents to use their rewards to change the culture to their own advantage (someone relying on storytelling might want to remove the decision records). We then ask what the final culture looks like. We can analyze how well the reward distribution and eventual culture align with our organizational goals. This is often done using evolutionary computational approaches such as genetic algorithms and programming. This is always only a simulation, as there aren't closed-form solutions for any but the most trivial of cases.

We can also run the previous game with actual humans, if we treat our organization as a source of data and add the post-mortems of other companies. If we frame the results as if we all had been playing a game, we can then measure how these situations played out.[75] This is always flawed: post-mortems never contain complete details, there are many contaminants, and the number of examples is always in the realm of small numbers. Nonetheless, we can sometimes extract potential hypotheses that can be later tested. Using external data in this manner is also known as taking an outside view of our company, with the intent of questioning our own internal sociological assumptions.[76]

For an example of the type of problem we might want to subject to either simulation or an outside view, we might come to suspect that in our culture, advancement is driven by the growth of a fiefdom, and that this could be undesirable. Sometimes high-level leadership encourages this pattern as a form of training. A potential leader gets some responsibility, and their rating at their next review relates to how they grew their domain. If this growth aligns with delivered customer value, there is no problem, but almost always it doesn't. It often generates a proxy target for employees that can run counter to desired outcomes. We can model these situations as games and observe how they play out. Or we can bucket external companies into classes based on their strategies for this characteristic and see how they evolved. If we deem there is a problem, we can then pose the usual suggestion to fix such a case, which is to invert the responsibilities of the leader, and see how that plays out. For such a proposition, the fiefdom is removed, and leader is now tasked with strengthening direct connections between the customer and the developer, thus eliminating the value surrogate. We can then repose the game to show how this eliminates the distortion of the proxy while still growing our staff. The difference is that now the manager acts more as a servant leader. Other possible solutions naturally may exist as well.

In this example, we have taken a risky stance, as we presumed the results of the game and outside view. Modern theory favors servant-based leadership over fiefdoms, but our experiments could show otherwise, which might be interesting. We must never assume that we know the answer. If our experiments produce results at odds with prevailing theory, this might tell us something about our organization or our environmental conditions. It could also overthrow the paradigm. We must be careful to not make snap judgments, as the exceptions tend to be the interesting cases.

We can also pose games to better understand the needs of our individual actors, rather than analyzing the game itself. This falls more in the domains of confrontation and conflict analysis[77] and drama theory.[78] Here we try to understand the positions and relationships of agents and determine how to resolve their individual issues. This can be interesting when analyzing how our organization functions. For example, in a software company, we might consider the roles of departments: technical teams might feel cut out of decision-making, while other staff might feel slighted in turn by the attitudes of engineers. This frustration can then drive reactive behaviors, which undermines our efficiency. Understanding the root causes of these frictions allows us to heal rifts, which can reinvigorate our teams. Sometimes the best solution arises by addressing the needs and restrictions of the agents, rather than changing the game's rules and conditions.

Normative Decision Theory

In normative decision theory, we go away from groups and ask how and why a single rational decision-maker makes choices given an uncertain world and probabilistic outcomes to actions. We assume the decision-maker has unlimited compute time, so we do not consider fast, approximate solutions. This gives us the ideal decision-maker. While the decision-maker is rational, it need not be the case that the other agents in the world are also rational. To make the best decisions as a golden standard, the decision-maker must understand how people at least probabilistically behave. The norm used in such decision-making is usually simple; normative decision theory rarely considers the full complexities of human perception of value which we discuss later. Oftentimes, the norm used is some variant of profit diluted by time.

Decision analysis is the corresponding practical field. Since the 1980s, many companies have invested in tools to support decision analysis to better guide senior decision-makers. This field is often subject to the problem that the inputs to its algorithms appear sounder than they are. Probabilities from data can be out of date, insufficient in quantity, or surrogates for the actual subject of interest. Probabilities from experts are frequently more qualitative than quantitative, especially at the tails of probability distributions, where humans often distort estimates near 99% or 1%. Oftentimes, possible choice options are omitted due to human blind spots. Decision analysis systems can lead to false senses of security. Nevertheless, if we are mature about their use and understand their limitations, they can be useful exploratory tools.

As we've mentioned previously, our decision-making system parallels the scientific method. A core of our process is iterative hypothesis testing. This isn't by accident. Normative decision-making itself is linked to hypothesis testing. A decision is a judgment of value that we make, which after it is ranked with other options causes us to make a choice. In 1939, Abraham Wald noticed this. His subsequent work on differentiating between a null and an alternate hypothesis improved scientific falsification. He also discovered the sequential probability ratio test, which has been used in computerized testing to ask questions until a threshold is reached, which then fails or passes the examinee, rather than requiring a fixed number of questions. In a similar fashion, we might consider sequences of tests to determine whether a feature is adding value or not; this allows us to minimize the consumption of test subjects to validate our features. In many companies, there is a concern about exhausting the interest of customers in our product by premature exposure; also, many companies fear NDA breaches, which are less likely with fewer testers. Thus, there are many reasons we might desire an early signal.[79]

It might or might not be obvious, but in normative decision theory not all our decisions immediately capitalize on value. Many enable greater gains later. We accept that we possess uncertain knowledge of the world and of the outcomes of actions.

There are two types of uncertainty that we might face: epistemic and aleatory. If we have gaps in our knowledge and those gaps can be resolved, then we are dealing with epistemic uncertainty. If we are dealing with irreducible uncertainty such as the result of a dice throw or other random process, we are dealing with aleatory uncertainty. Some gaps of knowledge are theoretically knowable, but practically cannot be uncovered due to expense — in that situation, epistemic uncertainty is effectively aleatory. Early on in development, we often prefer actions that resolve epistemic uncertainty over immediate value creation. We do this where greater knowledge fosters greater performance later. For cases of aleatory uncertainty, however, our only option is to make ourselves more resilient to negative probabilistic outcomes and more prepared for positive ones.

Stated as such, normative decision theory parallels the probabilistic robotics solutions to the SLAM problem (Simultaneous Localization and Mapping[80]). For the more technically inclined reader, it can be useful to seek parallels between how robotics and machine-vision specialists balance strategies between knowledge and execution.[81]

This loop also underpins modern software-development practices. It used to be assumed that since the cost of fixing a fault increases over time, it was necessary that we get everything correct up front — the problem of software development was then one of shuffling tasks to minimize critical paths.

Now, however, software development assumes that we begin not even knowing what the question is, and that we must first increase our understanding. Once we've understood the customer's order, we then execute concurrent engineering practices (which we'll discuss further in Part III).

Descriptive Decision Theory

In the future, perhaps robots will explore and exploit the world in an efficient manner; once they take over, normative decision-making might be the end of the discussion.[82] Until then, we humans must deal with our systemic flaws in perception and analysis. It had been long thought that humans could be trained to be rational beings. The reason why humans suffered errors was just that they lacked education. Even acknowledging the uneducated, we assumed cognitive errors would average out.[83] In retrospect, this seems naive (but this is hindsight bias, where the outcomes of decisions create a narrative that causes us to believe that the results of choices were more certain at the time than they actually were — in other words, that the outcome was predestined and obvious, even though many other outcomes could have been equally or even more likely).

Our brains developed to solve the problems of our ancestors, including substructures that still resemble parts of reptilian brains.

Power was constrained — our brains evolved to operate at about 20 watts. That's a bit more than required for a modern household LED light bulb. To survive, we needed lightning-fast reactions to glimpses of tigers through tree leaves, but we also required the capacity to store complicated social structures and histories of favors and slights with our fellow humans. Perhaps most perniciously, it's even been suggested that part of what transformed us into modern humans was an evolutionary disruption that made us into storytelling creatures, with a narrative understanding of existence.[84] This could explain why some of our cognitive glitches are so deeply embedded. While there is some evidence of a similarly narrative understanding of relationships in other species — especially prosocial animals such as baboons — it is unclear whether our experience is a graduated refinement or a fundamental break with our fellow creatures.[85]

Optical Illusions

The realization of our inherent cognitive flaws began first with research into optical illusions. Gestalt theory provided an initial systemic framework for inquiry into the linkage between signals measured by our senses and our perceptual modeling of the world. Researchers throughout the twentieth century documented numerous visual quirks.[86] The most interesting of these glitches are the ones that we cannot overcome even after we are made aware of them. The checker shadow illusion is a modern constructed example[87] as shown in Figure 1. Note the image on the left. Consider the square with the A on it and the square with the B on it. Both are the same shade of gray, as we prove by the image on the right. Nevertheless, even knowing this, we continue to see the squares for A and B on the left as different shades. Our brain filters and translates the image without our conscious awareness.

Deep Management

Figure 1 Checker Shadow Illusion 1995. Edward H. Adelson (born 1952), Professor in Vision Science at MIT.[88]

This mistake does not occur in the eye. Our rods and cones measure the correct values. As the image runs through multiple layers of processing in our brains, we unconsciously inject these perceptual adjustments.

A similar enigma took the Internet by storm some years ago: "The Dress." Here an image of a dress appeared to some people to have bands of white and gold, and to others to have bands of blue and black. The correct colors were blue and black, as it was confirmed to be a royal-blue lace bodycon dress by the retailer Roman Originals.[89] We perceive the dress differently depending on our assumption of external environmental lighting. If we assume yellow daytime lighting, we resolve the dress as blue and black. The dress will appear white and gold, however, if we assume shadowy blueish lighting.

The light that arrives at our eye originates from a mixture of environmental lighting and the properties of the object's surface, not the object alone. Thus, for us to perceive a stable characterization of the object's visual properties, our minds automatically factor out external lighting. Using cues from our lighting environment, entirely without our conscious awareness, we filter our perception. When viewing a picture, however, external lighting conditions can be hard to reconstruct. Our minds unsurprisingly fail to extract the correct perceptual qualia.

Metastability supplies another common case, where an image can be interpreted differently, depending on assumptions we make about foreground and background. See Figure 2, for the well-known Rubin's Vase. Here, depending on whether we view black or white as foreground, we will see either two faces or a vase.

Even though we primarily cite examples from the twentieth century, when these ideas stabilized, there were earlier versions. Hume and Kant among others considered these issues when examining the rendition of their internal minds as they perceived them.

Figure 2: An example of Rubin's vase, by Martin Janecek

Once we realize that we can be deceived even at this most basic level of perception, it becomes easier to recognize that other misperceptions can afflict us as well, especially when we evaluate high-level concepts. How deep might the rabbit hole go?

Amos Tversky and Daniel Kahneman began to wonder this shortly after they first met.[90] They examined their own minds to establish their own gaps and went out to experiment with other people to see how tangled we really were. In their initial work, they identified three key biases: availability, representativeness, and anchoring and adjustment.

Availability Heuristic

The availability heuristic arises when we substitute the ease of recalling something for its frequency. For example, shark attacks stick out in our mind, so they're easy to recall. Thus, we believe that shark attacks are more common than is the case. Similarly, because terrorist attacks are traumatic and they are broadcast widely on the news, they appear far more likely. People who are anti-immigrant often cite anecdotes of crimes committed by lone individuals: such incidents are chosen for their peculiar uniqueness. Their luridness causes people to recall them when we talk about immigration reform. A similar issue arose in the 1980s for the United States, where parents acquired a heightened fear of child kidnapping, due to high-profile cases in the nightly news and evening gossip shows. Such crimes were in decline for the years over that period, which has continued to trend as such for most years since. Meanwhile, death by diabetes is not newsworthy, so is comparatively unavailable.

Availability can arise in surprising ways. Another early experiment by Kahneman and Tversky went as follows: given a piece of text, is it likely that there are more words beginning with k, or more words with k as their third letter? Because most people presumably index words in their brain by the first letter, it was easier for people to recall examples where k was first, the word know for example, as opposed to the third, as is the case with ask. As it happens, in most texts it is the third position where k is the most common.

How we are asked questions or how we pose possible futures affects the likelihood we ascribe to them. We can slant our entire decision-making process in this way.

Representativeness Heuristic

The representative heuristic describes the errors we make when we assume that similarity indicates a correct judgment, without considering base probability rates or other countering facts. For example, some situations are extremely rare, so that even if we see something that resembles that situation, it is still probably the case that it is something else. By default, we don't consider that. As an example, if a disease's base probability rate in our population is extremely low and the test for it is inaccurate, then we shouldn't be worried if we take the test and our doctor says it came back positive. Our probability of having the disease is now higher than the base probability rate, but it remains unlikely. Presumably the doctor will now order a more precise test.

Tversky and Kahneman posed a similar scenario known as the taxicab problem. Here, there is a Green and a Blue taxicab company, where 85% of the cabs in the city are Green, and the other 15% are Blue. A person tells us that they saw a Blue taxicab in a hit-and-run at midnight, but it is known their night vision is inaccurate — they only get the color right 80% of the time. People given this example systemically overestimate the probability that the taxicab was blue.[91]

The law of small numbers comes into effect in this heuristic as well. When we have an experimental result from a small group of subjects, we overestimate the strength of that conclusion. Notoriously in scientific research, when we repeat an experiment with another small group and get a different result, rather than concluding that not much can be said as neither sample was large, we instead attempt to find some explanatory factor to differentiate the groups, as if both experiments were sound. When this type of scenario was posed to actual researchers by Tversky and Kahneman, this was the most frequent response, rather than suggesting that we should try again with a larger sample.[92]

In another illustrative case, there is the Linda test. Here a description of Linda was given that keyed into stereotypes of

Deep Management

feminists in the 1970s (when the experiment was done). In the original experiment, it was asked which of ten possible cases described Linda, where one was a bank teller, and one was a bank teller who was involved in feminist causes. People systemically said the second case was the most probable. This is ridiculous as the first includes the second. Kahneman and Tversky even went so far as to run the test with only the two possibilities and no other distractions, and still got a majority picking the second case.[93] We follow specificity.

Kahneman and Shane Frederick later grouped the availability and representativeness heuristics along with others into a subsuming heuristic called attribute substitution.[94] Where the actual target is less accessible (perhaps due to the computational challenge of the problem), this heuristic will replace the target by an associated attribute that is accessible, perhaps due to it being simpler, part of normal perception, or because it was primed by the environment (something made it more available, for instance if it was something we just heard on a podcast).

These errors afflict any type of diagnostic evaluation. In engineering, an example would be whether something is a compiler bug or not. Compiler bugs do occur — they are not so rare as sometimes cited in university compiler courses. Nevertheless, they are unusual. If we are diagnosing a case of a compilation error, it's more often the case that eccentricities in the language generated the fault — some languages can have exotic corner cases. If it's a case of incorrectly emitted assembly code, it's more often that there's a subtle logic error. Or it could even be a rogue memory write. People are too quick to jump to the conclusion that it's the compiler at fault. Nevertheless, sometimes it is the compiler — we saw one or two legitimate cases per year across a floor of a hundred engineers.

Similarly, we can grossly miscalculate results from data analytics. People receive results from a single ten-person playtest and upend months of design. That test can tell us many things, especially if the problem is obvious, such as an impenetrable interface to the game.

When we attempt to establish more refined judgments, however, we need to remember that ten people is far from representative of any category.

Nowadays, the ubiquity of data analytics aggravates this problem. We do have data scientists and technical individuals well versed in the problems of analysis, but many results are broadcast directly to managers, who often act without personal training or validation by experts. And that's ignoring the problem that even data scientists can fall prey to these errors if they're rushed!

Anchoring and Adjustment

We've already discussed utility and how we might perceive it. In earlier chapters, we mentioned that our perception of the status quo can change based on outside events. Consider some chimpanzees in a row of separated wire cages. If they all get cucumbers, the chimpanzees are content. Give one of those chimpanzees a banana, however, and suddenly the other chimpanzees are enraged — they hurl their cucumbers out of the cages, sometimes even at the banana-eater, preferring nothing to what was once acceptable.[95] It turns out we're just like chimpanzees.

This can be a difficult bias to avoid. It's known, for example, that if we mention unrelated large numbers early in a negotiation, we can bias the result — especially if there is no clear reference for what the price should be. If we are negotiating for an object we commonly buy, we're not likely to be budged much by this heuristic. But if we're figuring out the price of a unique painting at an auction with no comparable examples, then we're at risk (consider the Banksy painting "Girl with a Balloon" that started to shred itself after its sale,[96] how much is it worth now?).

In a simple experiment, Kahneman and Tversky showed this by asking students to multiply one of two sums 1x2x3x4x5x6x7x8 and 8x7x6x5x4x3x2x1. The students were then asked to provide an answer before they could reasonably have produced the result. For the first case, the median was 512. For the second, 2250 (40,320 is the correct answer). Thus, it was sufficient for the number eight to be first to result in a guess four times larger. In another example, people spun a casino roulette wheel set to stop at either 10 or 65. The subjects were then asked what percentage of countries in the United Nations are African. Those who were stopped at 10 guessed 25% on average. Those stopped at 65 guessed 45%. No one realizes this is happening to them — it's as if it were an automated reflex.

This can lead to all sorts of bizarre estimation errors. In innovation, there often are few comparable examples, and we don't know how things will play out. Random noise can bloat or shrivel estimates of cost. The cost of a software product upfront is a notoriously difficult value to compute, which is why many just deliver the highest value features first until the money runs out.

Anchoring also generates bias based on age, LGBT+ status, sex, race, nationality, appearance, or any other distinguishable key.[97] It affects not only compensation, but whether our work is viewed as credible or not. Some female scientists change their first names to androgynous forms, especially in disciplines historically associated with men. Many transgender individuals report increased difficulties in finding employment or getting equivalent compensation after they openly transition and change their names. Age-ism is well reported in some fields such as tech. Minorities have reported discrimination when their name is stereotypical of a category, such as name variations more common with African-Americans in the United States. Even for something as simple as booking an AirBNB, this has arisen.[98]

This bias occurs unconsciously, which is part of why it's so insidious. People who believe they are unbiased fall prey to it, as it happens beneath their awareness, just like the roulette wheel affecting our guess for percentages of African countries in the UN. When challenged with evidence of this bias, we often feel uncomfortable —

a result of cognitive dissonance, which we discuss later. This, in turn, drives us to seek out alternative justifications for our actions.

The Filters of Reality

We've only just started to expose the faults that afflict us, but what we've seen so far should warn us how easily we are deceived and how hard it is to recognize that it has occurred. Our understanding of the world is faulty. The choices we enumerate are influenced by unrelated events of the day. The answers we produce are sometimes noise generated by automated reflexes. These are the filters of reality, and since we have only ever seen the world through them, the filters do not seem to exist.

Daniel Kahneman explained this via the acronym WYSIATI[99] (what you see is all there is). More precisely, it's what we think we see that is all there is. Our conception of reality is only a model that we have constructed in our mind, mostly unconsciously. It is a story we have formed. Because it is specific, it is compelling. It can make some futures seem impossible and others trivial, regardless of the truth.

As we learn more about our cognitive errors, however, we can start to develop tools that guardrail us. Even in cases where we can't resolve the feeling of certainty we get from an explanation; we can at least know that we are overestimating its probability of occurrence. Skepticism can provide an entry point to correct our assumptions.

Framing

At this point, we have enough in place to discuss framing and how it impacts value. Since the purpose of our decision-making system is the maximization of customer value, we should do our best to understand how our customers perceive our product.

The models of value that we discussed earlier assume that people view value consistently. These models had already long since incorporated some human factors; after all, Bernoulli built his model to explain deviations from expected norms. It was thought, though, that at least an individual's estimate of utility was stable. Sure, we don't place the same value in pepper that a fifteen-century peasant would, but we view the value of pepper consistently over reasonable spans of our life.

Tversky and Kahneman changed this when they made the statement that we don't care about utility, but rather about perceived utility. This seems obvious but had been excluded from economic models. Again, perhaps hindsight bias on our part. Before we had come to understand cognitive error, the difference might have seemed unimportant. Once we understood the many ways that our perceptions can be altered irrationally, however, we came to realize that perceived utility is a far harder objective to pursue than fixed utility.

The problem is that our perception of value can change in real time. What we hear in the media and from our neighbors can shift our estimation. Irrelevant details can alter our view. Marketing has used this for recorded history, but now we know that these faults are baked into our cognition, not just faults of education and failures of clear-thinking.

This can result in non-intuitive behaviors as we mentioned before in the chapter *Seeking Customer Value*.

Consider again this example: we offer a game that a customer enjoys. The customer wants us to add a feature, and we deliver it; the customer views the feature as solving their problem, so it is a positive value. Except now our product plus this feature resembles more a new category, and the customer now rates us as a whole relative to this new space — this can cause the customer to consider our product to now be less valuable than it was before, even though they still consider the new feature to be a positive gain.

This isn't a toy case. It can happen when indie games begin to look too much like AAA games, or when singleplayer games add multiplayer or GaaS services. A solid product plus a well-received feature now shifts to a new categorization; the customer then views our product as a solution to a different problem, even though they aren't aware of it. In this new space, we are sub-par, so our product is less valuable. In our next chapter *Consider the Hideout*, we discuss an example of this in more detail.

There's more to this story as well. So far, we've only discussed how the customer views the project at a specific point in time, but we usually don't think of the value of our products in that fashion. We'll get back to this idea shortly.

Prospect Theory

Let us take a step back and follow up on research for how people establish value in the moment. Daniel Kahneman and Amos Tversky had already established many fallacies; now they wanted to make inroads against *Homo economicus*. They chose the classic utility functions as their target.

Prospect theory proposed that we view utility not in absolute terms but as losses and gains relative to a status quo, with losses weighted more strongly. We make judgments (sometimes without being aware of our reasoning) and then rank our options from greatest gain to greatest loss. This isn't necessarily automatic; we might struggle a bit, feel out possible futures, and then maybe reconsider a previous option. In the end, we select the best.

That these losses and gains are relative to a status quo is the key point. This is where perceived utility enters. A trader might receive a 500,000 USD bonus, but if they expected a million, that's a loss. Or if their co-worker got a million, that also can be a loss. The status quo is set by external factors. Before they found out their co-worker received a million, they were ecstatic. But after they found out, they're crushed.

Through experimental studies, prospect theory further established that we emphasize losses more than gains, with roughly a 2-to-1 weighting. This is critical when we consider choices that have some probability of gain and correspondingly of loss. The gains and losses are weighted before being combined into a perceived utility. Again, it is the perception of loss or gain that matters.[100] Shortly, we'll also discuss some complexities with respect to guaranteed versus probabilistic losses and gains, which we view distinctly.

Prospect theory can explain some notable behaviors. The Disposition Effect, for example, was noted by Hersh Shefrin and Meir Statman in 1985, when they realized that investors were behaving irrationally. They discovered that traders held onto stocks when their value declined but sold when stock values rose. This is despite the historical evidence that it is usually the case that rising stocks continue to rise and falling stocks continue to fall. This was a clear inefficiency in terms of investing. What came to be understood is that investors liked to lock in gains but hated losses. They held on to the losers in the hopes they would later recover. They sold off the stocks that gained, because future gains were perceived as less valuable relative to the possibility of a subsequent drop. This was eventually explained in terms of the utility model offered by prospect theory.

It should be noted that our perception of value becomes more complex when we consider probabilistic spreads of payouts. Prospect theory is posed in terms of recognized gains and losses. When we are presented with a probabilistic payout where we have some percentage of losing nothing and some percentage of losing something larger, our view of risk changes relative to a fixed loss. We tend to be more willing to take riskier bets. Here, given a guaranteed loss, we will often take a probabilistic bet where the best-case scenario is less of a loss, but the average is lower than the guaranteed loss. This is the opposite of our behavior with gain, where we would rather take a fixed payout of lesser value than the average gain of bet. This makes sense with prospect theory when we mix it in with other biases — what happens is that we are using an asymmetric filter on our utility function, where the filter is the spread of probabilities versus gain.

We also know that human estimations of tail-end probabilities near zero and one are biased away from their actual likelihood, so that the filters are even more deformed when large payouts or penalties are at the edges — and that's ignoring the distortion that can arise from the availability bias, where we have heard of the case occurring at least once, which makes the rare condition seem dramatically more probable than it is.[101] Lottery wins and being struck by lightning would be examples.

What Is Happiness?

We've spoken as if value were something that exists like a score. I eat a sundae, and that provides an amount of happiness for me, just like a happiness dollar. So far, the assumption has been that our lives are a summation of this happiness accounting.

But happiness viewed from when? How do we measure the value of our life, and at what point do we measure it? Is happiness a summation of events? Or is it something else?

Even over short spans of time, our brain reinterprets our evaluation of delight and suffering. Daniel Kahneman became interested in how we view happiness and regret; to explore this topic, he and fellow researchers did many experiments to determine how we perceive these experiences, especially after the fact. In one experiment,[102] he took a group of subjects and exposed them to pain via cold water. For one trial, they put one of their hands into a tub of water at 14C for sixty seconds. Then they put their other hand into a tub of water held at 14C for sixty seconds, which then gradually warmed to 15C after thirty seconds. In both cases, the participants had a dial that they used to continuously indicate their discomfort. Clearly, the second trial as a summation involves greater discomfort — after all, it includes the first case trivially. Still, 70% of participants preferred the second trial. The specific point is that the final experience often frames our recollection of the entirety. Subsequent work has supported this finding of the "Peak-End" Rule and has even led to changes in terms of how some medical procedures are done. It's also a key design strategy for games, fiction, and movies! End on a high note.

How do we then package our estimation of value? Is it just the sequence of positive and negative events, or is it estimated from some key point — for example, the moment we exit the game? Or is it the day after when we think back on our game experience? We might even ask the larger question: do we experience happiness in the moment in any long-term meaningful way, or is it only our recollection that is significant? We must remember, we are delivering value, but it is only after the experience that the customer considers whether it was worth it and whether they want more. This evaluation of after-the-fact worth drives them to either spend more on our product or purchase our next offering.

Kahneman's experiment was only over a short span of time, so we might choose to reject it as meaningful. However, the same effect occurs over the long-haul as well. We know this from everyday life. Consider how we view the long, happy experience that ended poorly. Many divorcees, for example, remember their marriages with bitterness, even though it was good for most of its duration — after the split, they rewrite their history. Some regret years of happiness only due to its outcome — after the fact, they often don't even remember those years as happy.[103] Similarly, an artist might struggle, starve, and suffer miserably for years, but then just before they die, their work is discovered. Suddenly, everything is seen in a different light, and it all becomes meaningful.

It's also well known that we can alter our recollections. Recalling memories reconsolidates them, which transforms them, although we are unaware of the change (just as with anchoring). This can be used as a treatment: sometimes PTSD patients are asked to replay their traumatic experiences, but this time overlay in their mind a story about how the events could have played out differently but didn't. Sometimes people imagine being sent back to comfort themselves. Nothing changes in terms of what happened, but now their perception of helplessness is mitigated. Experiencing negative events again can allow people to change their trauma to a different category, where they were unlucky instead of powerless.[104]

While this example concerns traumatic experiences (and only a few games have been that traumatic), it has broader relevance.

Everyone who works in AAA game development, for example, knows the frustration of negative reviews by players who've played their product for hundreds of hours. The players were happy to sink tens of hours in, but now they're bored, or they don't like a change, and suddenly our game is the most awful one they've ever played. Meanwhile, this other game they played for an hour is the most amazing thing ever.

What then does all of this mean for our delivery of customer value?

The Reality

In the end, there is no easy answer. We still must find some way to work. If we have happy customers who engage more with our product, then that's enough.

There are practical problems that we can be wary of, as we've mentioned. If our product starts looking too much like it belongs to another category, we should be wary that we might start to be compared to a different set of competitors.

As another example, while many products fear jump-off points as they can trigger the loss of players, perhaps it's better to provide off-ramps rather than exhaust our customers until they hate our game —

and thus remember it only as a waste. Alienated players move on, but satisfied players might return in the future or for our next offering.

For games, the natural beats of the product are good reconsolidation points. We already polish these as they're the most memorable and tend to define the entire game experience in our memory, but perhaps another motivation is to make sure that those who drop out of our game end on the highest note possible. Similarly, perhaps we should be careful with cliff-hangers. They can keep players engaged, and that can be good, but not if it drags them onward only a bit more to lose them in a lower quality period. We need to consider pacing.

In practice, we mostly establish feature value as if we were summing incremental value. The legacy of our product should also have a place in our strategy. We should ask how these features might dovetail into the experience of our product or service over time. If we can do both, we will deliver value incrementally and project a quality brand into the future.

Cognitive Dissonance

The previous biases we've discussed distort our understanding and interpretation of what we've seen. Cognitive dissonance explains how our current model of the world resists or adjusts to conflicting external evidence and influences. Despite its negative side, cognitive dissonance no doubt arose as part of our mental defenses, providing a shield of incredulity against other people's beliefs. After all, if we've established that the blue mushrooms are good and the spotted ones are evil, it could be life-threatening to adopt another person's view. If our social cohesion as a tribe is founded on us being the descendants of a local river god, someone else's sun god could shatter our coherence. While cognitive dissonance is an old feature of our brains, our modern global information sphere combined with the conceptual turnover induced by technological and scientific advancement has made cognitive dissonance and its reactions everyday experiences. We see stereotypical responses every night on the news media or from our friends reacting against another group's political line.

Leon Festinger posed the first version of this idea after he studied a UFO cult in the 1950s. The cult leader preached that aliens would descend to her house at midnight on a defined day and bring all believers into their spaceship, and from thence to a utopia in space; meanwhile, the rest of humanity would be annihilated in a flood. Based on his team's observations, Festinger argued that we strive to match our internal model to our external actions and our perceived world state. We do so because we suffer mental tension until discrepancies between perception, action, and internal state are resolved. This can lead to decisions that seem insane to an external observer. In Festinger's book *When Prophecy Fails*, he documented what happened after the designated night of rapture arrived, but no aliens showed up nor did any apocalypse occur. Some of the cultists drifted away, as one would expect. But strangely, those with the most invested in the cult became even more entrenched. They reinterpreted what happened to align better with their internal model — they believed that their dedication impressed the aliens so much that humanity was spared, and thus no ascension was required — the cultists could then continue to spread the word.

Similar events have been noted before. In the Great Disappointment in the United States, the Millerites believed that Jesus Christ would return on October 22, 1844, whereupon the faithful would be raptured and Christ would purge and cleanse the world. The day came and went, and people reacted much the same way as the cult in Festinger's book. Some went their own way quietly after the Great Disappointment. Some stated that they had made a mistake in their computations and that the actual rapture would occur later. Eventually the group that gave rise to the Seventh-Day Adventists interpreted the prophecy to refer to an event occurring in the heavenly plane instead, which they asserted had happened on Oct 22, 1844 as expected.[105] We simply could not perceive it here on Earth.

The tension we feel when our internal model does not match external life can be intense.

We take several approaches to resolve this crisis. Sometimes, we change what we're doing — the case where the cultists drifted away. We can also justify our behavior by altering the nature of the conflict, so that it no longer applies — sure climate change is real, but it's only a problem for low-lying islands or at worst those places in Louisiana below sea level. We can inject a new idea, which then resolves the conflict — it was a heavenly event only. Or we can outright deny the information.

For example, I might know that smoking is harmful, but perhaps I smoke. I could stop smoking, which resolves the conflict. I could justify it by saying that I only smoke occasionally, so it isn't really a problem. I could switch to electronic cigarettes and say that now there's no issue. Or I might deny that smoking is harmful.

For our purposes in management, cognitive dissonance arises most often when we want to resolve the afflictions of organizations. Or when we need to recognize our own afflictions! One impact of cognitive dissonance is that those suffering from it filter out information that conflicts with their model; they also latch onto anything we say that is accidentally erroneous. We must be careful when approaching a project with entrenched views, especially where those views are tied up with team identity. Dealing with cognitive dissonance requires mental judo, where we must avoid triggering others' defenses while simultaneously shifting them onto a better path.

To resolve our own cognitive dissonance, we can use the tension to tell us where to direct our investigations. It's not that our cognitive model is necessarily wrong, but it is where our model is challenged that we are most likely to filter and reject information that runs counter to our views. We should consider these conflicts to be opportunities to seek out the truth.

We'll discuss this topic more in our chapter *Dealing with People* in Part IV, where we cover how we resolve dysfunctions in projects and bring our system into wider use.

Debiasing

Once we accept that we are flawed, what can we do about it?

The most valuable step is to be aware that we are biased at all! It is often shocking to us how easily we are fooled. Once we are aware of our faults, however, we can reflect on our choices, which is the first safeguard we can employ. When a gut instinct rises, we must stop and consider it. When we start to fantasize how a choice leads to an enticing story of our future, we can pause and step outside ourselves to realize that the siren of narrative has caught us.

At the end of every day, it is worthwhile to make a habit of reviewing our decisions and examining whether various biases might have been at play. First, we must detach ourselves from the outcomes and our involvement and observe ourselves as if we were consultants brought in to evaluate our organizational health. Are we making fair estimates of likelihood? Are we where we say we are? Where should we be more uncertain? If we now suspect our choices or if we have encountered new questions, we should write them down once we have explored them in our mind. The time to engage in such introspection can seem challenging to find, but it pays off more than longer hours at work.

Nudges[106] are also a common approach to sneak past our cognitive faults. The trick about reflection is that we must trigger it. But we know that many cognitive faults occur imperceptibly. We can train ourselves to catch these glitches to some degree, but there is never a warning light. Regardless, we cannot fairly expect every one of our employees to be masters of self-introspection. For any number of reasons, they might not value the skills or have the time.

Thus, it is worthwhile to consider methods where we shift employee behavior in positive ways. For example, the default choice is the one we take lazily. If we make sure that the default choice is the one that is preferable for the organization, then our employees will often take that path, only overriding the default when it is necessary. As a simple example, when engineers want to submit code to the mainline, the default is that their submit will be rejected if the mainline is already broken. We need to be able to override this behavior for a fix to resolve the issue, so there is an option that requires some effort from the engineer to enable. People still might cheat and use this means regardless, but they know we'll track it and it takes effort, so they're more likely to just wait. Ideally, a nudge should be a behavioral shift that our employees agree with, and would want to engage in.[107]

For another case, in our decision-recording application (if we have one), we might display UI screens with tips for common biases before users commit a choice. For example, remind them that something that looks like a rare event might be better explained by a more common cause we haven't considered yet. This could trigger a moment of reflection.

Another common approach is reference-class forecasting. This is the outside view we discussed earlier. Part of our problem is that we often evaluate our choices from the inside — by which we mean that we consider what software we need to build, what problems we need to solve, and what our plan should look like. Reference-class forecasting is an approach to invert this. We look outside the company to find external examples of similar decisions and see how they played out. A problem here is that we often lack enough information or examples to use this for sound decision-making. It can, however, help illuminate self-deceptions. If we think something is easy, but we know that many other companies have struggled with it, then this can point out a flaw in our assumptions.

In the end, we can never make ourselves unbiased. We can mitigate some of our errors and purify our thinking to some degree.

We can have our co-workers check us and point out where we've gone astray. Our processes can guardrail against our worst mistakes. Our tools can nudge us back onto the path.

If the shields we put in place to constrain our errors slow us down too much, however, we will need to prune them. There is a balance between moving fast and being sound.

7

Consider the Hideout

When we advocate pursuing customer value and magnifying it to high resolution, sometimes people don't grasp what we mean. We require value to be an obsession; we never stop striving to illuminate our customer's needs. Many people focus on the product itself — this is akin to focusing on the oven rather than customer's desire for hot pizza. Or they think of the customer in terms of population segmentations for marketing, but that is treating the customer as a resource for exploitation — again, not sustainable.

For those rooted in product development this obsession is old news. This is seeking to the root cause of business success over the long term. We listen to the customer without judgment, and then we seek to understand the customers' needs at a deeper level than even they might be able to articulate.

To clarify the types of questions we should ask, this chapter expounds a specific case. This is a constructed example that blends considerations from multiple games. It shouldn't be considered as a representative analysis of any specific game, whether one we have personally worked on in the past or otherwise.

The example feature we will consider is that of a player character's home base or hideout. In games like *Star Wars: Knights of the Old Republic*, this hideout was the player's ship. In *Dragon Age: Origins*, this was a camp site. In *Dragon Age: Inquisition*, it was a castle. *Fallout 4* had your primary home village. *The Division* had the warehouse. *Anthem* had Fort Tarsis.[108] Each of these types of bases serves common needs for our customer.

To frame our case study, let us imagine our game is a science-fiction tale, where the players are renegades in a large section of the galaxy dominated by autocratic empires. The players strive to live free under the empires' radar, surviving by preying on AI-operated merchant ships while dodging the combat vessels that defend them. Early in the game, players cobble together a hideout in the asteroid field of an unpopulated and uncharted star system that happens to have a forgotten interstellar waygate from a previous war.

Our game is meant to be space travel and ship-to-ship combat primarily. The viewpoint in space is a camera outside our vessel, not from inside the ship. Our core game loop is to take the waygate into a hyperstream and then go to an interesting star system where we seek rich prey and battle empire ships for our survival. Other players can be allies or enemies. The game is a GaaS (game as a service), has a back-end for transactional services, and runs on dedicated servers.

In their hideout, the player can build a pirate town populated by free-loving peoples. Merchants buy loot and sell weapons. We can build a shipyard that fixes our vessels and allows us to build larger hulls. Taverns keep our people happy and provide a source for new crew. Some citizens mine valuable elements from within the system, or they operate oxygen and food farms to keep the town sustainable. The player thus becomes both a space-faring pirate captain and the

Deep Management

mayor of a free-wheeling utopia for those seeking a better if harsher life.

There are many ways the above feature can be realized. As we will discuss, different players will prefer distinct solutions. We must align our design with their problems.

Why a Base at All?

This should always be an upfront question. The cheapest feature is the one we never do (which relates to the policy of deciding late — see Part III). Not only are unnecessary features wastes of resources for development and maintenance, they also clutter our users' experience.

While Blizzard's *Overwatch* does have a waiting room between matches, out-of-match management activities occur in user interfaces that aren't part of the fictional world. This is true of Blizzard's *Heroes of the Storm* as well. These games, though, have no sense of an embodied player avatar. While a player might prefer particular characters, they're free to switch — even between rounds of a match if they believe doing so will improve their team's chances of victory. For our game, the choice of a specific ship hull can fill that role of adaptability, but the pirate captain always uniquely embodies the player.

For many games, a base makes sense. Firaxis Games' *XCom: Enemy Unknown* has a hidden base from which the players launch missions. They can also use it to improve the capabilities of their team and shoot down alien vessels. In *The Division*, the warehouse is again an upgradeable location that allows the player to make their own mark and upgrade their gear. Games such as Blizzard's *World of Warcraft* and EA Bioware's *Star Wars: The Old Republic* have had personal bases at various times (for *The Old Republic*, the longest standing version of such a base was the player's personal ship). Those games along with Bungie's *Destiny* also have shared social spaces that offer a hub for missions, buying and selling, and story development.

In our game, we don't want the player to feel like they're just a ship in space. We want to have the experience of being a pirate captain. We allow them to buy and pilot new ship types, so a base gives the player an identifiable core. They can express advancement through upgrades. And we can also express the pirate captain in some form as an embodied avatar in the hideout, depending on how we choose to implement it.

For our decision-making system, this is only the hypothesis that commences the loop. We've posited this as a story, but we need to prove it out. What should the hideout look like? What are the aspects that our players enjoy? Most importantly, who are our players and what do they want? As we'll see later, different propositions for our customers imply different resolutions to problems.

We can consider the expected game loop. The player leaves their asteroid base and engages in activities in a distant star system. After they complete an activity, do they wish to return to the hideout, or would they prefer to continue onward? Some games require the player to return, which can be an error of design. The hideout should offer the player something that entices them, but they should be free to continue if they wish. Our design should align with the needs of the player, not the player with our design. If they never want to return, then clearly, we haven't justified the feature. Perhaps the game would be better off without it.

Possibilities for the Hideout

We must now flesh out our proposed feature. Two key propositions must be evaluated: first, whether the hideout should be a navigable environment, a standard 2D UI, or an advanced UI embedded in a 3D world; second, whether the hideout should be a mostly offline or an entirely online experience.

Deep Management

Navigable World

While our game is about space travel with a viewpoint exterior to the ship, we could have our pirate captain walk around the hideout as a navigable space. We could assume some form of technology that generates gravity, or that the base uses spin to induce an equivalent. This makes navigation simpler for players. While we don't discuss it here, it could be interesting to consider a zero or low-g version as well. It could also be interesting with spin pseudogravity to make it a smaller space, so the player can look up and see the other side of the hideout above them. We should not lose our focus on the customer here, however, and remember that player comfort is a critical need.[109] If we induce nausea in our customers, they will not like our solution.

There's a clear argument for allowing players to move about the hideout space, as it could embody the character's advancement in the world. Allowing players to wander also exposes the scale of their space vessel — given the in-game viewpoint cameras, our ships might seem like toys otherwise. When a player stands next to their ship in the dock, however, the space vessel's enormity can be realized.

Let us consider how the experience of the hideout might play out for the player if this direction were taken. To start, the hideout is a separate level. In some games, the home base is embedded into the world. For our case, we have no interest in expressing the size of our galactic sub-section and we use waygates to warp around anyway. We have no gameplay involving flying in our own personal star system, so when the player arrives at their hideout, they start in the docks next to their ship. The player can then walk out into the main hub of the town and go to whatever building they want.

User Interface over the World

For the user interface overlaid over the hideout, there are two main versions with different levels of realization.

The first mode is the lighter one, and more directly akin to that of *XCom: Enemy Unknown*. Here we provide a flat 2D visualization of the hideout. For *XCom*, this menu corresponded to a vertical slice cut through the player's hidden base. For our pirate hideout, it could be the same, or a circular hub, or perhaps even pseudo 3D, with a background and a hideout layer over the top, as is the case with Red Hook Studio's *Darkest Dungeon*. As with *XCOM*, some buildings when clicked would take the player into a 3D cinematic stage for higher-resolution interactions — perhaps a cinematic scene starts, where the player captain appears in the tavern before the bartender and can pick between speech options to determine their next steps. In cases without story, it might make more sense to go straight to a standard UI, as with a merchant's buying/selling screen.

The second mode is still a user interface in functionality but is embodied in a 3D world. The camera focuses on whatever building we currently have selected and does a transition whenever we switch focus — flying between destinations or doing wipes or dissolves between scenes. Compared with the navigable hideout, there are many visual shortcuts that can be taken with assets to make them lighter in this version, while still offering a 3D world. Players are much more constrained in terms of what they can see and how close they can get to objects, so less textures and mesh data is required. Also, some lighting situations are simplified, as we can prevent complex situations from being viewable.

General Hideout Traits

In all versions of the hideout, navigable or UI, many of the buildings start as blank lots and then can be upgraded to offer increasing levels of functionality. Perhaps when the game starts, the

Deep Management

hideout isn't even full size — just two derelict, broken-down space-station chunks rammed together! The functionality offered at this point is minimal. Once players get some loot, they select what they want to upgrade first. Maybe for the first version of the shipyard, they jam a derelict merchant freighter into the side of the station to offer more space, which also allows the player to build a new ship with a different hull. Further upgrades offer more weapon types and hulls and improve the appearance of the jury-rigged shipyard.

For the 2D UI, this is just an image replacement. For the 3D user interface, we substitute new meshes and textures, plus potentially lighting data. For the navigable experience, we generally have the same new data as for the 3D UI, but it is higher resolution. We also might need new path-finding data if a building now blocks us — or we might have fenced these areas off from the start. Maybe for the 3D versions, there are also new NPCs related to the buildings with whom we can interact.

Multiplayer versus Offline

While we are describing a multiplayer game, we haven't discussed whether the hideout itself should be multiplayer or not. This isn't a trivial question as the options cater to different players. Again, in Blizzard's *Overwatch* out-of-match activities are all handled by back-end transactions, not as actions within a playable space. In Bungie's *Destiny*, on the other hand, all activities are in the station with other players.

The question then is should the hideout be shared by multiple players or not. For the game we're describing, this generally means backed by a dedicated server or not, but technically a different network topology like peer-to-peer (P2P) could be used. We should note that while we say there is an off-line hideout mode, the hideout is still connected to the back-end services for transactional activities like buying and selling, completing and issuing missions, and so on.

Our key issue here is what do the players want? Regardless of cost, there are unavoidable negative consequences to having a heavyweight hideout — for example, load time and travel. There are also compelling positives. What do the players expect? To just buy/sell/upgrade? To engage in laser gun duels? Like Firaxis Games' classic *Sid Meier's Pirates!*, do we need dancing to impress the sector governor's daughter? Do we expect to share our hideout experience with other player captains, strangers or otherwise?

The Value Propositions

Having defined possible directions, let us consider hypotheses about how different customer archetypes might engage with these feature sets. For the propositions we've defined, some players will find that a particular choice ruins the game, whereas others find it compelling. I've specifically avoided cases where customers either find the feature neutral/good, or somewhat good/excellent. Obviously, if all customers dislike a feature, it needs to go.

We will be considering the impacts of loading speed and walking time, and offline versus online hideouts. We will end with a discussion of how the hideout can be a case that exposes irrational customer estimations of value.

Loading Speed and Walking Time

A key question concerns how a player experiences our game loop. How often do players transit to the hideout? All the time? Rarely? Can players avoid going to the hideout altogether? Later we will consider how the organization of activities affect the player experience.

One reason why *Overwatch* has no hideout equivalent, is that *Overwatch* players just want to get into matches as rapidly as possible. Team-based PVP is where *Overwatch*'s value is located.

Deep Management

Players don't want to loiter in their own *Overwatch* tower. The "business" side of the game — buying skins for their favorite players, unlocking loot chests, and so on — is all handled through rapidly reachable UIs (which often have a bit of 3D pizazz to make them pop). Players get enough of a break waiting for the matchmaker to set them up for their next game. The longer the break in between matches, the more likely the player is to end their game session.

We might also consider the case of CCP Games' *Eve Online*, which after their release added a space-station experience in their expansion *Incarna*. Before this expansion, players were only embodied as their captain in the form of a UI portrait. *Incarna* made them into full 3D avatars that could walk around inside navigable space-station interiors. By and large, the player base met this feature with a shrug. People didn't play *Eve Online* to walk around space stations. Players viewed it as a low-value waste of time and so they didn't engage. Social interaction occurred through other venues. The value for these players lays elsewhere — the space station was a distraction.

For many games, however, such a feature worked well. We need to consider why these different consumers placed more value on these features.

An effective distinction is often this: the higher the level of realization we require, the longer the load experience must be when one travels to the hideout. Navigable hideouts require the greatest load times; on PS4/Xbox One era hardware, it can often be around a minute. The 2D hideout is much less, and sometimes can be kept always loaded. The 3D UI hideout sits between these two extremes; it requires less realization than the navigable hideout, but probably too much to store in memory all the time.

Thus, we must consider how our player wants to experience our game. If the player faces a one-minute load every time they enter the hideout, having a hideout at all can be a negative experience if we force them to return between maps or to complete missions. Such customers might demand that we move the functionality in the hideout into the star-system maps or into an out-of-game UI experience like that of *Overwatch*. For such a player, the hideout is waste. The 2D UI hideout, though, might be fine as it has a faster response loop. Maybe we test, and we find out they don't mind the stage loads; otherwise, the hideout is in memory, so it's instantaneous. Or perhaps the faster load into the 3D UI hideout is low enough compared to the navigable hideout, given that they appreciate the higher levels of realization.

Another player, however, might prefer being able to walk around as their captain. Immersion in games is a powerful experience. They might enjoy hanging out in the hideout and watching the NPCs. For them, the load isn't a big deal, because they might spend the next ten minutes there. Perhaps they need to plan their next outing. In a survival version of our game, they might need to analyze their burn rate and calculate how many supplies they need and should put at risk for their pirate run. If this all takes substantial time, the time spent on each load isn't so bad.

We need to engage with our players and understand how they experience our game. If we want to favor the team-based PVP crowd, we need to bend to their preferences. If we decide the resource-limited survival game players are our base, then that becomes our litmus test. If we attempt to cater to everyone, we will not be able to understand the value of features to anyone. We lose the ability to establish which feature provides more value. And that harms the perceived value of our products.

Loading speed isn't the only issue, however. For the navigable hideouts, we must walk between the various stations we interact with. Thus, not only do we need to load into this world, we then need to walk to the merchant. The same players who dislike load times generally dislike wasting time walking. The players who prefer immersion, however, find that walking has value in and of itself — if the added time isn't excessive.

We should analyze this case for our players by using an approach akin to value-stream mapping, which we discuss in Part III. Here, we

Deep Management

consider the value of moment-to-moment gameplay as a first cut (remembering, of course, how our mind can transform our recollection of moment-to-moment value). Time spent loading is negative value to the player. Walking around the hideout can be negative, zero, or positive, depending on the player we are modeling. The other activities all presumably have value. We can then consider for different models of players how our value proposition for a version of the hideout plays out. If 10% of their time is spent doing zero or negative value activities, that's bad design — certainly the lower the percentage the better. Many would call me out for such a high value! If the player gets to what they want fast, that's good design. If they spend lots of time indulging in the offerings of the hideout, then the navigable hideout can be a feature suited towards our game, although development cost could still be a factor. We might find, though, that it is an unsuitable feature even if it were free.

In Bioware's game *Anthem*,[110] at least at launch, Fort Tarsis suffered from the exact problems we described above. Story progression forces the player back into the fort and requires seeking out NPCS spread across the map. Many players noted that this breaks them out of the game flow, when they would rather just continue playing in the open world. They introduced a shared player space in front of Fort Tarsis called the Launch Bay to mitigate this, which provides access to key vendors.

The fort also posed a problem in terms of development costs. While the world of *Anthem* outside the walls gets positive reviews, the fort itself is often described as lifeless. Bioware took on an extra chunk of content and appears to have lacked enough capacity to implement and optimize functionality for a fort experience that popped. No doubt they preferred to focus their polish efforts on the open world. Unfortunately, the lackluster quality of the fort aggravates the problem of being forced to return.

This has led many players to pan Fort Tarsis. They comment that they'd rather skip the load and just continue with the next mission.

While there are story elements that occur in the fort, to some players those elements aren't sufficiently compelling. They'd rather blow up more enemies in the open world. Since *Anthem* is also a co-op game, time in the fort can also result in friends waiting for the other members of their group. Everyone must finish their accounting activities before they can head back out.

We must ask every experience we offer to pull its weight. When it can't, we need to dig out the root cause of why it is failing. If we can resolve the root issues, then we must do so. If we can't, then we need to stop, step outside ourselves, and ask what we are doing. Either the feature should not exist, and we cut it, or if it must due to customer expectations, some resolution must be found. If we don't ask every experience to answer for its existence, our players eventually will.

As much as possible, every hypothesis about our customers should be based on empirical tests. We might begin with theory crafting, but until we expose our scenarios to players, we are building on sand. Our measurement systems should be giving us feedback from the earliest stages of development, even if our feature is only a mock-up in game. It is a cycle, as we interact with our players to determine who they are and what they want, and then expose them to possible outcomes to see if that matches. That in turn can show us that we haven't yet understood our players' needs. Once we are live, we need to continue to track how much time they spend engaging in these activities to see whether they warrant further investment. It might be that this also suggests we should cut a feature but bear in mind the disproportionate weight players ascribe to removed functionality — oftentimes, we are stuck with what we ship with, even if it appeals to only a sliver of our player community.

Deep Management

Offline Versus Online Hideouts

For the navigable hideout, one pitch might be that it is purely the player's base and no one else can be there — this mode is only online for back-end transactions like merchants and mission acceptance/completion. While we're mostly ignoring cost in our discussion, if players spend a great deal of time in the hideout, this can reduce our expenses for supporting online gameplay via dedicated servers. That can be a bit of a red herring as an argument, however, because our game is primarily out in space, so we should aim to have little time in the hideout anyway.

Another pitch might be that the player encounters other captains in the hideout. One variant could be that we each see our own version of our base (so collision meshes would need to be identical regardless of upgrade level), but we are visible to each other. This can be a bit weird in that each of us sees our individual hideout while interacting, but it is often accepted as a compromise. The other common alternative is that the pirates live in a common city, where progression isn't visibly expressed in the hideout generally but rather shows up by merchants not displaying options we haven't unlocked. Or we combine modes and have a shared space for most of the functionality, but individuality is expressed in a uniquely owned set of rooms or the inside of our ship.

A negative side from the player point of view is that these social arenas often require some form of matchmaking. Players need to be scheduled on to dedicated servers, and dedicated servers have maximum capacities. In the worst case, it might be that there aren't enough hideout servers to handle the demand, so players queue to wait until either a new spot opens, or new hideout servers get spun up. Thus, the same players who dislike long loads might dislike this feature. They just want to get into the hideout and get out, perhaps in less time than it would take for matchmaking and loading to finish.

Some players also dislike other people. They might enjoy seeing other captains out in space but prefer their home base to be inviolate.

Odd as this may seem, some MMO aficionados prefer not to interact with others. They enjoy seeing people out in the game space from a distance, but that is all.

For other types of players, the possibility of interaction is a rich one. They can meet others, form groups, brag, show off their awesome outfits and character customization, gossip, role-play, or engage in any of the other myriad interactions people enjoy in multiplayer spaces. This creates an entirely new type of customer that we might not have considered. Here, we have players who enjoy spending time socializing, and so while they go out to hunt in distant star systems, they might be even more invested in the hideout game. Maybe they'll want to have laser pistol duels, dance-offs, or be able to play dice for rare metals with other players! If we favor these customers, it means we need to reevaluate our value propositions for hideout activities.

After all, maybe the real value for our players is to see their stolen lace-and-silk pirate dress on their avatar, and they don't care about walking around. Perhaps they only want a customization room. Or maybe to perceive value, they need to wear their outfits in a shared world, because their stuff is only worthwhile if other players can see it (and envy it). Bioware recognized this in *Anthem*, as Fort Tarsis is by default a single player experience. They added the Launch Bay feature to offer players a chance to show off while readying for another run.

Thus, we can frame this discussion as we did for load times and the time spent navigating the hideout. We again focus down to determine the nature of our players and match the features to their needs, potentially learning more about them as we go.

There is something special about the offline/online case and the meaning of value, however, that we need to point out, especially given that we've already talked about the irrationality of human perception of value in the previous chapter. When we create a navigable hideout meant to be off-line only, there is a risk that we remind the player of other games with similar features. Some of these games have shared bases. This can ironically cause a feature that is viewed as positive to cause the entire product to be viewed negatively.

The Problem of Anchoring

Normally, we'd expect that if we added a feature that the customer wanted, this would always be perceived as beneficial. That's a rational expectation. As we discussed in the previous chapter, however, this isn't always the outcome.

The problem is, users perceive value relative to a framing that compares the product with others in the same category. If the user perceives our product as belonging to the same space, their perception of added value from a feature will be rational. If, however, that feature causes our customer to perceive that our product now belongs to a different category, we can end up in the situation where adding a feature that the customer values now makes the product appear less valuable holistically. This occurs because the problem we are solving has shifted beneath us.

If adding the hideout as a navigable experience reminds the players of social hubs in other games, and we choose to not make our hideout a social space, the lack of other players could now become a severe defect. With a non-navigable hideout, it might not have been perceived as such, as it wasn't as comparable. By edging too close to another category, we induce unexpected demand.

Thus, giving the player something they want can cause them to reevaluate the entire product as worse than it was.

That this happens is sometimes surprising to developers, but we see it all the time in game reviews. AAA games are reviewed relative to other AAA games. Meanwhile, an indie game created by two people with a niche audience might get far higher ratings than a vastly more feature-rich AAA game. The reviewers and users weren't rating them relative to each other. As consumers of reviews, we don't want them to; if we're engaging with an indie game, we want to know how good it is within that category and how well it addresses its key niche experience. When that game begins to resemble a AAA game, our view of the product flips; we now want to know how it rates relative to other AAA games. Partially, this happens because the audience shifts, but even with the same fixed audience this can happen. As we discussed in our previous chapter on *Game and Decision Theory*, we humans estimate utility relative to a reference point, and that reference point can be adjusted by external conditions.

Pragmatically, perceived customer value is the only thing worth pursuing. We can't argue with our customers. This means that we must be aware of the context in which our customers evaluate the features of our product. It's often best to steer clear of spaces that will drag us into competitions where we lack resources to compete. Even if that feature is something our players want.

What's the Final Answer?

Well, we won't be answering that in this chapter. In fact, we can't! There are no doubt wrong answers for all customers, but the right answer depends on the customer we wish to pursue. Do our players want to indulge in the hideout, or do they want to get in and then get out? Do they value a social arena outside the depths of space? It depends. Some people hate what other people love. We must focus on delivering a perfect experience according to our Razor first, and never compromise our customers.

It's even possible that we've gotten our proposition backwards the entire time! This is something to be sensitive to. The market for space-battle games could be limited. We might need to invert our offering and pivot to new customers. Such a game could center on the hideout with piracy now as a side show. Perhaps there is an engaged audience that wants to relax after work or when their kids go to sleep — they don't want constant explosions, but quiet beauty. We abandon the asteroid-base idea and move to new environs, allowing our game to be a staycation with bright, HDR-lit, alien vistas. Piracy remains a spice, but no longer needs to deliver a core experience. It's just a fun way to break up the game and get some resources to improve our new virtual home. The core of our offering then becomes a space *Stardew Valley or Animal Crossing*. Or maybe we give up on the piracy altogether!

Obviously, this is only a possibility, intended to remind us that we must listen to our customers. The space game could be exactly what's needed; if we see our customers in high resolution, we will be able to see whether this is true or not. For most developers, their potential audience is a non-differentiated mass of individuals with varying unrecognized and conflicting desires. This causes us to fixate on the product as a platonic ideal instead of as a solution for people's needs — again, the story of the master oven versus the desire for pizza. When we can't see the people we're trying to help, we fixate on what we're building. When we see them in detail, however, we can separate out the needs of different groups and find the audience we want to engage with, rather than throwing some product at all of them at once. If they need a full space-piracy game, we create that. If they want a hideout game, then that's our product. Whatever solves their problem.

8

Twisted Reflections

It is easier to fix teams that recognize their own limitations. It is harder to fix teams who have over time constructed warped structures atop an idea that is true, where that truth gives the team its sense of worth.

There is a classic story. A scholar visits a wise master to learn Zen. The master pours tea for them both. With the visitor's tea cup, however, the master continues to pour even after the cup has started overflowing. When the visitor points this out, the master says that it is easy to fill an empty cup with fresh tea, and impossible to add fresh tea to a cup that is already overflowing.[111]

Established teams and organizations are often averse to accepting change, even when clear signals warn of problematic behaviors. Change, after all, means that we have been doing it wrong, else why would we need to change? This is hard for the ego to bear. Teams that are either new or young, meanwhile, have not yet committed to a mode of thought, so can be much simpler to handle.

When a team's self-view is founded upon a seed of truth, but a dysfunctional network of behaviors has grown atop it, that team is suffering from a twisted reflection. Cognitive dissonance will cause the team to mistake criticism of the dysfunctional network for an attack on the core seed. Since the core seed is true, they can defend it, and thus conclude that they have rejected our argument, even though we never asserted that the core truth was false. Since failure is sometimes out of our control, the team after rejecting our cure can then maintain that their problems were only bad luck, not a flaw in their approach. They often believe that adopting our approach would increase their rate of failure.

A twisted reflection is distinct from other simpler misperceptions. There is a similar affliction that occurs when something that we perceive can be taken ambiguously. A simple case would be the Rubin's Vase image we have discussed previously, where the black-and-white painting can be taken either as a vase or as two faces staring at each other, depending on whether we take black or white to be the background. This is a case where there are two equally valid impressions. If a team is seeing only one state, we can work to show them the alternative; since both are correct, we do not threaten their world view.

For this to work, we must see as they see. We described in chapter 6 the case of "The Dress." Here, a picture went viral after people discovered that they disagreed vehemently about whether the dress had gold and white bands, or blue and black bands. Depending on how our brain interprets the external lighting conditions of the picture, we see the dress either way. If the team sees the world the wrong way, and we see it the correct way, but we do not recognize that it is legitimately possible to perceive the world as the team does, we will be unable to remedy their afflictions. If we understand that there are two views and how each arises, then we can solve the crisis.

For this case, there is no true seed for the team, only a misperception that we can refute.

A twisted reflection is a harder case than either of these, as there is a valid truth upon which dysfunction has been built. The view of the team is partially wrong, so it not the case of Rubin's Vase. Nor is it the case of "The Dress" as the seed is true. This is a trickier situation, and one where we can paint ourselves into a corner if the team rejects our initial arguments. If we understand how to solve twisted reflections, however, we can deal with the other two cases as well.

Later in this chapter, we'll describe some specific cases of twisted reflections, but first let us consider how to break them apart. It isn't easy, and it requires that we gain the trust of the team. We are being brought in from the outside, and that is by default an adversarial role. Our beginning is thus unstable. If the team feels that we challenge the truth of their core premise, they will dismiss us as being in error. From that point, it is hard to recover. We must also be careful not to take their side too closely, as this could make us appear inauthentic when we later point out their dysfunction. If they believe that we were dishonest with them from the start, they will reject us. We must avoid going native. In between these two extremes, we can maintain our status as outsiders with no agenda to push. If they are not threatened, they will be slower to react against us, which can give us the time necessary to engage them.

First, we must get the team to understand that there is a problem symptomatically. At this point, we don't yet explain the cause. Even if they resist and argue that many teams struggle with their customer definition, if they have repeatedly failed, they will at the least acknowledge that this is a problem, even if they still believe it is a common one. If the team from the start believes that there is no issue, we cannot make headway.

Once the team agrees that the situation could be better, we need to ensure that we support the seed of truth that they uphold. Celebrate it even. Make it such that they feel dissonance if they try to dismiss us by using that seed against us. It is important to do this before we address the affliction, as otherwise they might lock us out. Then we need to make sure we understand the dysfunction. We cannot move forward unless we have come to grips with it, or we will make the situation worse. Oftentimes, the problem is that the seed of truth was viewed as a core team principle, but there were no other principles to constrain it. Thus, the truth was driven to extremes that make no sense. In this case, the solution is to start injecting those other principles, which need to be obvious enough that the team accepts them. Then we show that the dysfunctional behavior is occurring because there are multiple truths, but we are paying attention only to one. In other situations, a truth is placed into a context where it can be perverted, often by hidden incentives to agents within our organization. In this case we must show the team how this can occur, so that they can build guardrails to prevent or detect misbehavior while still benefiting from the core good. This is the case with the twisted reflection that can arise out of KPIs (Key Performance Indicators).

Examples of Twisted Reflections

Let us consider some common examples.

Consider this: high morale leads to superior productivity. This is well backed by research. On average, high-morale teams perform superior to low-morale teams, and the margin is substantial. This pillar alone, however, can be taken to extremes if not bounded by other principles.

Sometimes management will conceal information from their teams, fearing that realistic appraisals of problems will damage morale. In team meetings, negative feedback is suppressed — everyone should always be positive. In one case I have seen, at the end of every leads meeting, all attendees needed to give a thumbs up or a thumbs down regarding their "mood" for that week on the state of the project. Those who put their thumbs down would be pressured outside the meeting to conform. The only proper result was all thumbs up. Even when the project was clearly in a poor state, it had to be this way. The idea was, this would bolster the morale of the leads which would trickle down to the floor. There was enormous pressure to not be the person who gave a thumbs down, no matter how challenging or problematic that week was, or how much the leadership team needed to address a systemic issue.

The argument for this was that this is how a positivist culture works; the truth is that this isn't positivism at all. This is where the twisted reflection occurs. A positivist culture is one that recognizes problems and challenges but asserts that no problem is unsolvable. For a positivist culture to work well, information must flow freely, and we need constructive feedback — if we do not see the problems, we cannot fix them. Constant and unrelenting self-improvement is the mark of positivism, which requires self-awareness. In positivist teams, members know that they have access to the best information possible, so that if a solution is reachable, they have a chance of achieving it. Team members pull together with management and even in hard times, camaraderie prevails.

With the twisted reflection, there is an attempt to deny the existence of problems. Top management wants to prevent anyone from thinking the leadership has made mistakes. After all, in this view, the problems belong to the domain of high leadership, not the project as a whole; the team leads need to keep in their own lane and do their assigned tasks with a positive attitude. However, when the team sticks their thumbs up at the end of the meeting, far from being left in a good mood, they are left alienated. Even if outside of the meetings they discuss their concerns with their peers — thus they rationally know others share them — while they are in the meeting and see everyone else put their thumbs up, they get the feeling that they alone see the issues, and thus perhaps it is a flaw in themselves, not in the project. This affliction corrodes and demoralizes teams, despite being founded on the premise that high morale is good. Our staff are made to doubt their own expertise and experience. They can even be made to doubt their recollection of past events.[112]

It is difficult for a management team that has fallen into this affliction to escape. To do so, they must learn to trust their team and treat them as equals — effective principles to counter this affliction are humility, trust, transparency, and root-cause analysis. This affliction arises when management views team members as a means to an end, rather than as ends in themselves. Rather than engaging with their team members, management views them as tools with statistics such as morale that must be controlled. When management is faced with the damage they are causing, they will argue back that the alternative will demoralize the team, potentially destroying it. If we force leadership to enact transparency, sometimes they will exaggerate conditions to induce fear, thus trying to make their own prophecy come true. To reference a common development metaphor, they will claim that we cannot let the team see the sausage being made.

To be fair, the team doesn't need to see every twitch in leadership. We can filter out the noise. Our teams are always trustworthy enough to handle the signal. If not, that is a team that should be shut down. To get that message across to top management, however, can be difficult. This affliction arises because managers sees a specific kind of world where our argument seems insane. We must try to re-educate them, but if this view has become so entrenched that top leadership undermines necessary changes, leadership will need to be switched out. With patience the team can be saved, and good teams are quite valuable.

While we have stated that the thumbs up/down approach is bad, there are related practices that are not problematic. First, the thumbs up or down itself isn't bad if it's meant to be an actual signal. If we use it to ask who needs help this week, we can use this as a jump-off point to get down to the floor and smooth out issues. After all, on any given week we should expect that some of our teams are encountering more challenges than usual, while others are enjoying a smoother run. With such a policy, we should see quite a few thumbs down every week. If someone has a problem and they don't signal it, that's an error on their part. When people feel safe to say they are having a rough week, we are in a healthy climate. If we almost always see thumbs up, however, we know there is a dysfunction.

Cheerleading meetings are another approach that has validity. Here, we aren't projecting that everything is great, we're just getting hyped. Sales teams often do this. Here people might be asked to let forth their barbaric yawps[113] amidst their peers. While this isn't something we personally enjoy or advocate, we don't think such practices are meant to warp the team, but rather to pump up their energy for high-intensity activities. The distinction can be subtle.

Since it is related, we will note another fallacy, where management mistakes correlation for causation. This is more akin to "The Dress," in that we see something that we believe is true, but if we were more careful, we would recognize that it is mistaken. Again, we start knowing that high-morale teams are superior in productivity. Sometimes, if people have been on high-morale teams, they will note that such teams often work more overtime. Whether this is good or bad is a separate consideration (see our later chapter on *The Hero Complex*). Let us assume for the moment it is good. What some managers will do then is institute policies of mandated crunch, using the logic that since they noticed crunch on high-morale teams, crunch cooks up greatness. The reality is that high-morale teams feel a sense of purpose, and so often push themselves hard. Mandating crunch on damaged projects results in low-morale teams. This can be a hard mentality to break, as top managers will cite anecdotal evidence. Moreover, both Confucian and Protestant ethics (among others) maintain that hard work is moral. What we must do in this case is raise our principle of root-cause analysis: before jumping to death marches, let us figure out why our team isn't high morale and resolve that first. Then the team will have purpose and our primary concern will be whether letting them crunch on their own accord is wise or not.

Let us consider some other common twisted reflections.

We mentioned one earlier in this book: the notion that the team is more important than the project (in the chapter *Seeking Alignment*). We won't belabor this discussion too much as we've already covered it but let us take a moment. Here, the true pillar is that great teams deliver more value over the long term, whereas focus on a specific project can damage the team. Thus, preferring the team is usually the correct bet. As we pointed out, though, the team exists to solve problems in a class, not arbitrary ones. The team is shaped by learning how to solve specific customer needs, not abstract issues of team cohesion. Thus, they must focus on the project's success to become a team that is good at solving problems within their space. While we accept some failure as we embrace risk, the team should always act to succeed. Management must then monitor and nudge the team when they believe there is a risk of burnout or other similar problems.

As a related issue, we might examine the question of whether failure is good. Here let us start by quoting Clayton Christensen: "Managers accept flaws, missteps, and failure as an inevitable part of the process of innovation. They have become so accustomed to putting Band-Aids on their uneven innovation success that too often they give no real thought to what's causing it in the first place.[114]" We begin by acknowledging the truth that if we wish to innovate, we must face failure. Because innovation and failure are related, however, we come to believe that failure is inevitable. This causes us then to believe that the problems related to these failures are inevitable as well. We fail to recognize that failure is bad, and we should be striving to reduce it, even though we should embrace the risks that give rise to it. The answer is to seek always to the root causes of why we are failing and do better. We will still fail, but less. There is no minimal frequency of failure that we must accept.

KPIs (Key Performance Indicators) are another root of a common twisted reflection. This is a twisted reflection that is often controversial when discussed with many leaders, even those involved in Big Data analysis.[115] As we emphasize throughout this book, having metrics is critical, but it is also important that we apply correct analytic techniques and consider that our metrics represent partial knowledge of the truth only. In cases of partial metrics, we must remember that there is room for goal distortion, especially where incentives for agents within our organization are tied to these numbers. As an aside, as per our discussion in the chapter *Game and Decision Theory*, there are game-theoretic analyses of these various cases in the literature, with their corresponding outcomes in terms of waste. Rob Austin's book *Measuring and Managing Performance in Organizations* is an insightful classic on this topic. We also recommend *The Logic of Political Survival* and *The Dictator's Handbook*, by Bruce Bueno de Mesquita, Alastair Smith, Randolph M. Siverson, and James D. Morrow: these last two books focus on a model of political survival derived from game theory and empirical evidence, which parallels our logic with respect to KPIs.

In the next chapter, we'll discuss this specific case more, but let us motivate the topic here. We'll consider one of the earliest canonical examples of this issue as discussed in the literature.[116] In the 1970s, there was a sustained period of unemployment in the United States. In reaction to this, job offices were set up by the government to help unemployed people find jobs. These offices were tasked with getting people back into the economy, preferably avoiding underemployment. The KPI used to determine an office's success and thus reward was how many interviews the office arranged. The outcome was that these offices did little to help people get jobs. In particular, the officers would schedule as many interviews as possible without consideration of whether an applicant matched the job requirements. The outcome didn't matter to the rating the office received. Every interview could be a failure. Fiscal incentives based on partial metrics gave rise to misaligned outcomes. Even the most well-meaning people can suffer this, especially if the negative aspects of their actions are unclear. They might justify their behavior to themselves: more interviews equal more jobs, right?

In this case, we began with a sound premise. Metrics are good. We then tried to set up a data-driven goal to incentivize good behaviors. Our measurement was partial, however. In this case, there were other aspects such as the quality of an interview which were not measured. Thus, anyone optimizing against the KPI would push only the tracked value via the most efficient means available. Now, this is a real-world case, but the solution is obvious. This is what makes this a great test example. Most real cases are far more convoluted. When people first hear about this, it's often dismissed. The people who generated the KPI didn't consider the problem thoroughly. Or the character of our teams needs to be such that people won't exploit these gaps. This is a dangerous assumption. Over and over again even top companies fall prey to this. Whenever there are metrics associated with agent pay-offs, this issue creeps in. This parallels the problem of the wish-granting genie and maintaining control over a superintelligence.[117] Vigilance and skepticism must be maintained.

In economics, this problem is known as Goodhart's Law: "When a measure becomes a target, it ceases to be a good measure.[118]"

We will discuss the factors that give rise to this problem in more detail in the next chapter. It is also a rich topic in business management literature. And, unsurprisingly, a core topic in machine learning and AI safety.

Let us now shift to the engineering side of development for another example of a twisted reflection. In software development, one generates a build periodically — many times a day in modern practice, preferably with every submit. If the build is unstable, this can impact the productivity of many team members individually. A build break can slow work on their specific task. As a result, the reaction sometimes is to firewall developers away from the build. People are encouraged to work on their own branches in isolation until their task is done. Only then do they push their work up to the mainline where it becomes a part of the product. We'll discuss this more later in Part III: Waste, when we discuss Agile and Lean practices, but this is an example of an anti-pattern.[119] Its resolution has given rise to modern practices such as ubiquitous automation and DevOps practices in general.

The key flaw here is that when we firewall our developers, while a single person's work is less impacted in the short term, the impact on the team is increased. It is well known that bugs are most easily fixed the sooner they are caught. Moreover, integrations are not trivial when code is overlapping — two distinct functionalities must be merged, oftentimes by a person who is familiar with only their own work. While work on a single task is sped up, the general health of the codeline is damaged. We substitute a relatively easy problem for the harder problem of integration, which often isn't even tracked — this is also related to partial knowledge, where we optimize what is explicit. Fixes on integrations are often less well thought out due to time pressure, and the general quality of the build goes down.

The proper process for most environments is working directly in the mainline and submitting daily — this is continuous integration. This involves strengthening automated testing so that people can have confidence that the mainline is always healthy. This increases general quality and resolves faults faster.

In some situations, it is necessary to do branching; we are not asserting that the above applies in every case. We need to consider our context. In many open-source projects, people do not work in the mainline, as that is not how those projects are organized. Typically, there is a small group of owners who validate pull requests. They bear the weight of integration costs because they don't want to expose the mainline to arbitrary submitters.

Nevertheless, in most environments, it has been proved a twisted reflection to insulate developers from each other, rather than investing in infrastructure and automation that gives increased confidence in the health of the build.

In all these cases of twisted reflections, there is a correct root idea. In each situation, though, our view is too narrow, and we accidentally divert the team and the project into the ditch by not seeing the bigger picture. Because of the good root, it is challenging to redirect the team. Humans rarely see nuances of truth, so when we try to correct behavior, the team will assert that we are trying to disprove the good root idea, when in fact we are not. To resolve this issue, we need to separate the good idea from the bad or show that another good idea needs to constrain the first pillar. In all cases, this is much easier if humility is a core value of our organization, as it allows us to take the outside view. Sometimes, if humility is at our core, we don't even need to bring in external agents to remedy the affliction, as the team can recognize it themselves.

9

The Specific Dangers of KPIs

An adage often stated is "measure what matters." There's even a book with that title![120] In our system, we've emphasized getting to the truth — to do so, we must compare our models with measurable facts. No theory can be validated without recourse to reality. We then determine how likely our model is to be correct with respect to other models. KPIs and OKRs (and other similar measures) can give alignment to employees, which is critical for avoiding waste. Our employees want to know if they've succeeded, and these provide an answer. A common complaint from our staff is that managers fail to establish expectations. Then at review time, we dock employees after we evaluate them subjectively against goals they cannot challenge. Clarifying targets is a good justification for using KPIs and OKRs, and we should employ them, but using them means we also need to consider how they can cause harm.

What also occurs as a result of the above adage is this modification: "What matters is what is measured." We mentioned Goodhart's Law last chapter: "When a measure becomes a target, it ceases to be a good measure.[121]" When metrics work as intended, we gather data, get to the root cause of failure, resolve the issue, and then check our data again, hopefully seeing improvement. When incentives are tied to metrics, however, an improvement in tracked data now has an alternative explanation as well: the employee might have pursued the incentive itself by modifying the signal. If everyone acted with perfect character, this would be less of an issue — our primary concern then would be that we might prioritize easily measured metrics over those that are either hard or impossible to measure.

Unfortunately, perfect character rarely exists. Even if we try to behave ideally, incentives can deform our decisions where immoral outcomes aren't obvious or are easily dismissed. And, of course, we often don't behave when there are rewards. If we know about the metric and its link to a payoff, it is often the case that we can tinker with the signal without resolving the issue. This can be overt and possibly a termination-inducing offense if it is clearly abusive, but more often the distortion is subtle. It can be as "innocuous" as prioritizing the fully tracked and thus flashy tasks, as opposed to the necessary but unquantified quality and support tasks. Given the range of employee personalities, one will find that there will be varying levels of exploitation, with the general trend normalizing to whatever people get away with (see Normalization of Deviance in our chapter *Never Tolerate Waste* in Part III).

To quote Tom DeMarco and Timothy Lister: "When you try to measure performance, particularly the performance of knowledge workers, you're positively courting dysfunction.[122]"

To be fair, Google was aware of this when they created the OKR system, although from blogged experiences of some ex-employees, it remains imperfect. Most practitioners suggest that the OKR reports not be tied to the reward cycle, to lessen the implied link. That is a good approach and one any adopter of OKRs should use. Not only does it sever the relationship, but it also indicates that we as an organization frown on manipulating OKRs. Nevertheless, the employees always think they know the game and how to play it. It's a matter of degree.[123]

This problem occurs because what was once a static measure of the state of the world has been transformed into a dynamic and recurrent system with a reinforcement learning function. This reward signal can often be decoupled from the correct solution. How easy this is to orchestrate depends on the KPI or OKR, but it is hard to prevent entirely.

In effect, incentive-based measurements define a game that our employees engage with every day — the KPIs constitute the scoring rules. As we discussed in our chapter *Game and Decision Theory*, the rules of the game define both our culture and our outcomes. Because the rules never fully cover or align with reality, it is inevitable that they distort results. People want to win. Thus, we need to consider what outcome we should expect when our staff push incentive-based measurements to their ultimate limit.

For example, we can consider DAU (Daily Active Users) as a measure of our customers' happiness. DAU can correlate with user satisfaction, but it can also reflect addiction. While some might consider our goal to be getting our products in front of users every day — in which case DAU is aligned — in our system of principles, we prefer to primarily solve our customers' problem, not the problems of our marketing department. Thus, we must be careful of a measure such as DAU, which can mislead us. We must favor that which is measurable, as anything else bears the risk of being subjective, but we know that there are additional quality and integrity issues that aren't tracked, often because it is difficult to do so. Like an iceberg, what it is beneath the surface can be the most dangerous part.

Even if we ignore the preceding issues, other problems remain, especially if we broaden our consideration to mass data collection on employees, rather than just the limited OKR sets that we agree on in our one-on-ones. While we advocate tracking as much data as possible, it is also well known that analysis over large data sets can trick us if we are fishing for correlations. If one has a data set with high enough dimension, it is inevitable that odd relationships will be discovered. For example, for a long period of time, it was noted that which league won the NFL championship was correlated with a rise or fall of the market over the next year.[124] Leonard Koppett discovered this in the 1970s. Up to that point, it had never been wrong. If we look at enough possible cases, some correlation will always be found. To cite a common meme from the Internet, we might also claim that a lack of pirates is causing climate change.[125] The higher the dimension, the more frequent these relations will be. Any data scientist already knows this, but employee analytics are often used by people who have no training. A manager might do a query and find out that all employees recently fired have also read Joseph Heller's *Catch-22*, whereas none of our top-performing employees have. That is not a relationship that stands up to scrutiny. If it does, it must be that there is a deeper root cause that gives rise both to reading *Catch-22* and to getting fired.[126]

As has frequently happened in the financial world, given immense data sets and huge incentives to find relationships, we sometimes create high-parameter models that fit every data point historically. These models, however, do not generalize. Even if one is careful with overfitting, there remains the risk that the model can only extrapolate from the view of the past that it has seen. Long Term Capital Management was a famous case of this. They built complicated models and strategies to estimate and exploit future price probabilities, only to then collapse in the late 1990s when they failed to predict the economic problems of post-Soviet Russia.[127]

Again, these big data issues are not problems for employee OKRs, where employees and managers agree together on a set of goals and measures. This is only a problem once we start exploiting our data collection systems. It is vital to remember there are many traps, and that we might lack the training to give proper weight to the conclusions that emerge.

Ultimately, there are two ways to handle this.

First, we as managers need to be humble and recognize our own limitations in terms of data analysis (unless we are specialists, but even then, it's best to be humble). We need to approach the data rigorously, and if necessary, bring in staff who have the knowledge to expose our blind spots. Data can sharpen our employees' contributions, but it can also rebound negatively. If we do a bad job, our employees will feel that not only are we treating them like robots, but that we are doing so ineptly.

Second, if we want to foster a goal-driven rather than a task-driven mentality — as we've advocated — we should remove the incentives from our KPIs and treat measurement solely as information to validate our models. This severs the recurrence. If our staff see themselves as owners, they will be motivated to take the actions that deliver value, regardless of metrics, which is what we would prefer. We then as managers need to spend more time on the floor to directly establish our employees' quality, so that their reviews can have sound foundations.

When we choose to be goal-driven, we must be careful. If we come in and hammer employees with bad reviews over lower explicit task completion rates because they have been acting as owners, we will convert those goal-driven employees back to task-driven employees. It takes extra effort in a goal-driven world to evaluate our staff. This is the siren call of the pure metrics-based approach — it's easier. It's just self-deceptive.

In the end, the problem here is that our metrics can only give us a partial view of the world, at least within innovative knowledge-based industries. We can monitor the production of identical widgets on an assembly line relatively easily, which is a factor in why Frederick Taylor's Scientific Management became so prevalent in the early twentieth century. If we want to create a product for a niche that doesn't exist, however, the most important part of the work is exploratory, creative, and driven by experiment — all of which are not predictable or easily measurable. In the end, we must be profitable — that is the representation of our final relationship with our customers. Intermediate signals and proxies other than value must be viewed skeptically. The larger our organization, the more plagued we will be with these surrogates.

What this means is that a modern manager needs to balance understanding of the measured world against those aspects of the world that are not being measured yet are critical for value. The manager needs to be able to project both hard and the soft evaluation criteria to employees. Meanwhile, our employees must be able to operate in a world where they must rely on their judgment and possess a broader view, as opposed to pursuing manager-defined goal posts.

Another useful method is akin to common practices in data science and is an on-going research topic in deep learning. When evaluating KPIs and what they mean, it is critical that we as the manager shape a story of what is happening beneath the surface, using the data but also considering the non-measured features. We must then test the story as best we can. Any non-testable story, of course, is useless. If tracking tells us that our rendering engineers are delivering massive feature counts, but we're hearing complaints from the art team, then we might need to reevaluate how we are measuring the performance of our rendering engineers — perhaps an intervention is required as well. Rendering might be knocking out features without doing the work to make them easy or stable for art to use. But complaints from art can be deceptive: perhaps what art wants is not in line with what design requires — design needs hundreds of units visible on the screen which requires short cuts for real time, but art cares only about high-quality visuals. Before cracking down on a team, we must make sure we've tested our story. There is nothing more frustrating than achieving our KPIs and being attacked for a non-measured output based on a false assumption. This will break trust between leadership and the floor, and foster a view that management is unaware of the actual requirements of the product. That is corrosive to morale and team cohesion. Good morale sustains productivity, after all.

The challenge, however, is that we as managers must spend more time on the ground with our employees to see what they are doing. If we operate purely by metrics, we can spend our time elsewhere. But if we do that, we risk unleashing afflictions that will damage the output of our value-producing workers to save our time as managers (and we need to be honest, our time as managers is rarely value-adding time — sorry). We must be on the floor, making the effort to understand what our employees are doing. If we are at a company where management lacks technical understanding, get technical managers. And get them on the floor. All our strategies discussed behind closed doors means nothing if they are not expressed as well-understood goals by those executing our plans.

Consider, though, what we now expect of a modern manager. They need to be team builders, they need to know enough about their field to be visionaries and leaders, they need to understand enough about data science to interpret and analyze the state of the world both seen and unseen, and they need emotional intelligence to manage expectations upward and downward. Although it isn't the direct subject of this chapter, the increasing demands placed on our managers are part of the reason why we must strengthen the system that underlies our culture. This can involve improved tools, increased learning, but mostly we must make sure that our managers can always operate at their best — this means ensuring that we remove distractions.

Despite the challenges, though, and the risk of twisted reflections, without data all we have are stories in our own minds without a relation to reality. This causes enormous waste if not addressed. We need data to falsify bad decision paths; often it is better to over-measure than lose potential knowledge.

Nevertheless, data poses many risks, including false senses of security. We must examine and re-examine our data with a well-developed storytelling and questioning mindset. We must realize that data can sometimes tell false narratives when we are dealing with high-dimensional data sets. We must remember that for everything that is measured, there are many more things that are not, some of which might be directly related to our success. Moreover, many of the things we measure are only proxies for the actual information we wish to acquire.

Data nowadays is valuable purely as a commodity, but it is only the strength of our interpretation of that data that can provide long-term customer value and strengthen the system that we've built for our teams and projects.

10

The Hero Complex

History and myth provide innumerable situations where humans faced problems beyond either their comprehension or control – the weather, aggressive neighbors, illnesses, storms, and so on. We feel at a primordial level that sacrifice can assuage fate. Thus, to placate magical forces, humans sacrificed their best livestock and burned their finest art. They even yielded up members of their tribe to satiate the hunger of these miraculous powers. This impulse resides deep within us, to seize control of the uncontrollable. When we pursue this urge, we accept the contract proffered –one that we surmised ourselves – and fail to look deeper for answers to our problems. Ritual bounds the limits of acceptable inquiry, especially ritual accreted over time to form our cultural foundation. In many companies, the act of sacrifice overtakes problem solving as the route to success. Unfortunately, the price of our sacrifices can sabotage us. Most twisted reflections bear within their heart a core of irony.

The AAA game industry, as with many creative industries, is competitive. Skilled and passionate applicants are in no shortage — at least young applicants. Most cultures prize hard work. If we value some effort, we must value total effort even more. Total sacrifice! When we are stuck in a difficult situation, it can become easy to believe our salvation arises from complete commitment, rather than by digging deep to find and resolve the problems that are stymieing us — especially when the problems cut against our world view or self-worth. It has become ubiquitous that teams in the game industry do hard crunches (there are some exceptions).

No doubt some of this drive arises from our desire to create something lasting, but some of it comes from fear. Our anxiety parallels the concern that our external actions do not match our internal concept of how a game developer should behave. When we work late every night, we create a shield for our ego. We get respect from our peers. Our failures are then excusable, for we feel that no one could have asked for anything more from us. It is not possible to do better or to give more. This is the false narrative built on top of the core truth that hard work enables success. Thus, we have the hero complex, another twisted reflection, and one that sometimes has dire consequences in terms of social, familial, and personal health for the game industry. And one that engenders inferior products as well.

Outside of games, the impact of chronic long-term stress has been well-documented. The neurochemistry associated with this degrades creative capabilities. When we are subjected to high levels of cortisol, we narrow our view — we select from fewer choices that are more conservative.[128] For our ancestors in the wild, this made a great deal of sense. If we see a tiger, we shouldn't spend time weeding through all the possibilities, but should immediately leap to a well-tried solution such as climbing a tree, even if it turns out that there were better choices. Stress floods our larger muscle groups with blood which allows us to flee faster, but it doesn't help us debug a critical late-night failure.

Within the game industry, there have been numerous studies about the deleterious impact of long-term crunch on team efficiency. Even though these studies are in some cases over fifteen years old and continue up to modern day,[129] it remains an ingrained belief that games require crunch. Books such as *Blood, Sweat, and Pixels*[130] glorify this by telling the story of hard pushes as if they were necessary to justify the art. It is the classic myth of the suffering creator.

What we know is that when crunch lasts more than two or three weeks, performance suffers a negative impact for each extra hour. Eventually, it would be better to work regular hours rather than crunch, due to the increasingly negative margins. Worse — and this to my knowledge has not been studied in games — the situation is more dire: from anecdotal evidence, people in crunch tend to focus more on completing the tasks they are given, rather than completing work that delivers better outcomes. It's been shown that people's judgment suffers under sustained pressure, so we must expect that increasing percentages of work are just waste. We rarely track whether our features are more mismatched or excessive with respective to customer need due to crunch. That less is more is a hard lesson to teach to producers driven by feature KPIs. Research has shown that stressed individuals seek shelter in hierarchical behavior, rather than exercise the open decentralized problem-solving that characterizes owners.[131]

It has been shown that forty-five-hour weeks are sustainable, although we wouldn't say that sustainability is the only metric. Many people advocate keeping slack time in schedules as a fertilizer for creativity.[132] We know that studios that engage in sustained crunches often have wasted time for their staff — excessive YouTube consumption, playing video games, long breaks in the pantry drinking coffee, showing up to work exhausted the next day, and so on. Some play is almost certainly helpful,[133] but as hours ramp up, people increasingly seek any form of escape. These behaviors become normalized. They are accepted as a price, even though they erode marginal productivity even further.

This problem affects managers as well. After all, if we're going to ask our floor staff to crunch, we as leaders can hardly do less. This means that our choices will be just as undermined as theirs. We become a caravan of drunk drivers struggling to keep together, but inevitably losing some people to the ditch. And maybe we end up in the wrong city at the end of our journey.

Of course, our gut tells us this is the right path. We know other successful projects have had crunch. Most game companies feel they must push. Moreover, to have even gotten where we are in our careers, most of us have had to make sacrifices to master our field. Society tells us this is the right path. And again, there is some truth: hard work is necessary to succeed. It's just a matter of how much.

Further, if we as managers inspire our teams to put in hard crunches, we know that will be taken as a signal of our own leadership quality in many environments. Our team knows that if they put in the late nights, they'll be noticed, and that too will be a signal of their heroism. In both cases, it gives a sense of security in an industry prone to lay-offs and sudden moves across the globe for work — especially for those in lower demand than engineers.

If we look at the research and our situation and recognize the need for change, how do we accomplish it?

The challenge here is that we must build our team's self-trust, while simultaneously maintaining the values of hard work, so long as we do so in a controlled fashion. One motivation for the system in this book is to give us a methodology that we can rely on. If we have faith that we are executing the system well, then our situation is as good as it can be. When we need to push late, we can for a brief period. And when it's done, we can sleep the next day. We can break the cycle and make our best choices.

Meanwhile, we need to keep our quality metrics public. When we push too hard and see them destabilize, it will reinforce that we have exceeded our limit. Build breaks have heavy downstream impacts that negate any marginal productivity gains the pushes added. Faults that are injected and show up months later can take days to resolve instead of the half hour they might have taken if caught immediately. Management will need to monitor their employees and send home early people who have pushed beyond their limits. Managers must also make sure that they themselves aren't pushing too hard. If their responsibilities become excessive as well, they will start to drop soft needs like spending time with their staff, and that can be fatal.

In time, our anxiety will lift. We might still be concerned about success or failure, but at least we know that we have done all that is possible.

Bear in mind, the practical cost of a hero culture can be enormous. Heroic hours often end with mass turnover in our staff. If our project fails, this is even worse. As we've mentioned, success can rewire our recollection of how hard a push was, but failure leaves us where we were. The cost of training new staff is enormous, especially as we need to integrate them into our culture. Worse, we could end up losing too many people, leaving us without enough experienced staff to bootstrap all our teams. Many employees who remain will require long cooldowns. Sometimes, they never recover, and hang around for a year or two before moving on, always verging on bad reviews. Among those who stay will be toxic individuals who disdain anyone working normal hours and glorify their 24-hour debugging sessions, regardless of whether they generated the bug themselves or not.

We spoke in our chapters *Seeking Alignment* and *Twisted Reflections* about the twisted reflection where we overvalue a team versus a project's success, but the opposite is also true. If we grind out our teams to pursue a single win, we will have a Pyrrhic victory.

For the most part in this book, we focus on what's effective from a pragmatic standpoint, as we don't want to cloud our discussion with external moral issues that everyone might not agree with. All our points are founded on the premise that our business will do better if we operate in this fashion. If that meant unpleasant things for us, that could be something we have to live with. In this case, though, we wish to point out that since it's clearly a negative to push in the fashion common to the game industry, it's doubly unfortunate as it also harms the quality of life of our staff and drives many talented individuals into other industries. This, in turn, causes the game industry to repeat its mistakes time and again. The survivors tend to be the ones most caught up in the delusion.

The fires of innovation are not best stoked out of the ashes of our burned-out creators.

11

Creativity

Creativity is the driver of innovation, but we treat it erratically. We can take creativity to many extremes,[134] some of which result in inferior decision-making. Two views of creativity often dominate: the creativity myth of the intrinsic genius, and creativity through grit.

The creativity myth of the intrinsic genius has not always been prevalent. It has come and gone. Even in Ancient Greece there was some dispute. From Plato's view in *The Republic* and *Timaeus*, the proper role of the artist is imitation. Everything exists already in its perfected form. Art is discovery not invention. For Aristotle in *The Poetics*, however, while on the one hand poetry operates in imitation of either of the low (Comedic) or the high (Tragic) aspects of our nature, on the other hand it is neither true nor false — thus it cannot be entirely imitation.[135] In many cultures it has been believed that knowledge exists in its full extent already, and is periodically gifted to humanity. In Hinduism, the *Vedas* always exists. The great rishi Vyasa who was the mythical author of its current version was given access to it rather than creating it. In medieval Christianity, similarly, divine inspiration entered the artist to guide their hand.

This metamorphosed in the Western tradition through the Renaissance into a view that some special individuals were gifted not with divine inspiration but with intrinsic gifts. We might consider the following example given by Kevin Ashton in his book *How to Fly a Horse*. Mozart wrote in a letter to the German Confederation's *General Music Journal* in 1815:

> When I am, as it were, completely myself, entirely alone, and of good cheer; say traveling in a carriage, or walking after a good meal, or during the night when I cannot sleep; it is on such occasions that my ideas flow best and most abundantly. All this fires my soul, and provided I am not disturbed, my subject enlarges itself, becomes methodized and defined, and the whole, though it be long, stands almost finished and complete in my mind, so that I can survey it, like a fine picture or a beautiful statue, at a glance. Nor do I hear in my imagination the parts successively, but I hear them, as it were, all at once. When I proceed to write down my ideas the committing to paper is done quickly enough, for everything is, as I said before, already finished; and it rarely differs on paper from what it was in my imagination.[136]

As it happened, however, this letter was a fraud, as shown by Otto Jahn, Mozart's biographer, in 1856. His actual process was one of sketches, hard work, getting stuck, and overcoming it.[137]

These stories hold great appeal — they excuse us from our own failures. Even so, in "mundane" areas such as business, popular counter stories in the same period argued that hard work could lead anyone from rags to riches, espoused by such figures as Ben Franklin, Samuel Smiles, and Horatio Alger, Jr.

This myth of inspiration has gradually been eroded in the twentieth century, but as a popular notion and one that pervades many areas of business — especially tech — it still has relevance. We cannot earn our inspiration; it must come to special people only when it is good and ready.

The problem here is that not only must we wait for inspiration, we must rely on these oracles to deliver it. All too often, these "prophets" abuse their status. Since they are the bottleneck of value, they are free to make exorbitant demands and denigrate the rest of our staff. Before them, we are helpless. If the Muses favor our creative mediators, we receive our gifts of innovation, and if not, we don't. Faced with a struggling project that cannot find its heart, management caught up in this belief system will shrug and argue that we must wait for a miracle. That is the only response when our solution comes from a black box.

The twentieth century began to overthrow this idea. Researchers began to consider our minds as processes. Behaviorism was a side track on this journey, where we chose to ignore internal workings of the mind. Researchers, however, eventually began to see our internal mental process as a topic of study subject to the normal rules of falsifiability. Once we began to see creativity as a material event instead of as a connection to a mystical universe of hidden forms, it became possible to consider its nature. What gives rise to it? What fosters it? What hampers it?

Most innovations do not appear to their creators entire from the mists.[138] Innovation is a grind. Ideas are cheap — it is execution that matters, and execution is not a direct path. Process and effort forge innovation; the final creation only seems inevitable to people who see it once complete. Creators are keenly aware of the many directions it could have taken instead.

The advantage to recognizing that creation is effort and process is that effort and process can be refined. Creators embrace problems and solve them. They do not trust inspiration. Many do not believe in their Muse.

As with most things we discuss in this book, however, there is a dark side to taking this notion too far — that creativity is solely the product of hard work. Once we recognize that creation is not the domain only of special people, but of anyone, we can embrace the notion that innovation is purely a process of grit. People who have achieved great things did so because they engaged in superhuman levels of effort. We must remember that there are good and bad paths to take when pushing forward. Work alone is not the final indicator of our success, and work driven too far and blindly can destroy creativity.

Mastery requires hard work. It is often stated that there is a rule of 10,000 hours to become an expert, although there are caveats to that, and it is an order of magnitude claim only.[139] When this is taken as a ground truth, however, then it is seen as the solution to all our problems. We stop asking whether there are better ways to move forward, especially when those methods differ from our past experiences. Followers of such a view assert that is foolish to challenge the inherent hardness of development, because it is an immutable truth that it must be this way. For example, it just takes nearly a decade to build intellectual properties (IPs), and it is done by the blood of the teams involved.[140] In such an environment, we should avoid being on the starting team! We noted a related issue to this last chapter in *The Hero Complex*. Oftentimes, believers in this view reject alternatives as theoretical — they see their own complex as pragmatic.

This is another twisted reflection. The afflicted have seen the power of grit, but they reject the notion of faster paths as naive. This is a defense of the ego as well, for as leaders they should have seen any such faster path. The magic of grit assuages anxiety. Hard work will get us there, and if it doesn't, then nothing could have. When someone comes in and suggests otherwise, they open the possibility that our bad decisions gave rise to the failures. That is frightening, especially when budgets for AAA games are blowing past a hundred million.[141]

This view is almost as toxic as the original creativity myth (but not quite!). Instead of the miracle of inspiration, it's the miracle of hard work. Faced with problems that need to be solved, when management is caught in the grips of this mental virus, they will assure the team that there are no issues — development is always magic.

Creation is hard. There is no shortcut. We need to put in the hours. But there are always problems that can be solved. There are always experiments to rule out decision branches. We can get features to users faster.

Moreover, too much hard work destroys creativity! We already discussed this in *The Hero Complex*, but as we said, cortisol — the neurochemical associated with stress — narrows our enumeration of options to conservative choices (typically the available ones most easily recalled by our memory). This is the opposite of creativity!

Two Modalities of Creativity

What we do mean by creative thinking? In antiquity, the word might have just meant someone who created something, like a new pot. Now we mean the creation of something that has never been seen before. Even within that constraint, however, there are different frameworks.

For instance, Pixar and Disney animated films follow a narrative structure with intensity peaks occurring at distinct points, using a common toolkit of twists.[142] Consider one pattern: the good character who turns out to be evil. In one variant, we as viewers of the movie start recognizing clues to the betrayer's nature roughly a quarter into the film, but the protagonist remains oblivious. Part of the tension is that we as viewers know the truth while the hero is blind. Around the halfway point, something warns the main character of the threat, but they brush it off which leads to a further escalation of action. Then around 75% or 80% through, the full reveal occurs, and the protagonist faces their most dire straits as they realize the truth. There is always just enough time left to turn the tables before the end. There are many details that can be built atop this framework, but the three-act structure of films is prevalent in the film industry, along with all its associated baggage. Games follow a version of this as well in many narrative single-player offerings. Most film and game writers would be familiar with Joseph Campbell's book *The Hero with a Thousand Faces*, and the concept of the Hero's Journey. Yet like the poet working within the rigid constraints of the sonnet, we consider how we function within these limits to be creative. In such a view, expression through well understood rules produces beauty. Our innovation is the flesh and nuance, not the bones, which are more the bass line of our composition.

Another modality of creativity occurs when we take something that is currently perceived one way, and then transform it into something new. Someone saw unused rooms in their house and recognized that there was a scaling way to rent them, empowered by the Internet and modern e-commerce, which gave birth to AirBNB and its competitors. Now our experience of world travel is completely different, where we rent from locals instead of relying on hotels and hostels. Uber and Lyft upended assumptions in similar ways.[143] Of course, as with many innovations, they have their antecedents in the past. Smart phones are probably more of a cultural transformation — one enabled by the realization that the screen was a better choice for the keyboard, and that smart phones were more computers than phone.[144]

For a more straightforward case, consider classic creativity tests such as the Candle problem.[145] Here, people are given a box of tacks and a candle with matches, and told to affix the candle to a door. The most common solutions are either to melt the candle to the door or to construct a base from the tacks. The "innovative" and superior solution is to realize that the box the tacks came in can be tacked to the wall itself and used to hold up the candle. This demonstrates the challenge we have recognizing that we have made assumptions about an object in the first place, which prevents us from seeing its potential uses — in this case, that the box could be more than just a container for tacks. This is known as the functional fixedness bias.[146]

To use the language from Don Norman's *The Design of Everyday Things*,[147] in this second modality of creativity, we see a new affordance for an object, that either adds or replaces existing affordances. An affordance here means the way an object projects how it ought to be used — for example, a doorknob is the way a door projects its usage.[148] To be valuable, this new affordance must enable us to do or perceive something that was not previously accessible.

In the first modality of creativity, the greatest expression of a twist is one that transfigures the story up to that point in terms of evidence that was already there but that we didn't recognize. Famous examples would be that the psychologist was already dead in film *The Sixth Sense*, or that the protagonist in movie *The Usual Suspects* himself was Kaizer Soze. Thus, both modalities can occur to various degrees in the same work.

This shift in perception has parallels elsewhere, for example in scientific paradigm shifts. Thomas Kuhn identified and popularized this notion in his book *The Structure of Scientific Revolutions*, although various notions of scientific revolution predated his work.[149] Science proceeds by refining and extending a core set of assumptions, which forms the paradigm. Within any paradigm, however, there are always anomalous observations, which are dismissed as insignificant. In the nineteenth century, for example, it was known that the precession of the perihelion of Mercury was not correctly predicted by Newtonian mechanics. Then a paradigm shift occurred. This transfigured our understanding of the world and later resolved the anomaly. Even though Einstein hadn't predicted the solution for

Mercury, general relativity supplied the answer. The new paradigm in turn suffers from new anomalies that are dismissed just the same, at least until another paradigm shift occurs.[150]

The theory of disruptive and sustaining innovation cycles in technology also parallels the argument of paradigm shifts. Here a specific type of innovation occurs, which involves a technology that can be used to solve a low marginal-utility problem for an established competitor, but otherwise is inefficient at their higher marginal-utility cases. The disruptor then improves the technology and gradually grows up the value chain until it is too late for the established company to compete.[151] The innovation here is often to recognize that some unrelated technology can be cross-purposed to another task, with the possibility of growing into and supplanting an established industry.

Threats to Innovation

Many companies engage in practices destructive to innovation. Some of these companies are quite successful despite this! Typically, when such institutions succeed it's because their past successes allow them to draw top talent from across the world, even though their processes tend to cause high churn with employees. In industries where there is an ample supply of young and motivated talent — such as the game industry — this is a situation one sees from time to time. For a related situation, the top Indian Institutes of Technology used to be poor in facilities and use rote teaching methodologies, but because the entrance exams had such enormous intakes with an extraordinarily high bar, the students who made it through the cull were guaranteed to be of the highest caliber, thus succeeding despite their environment. When similar conditions prevail in an industry, the same situation can arise.

Such a situation is never stable, however. This is a strategic weakness in the long term.

One common problem is that the cost of failures can be enormous. Some large game companies have been known to buy, burn, and bury smaller studios to meet revenue targets. If we work in such an environment, we might not want to risk exposure to that year's cull, even if success might mean large gains. If innovation exposes us, there's a risk we'll be targeted. In fact, the evolutionary basis of our risk aversion is born out of this: if the cost of failure is high, it is better to lose out on big wins rather than suffer a fatal outcome!

There are also psychological factors. It's been shown that while many companies claim to be friendly to innovation, actual practices penalize innovators. Even if we say that we embrace new ideas, it can be uncomfortable to do so. This can lead to preferences in promotions, which in turn leads to a management team packed with people who say one thing but got to their position by acting in another way. This is subtle to expose, as with many flaws arising from our cognitive biases.[152]

Further, many companies focus on task-completion rates. Creativity doesn't arise from knocking out easily quantifiable tasks. Innovation is unpredictable. As we mentioned earlier in this chapter, when we are under pressure, we generate fewer variations of ideas, all of which tend to be more conservative. This is a fact of our neurophysiology. Many figures nowadays recommend open time in our schedules to contemplate ideas. As Warren Buffett has stated, the only thing we can't buy is time.[153]

Beyond this, a focus on task rates warps the nature of the work we commit to doing, making it less innovative. If less than a 90% completion rate mandates an ominous visit from the top boss, there's an incentive to redefine the tasks we take on to make 90% more achievable, regardless of the value delivered to the customer. Even if the tasks aren't distorted, in such a case we prefer to load up on predictable tasks. Obviously, we need to burn through our mundane work as well; however, we need to avoid fixating on the more easily measured and predictable tasks (recall the chapter *The Specific Dangers of KPIs*).

Filtering Our Ideas

We should note that creativity is not only ideation. We need constructive criticism as well. Not all ideas are good, and even those that have potential are often cracked at the start.

Some companies build a group to vet ideas once they've reached a minimal level of maturity. For Pixar, this group is called the braintrust.[154] Many of their creative minds meet to appraise an early cut of a film — typically at this point a mix of storyboards and animatics with the proper length and temporary voice work. Often nothing is rendered at final quality, or at most a few test scenes for tech evaluations. In theory, the Pixar braintrust has no authority to edict changes; instead, they offer criticism about what works or doesn't. That they have no direct authority is critical to their method. It is the director's job to decide whether the braintrust is on to the solution or not — sometimes the braintrust notices a real problem, but the solution is wrong; the director instead finds some deeper issue that resolves everything.

As we mentioned, though, the braintrust only in theory has no authority. There is a hazard in that the people in the group tend to hold multiple roles. Sometimes those are explicit positions of power where a braintrust member is also a manager of the director, or they control resources, or directly green-light projects. In other cases, they are people of influence, whose opinion can sometimes be taken by others as law. Politics and personal cliques can also play a role, resulting in criticism that is biased, deliberately obtuse, or destructive. It's not clear that this problem can be avoided, but it can be mitigated. The key is that we understand the threat. Sometimes this means that certain people need to recuse themselves from the braintrust when they hold conflicting roles.

When we create a braintrust, we must emphasize to our staff that its criticism are not mandates. If the braintrust members are humble and project this well, then our staff will trust that they can stand behind a decision they believe in, as long as they did their part to take the criticism seriously.

In general, a braintrust is a wise decision, just make sure that it doesn't get corrupted.

We should also be wary of influential figures as a general hazard. We should be focused on delivering customer value, but sometimes in the complicated landscapes of large companies, managers are compelled to curry political favor. This can take the form of features added to the game to appease a potential champion of the project instead of serving customer need. This happens in projects where politics dominates entrepreneurship. For some leaders, it can be tempting to do this as they trade favors and negotiate for position, but if we are entirely within our organization, this is a form of profound waste (see Part III). It's never entirely avoidable, but politics should never be allowed to warp our projects away from value. Sure, business needs at times might require undesirable solutions — that is a necessary compromise. But pure politics should always be suppressed at an organizational level. We should engage in it only when necessary. If our project ever reaches a state where we are focusing on delivering work just to appease an internal figure, it is likely that we have entered a spiral that will destroy us. The time we spend handling this figure is time where our project deviates from the customer, which means our project will keep falling further behind. When the situation has reached this point, cutting the project is often the best choice.

A lesser version of this can happen even when the influential figure isn't trying to dominate the project and is making an innocent off-the-cuff suggestion! We've seen projects flip themselves in response to a comment that a high-level director later doesn't even remember, and now thinks is ridiculous!

The lesson here is that constructive criticism is core to corralling our creative vision, but that we must never allow it to be more than that — it must never take the form of edicts. Our customer is our primary driver, and we must reject any criticism that takes us away from that.

Life on the Floor

Floor culture is another key ingredient for a creative organization.

How does our staff encounter each other each day? On the one hand, it is important that people be able to communicate and bounce ideas off each other in a free and open manner. Sometimes this is used to justify open-office plans. As many employees will note, however, open-office plans are also noisy. These disruptions break people out of flow. It's been shown that a single interruption could require tens of minutes to recover from. In an environment of continuous interruption, people might never work at their best. This is one reason why some employees arrive early or stay late — to avoid the crowd — but that brings with it its own issues. We need to be careful that pursuing one advantage isn't costing us innovation and morale.

Employees should also be given windows of time each week to pursue creative ideas outside their scheduled responsibilities. This is in theory a waste, but if we engage our employees to try out risky solutions to our company's problems, we can often generate the revenue streams that will define our future. Moreover, creative time is hard to schedule anyway; as we mentioned earlier in this chapter, over-scheduling predictable tasks is a good way to kill a creative culture.

The research remains out on this, but I recommend a freeform approach. People should able to work some days from home and there should be rooms people can check out where they can work inside a closed office without disturbance. Communication to all creatives should be asynchronous by default only. If people play the Inbox Zero game, where they continually react to every arriving email, they will be interrupted all day. It's well established that leaving social media open primes us to watch for notifications. This prevents focus. After a push of high-efficiency work, people will need some downtime. This is where they can run over their mailbox, maybe after they get a coffee. There will be a need for an emergency synchronous alert system, but it should only be used by authorized individuals when there is a legitimate crisis.

PART THREE

Waste

12

Why Some Engineers Are Amazing

Can one great engineer be more productive than ten, or even a hundred average engineers?

This is an oft-made comment by some in tech[155] — Mark Zuckerberg and Marc Andreesen, for example. It is a comment that raises the hackles of others. Most of us distrust the connotation of great people and rock stars. Such a view justifies the *prima donna* demands of the elect, including the allowances for toxic behavior that destroys teams.

Bill Taylor once stated in response and as a call to pragmatism, "If you are building a company, would you prefer one standout person over a hundred pretty good people? Have we become so culturally invested in the allure of the Free Agent, the lone wolf, the techno-rebel with a cause, that we are prepared to shower millions of dollars (maybe tens of millions) on a small number of superstars rather than a well-assembled team that may not dazzle with individual brilliance, but overwhelms with collective capability?[156]"

Bill Taylor was right: we shouldn't pour money into people who disrupt collective wisdom with their egregious behavior. But that isn't the end of the story.

What do we even mean by productivity? There is a trap here. If we measure productivity by our task completion rate, then the difference between a great and an average engineer is not so large. But we have already established that the size of our task list is a delusion. Task lists represent platonic ideals of software products. We conceive of the master oven, with all its shiny features and doodads — everything we imagine the best ovens must have. What matters to our customers, though, is not the oven, but the pizza they're hungry for. Perhaps they don't even need a regular oven if it's just for pizza! What matters is the outcome and the experience. Our productivity is not our task completion rate; it is how fast we expose our customers' problem and provide a solution. The necessary work emerges when we are aligned with customer value. Everything else is waste. It is here where the great can vastly surpass the average.

Consider this case referenced from Lean Software Development: An Agile Toolkit:[157]

> Jim Johnson, chairman of the Standish Group, told an attentive audience the story of how Florida and Minnesota each developed its Statewide Automated Child Welfare Information System (SACWIS). In Florida, system development started in 1990 and was estimated to take 8 years and to cost $32 million. As Johnson spoke in 2002, Florida had spent $170 million and the system was estimated to be completed in 2005 at the cost of $230 million. Meanwhile, Minnesota began developing essentially the same system in 1999 and completed it in early 2000 at the cost of $1.1 million. That's a productivity difference of over 200:1.

That's an extreme but not unheard-of differential. In game development, projects sometimes founder for years. In the end, they might be shut down, delivering no value; or they might be forced to ship at low quality to capture whatever revenues they can, often far below desired targets. In some cases, a bad release gives us some revenue, but damages the brand so that it would have been better to not release at all. These problems arise due to avoidable afflictions, and while we can never guarantee success, the impact of great engineers on profitability can be enormous. It can be the difference between our margins being negative versus so large that our costs seem negligible.

To cut to the point, a great engineer is a master of the system we are presenting in this book. All great engineers are serial entrepreneurs. Many angel investors prefer that one (or even both) of the founders for start-ups be technical.[158] For media- and content-focused companies, creative leaders with similarly entrepreneurial mindsets should be sought out, although these companies should still embrace one technical head. Paired creative and technical founders can provide synergistic cores. The key is that these individuals originate from maker-based mindsets. Sales and marketing can always work with great products, but the opposite is not always true.[159] We aren't criticizing those with histories in sales and marketing; it is just that their training inclines them more to product exploitation and framing, rather than product development. In companies where no founders are from technical or creative fields, leadership often loses the capacity to understand what can be done, to gauge the reliability of propositions that they're offered, and to grasp how they can solve the customer's need. They retreat into politics. Eventually, customer value becomes secondary to image, perception, and stakeholder management. This is a profound form of waste. The correct path focuses on the customers' needs and their solutions.

On occasion, we have seen interviewers explore an engineer's capacity to elicit the customer's real need, but far more we see an emphasis on specific task-oriented skill sets. We hire engineers as if we were checking reviews on Amazon for a wrench. We assume that the engineer's purpose is to burn through our task list. This is the worst way to proceed. No great engineer comes from this. Can this person optimize a core loop? Can they prove something is NP-complete? These are useful skills and it is reasonable to test for them, but if we fail to test for the engineer's capacity to perceive the needs of their customer, then we are setting ourselves up for waste.

Why do these skills magnify efficiency to this degree?

Software development searches through an enormous implicit decision tree. A core skill is to establish the cost and value of a sub tree based on its expected features and architecture.[160] There is no oracle to forecast this, but if we can establish an engineer's process towards reaching value through decisions, we will establish how great an engineer they might be. Their process should be one of experiment, measurement, and validation through actual users. That an engineer can recognize their own assumptions can deceive them is a powerful sign of their quality. How expertly they can write an optimized search tree is interesting only in that it tests fundamentals. The scaling quality that takes an engineer to greatness is the judgment atop that foundation. A perfect software solution that serves no one's needs is worthless. If our interview process doesn't evaluate that capability, whether we hire great engineers or not is pure luck.

A problem we sometimes see in software development — certainly in games but in general as well — is that responsibility for value is shifted to top management, while the floor is responsible only for delivering "something." Typically, that something is a checklist of features. This is a view born from entitlement. We assume our success if we tick off the items. Development is transmuted into work, rather than understanding of our user. Indie game companies exhibit this flaw less, as they understand the challenges they face, but in larger AAA companies it becomes more common. Some engineers even justify this distance, noting that they aren't even working on the type of game they themselves enjoy (a great engineer cares not so much about whether a product is built for

Deep Management

them, but whether it is amazing for its intended customer). Teams that do not see themselves as responsible for customer value are teams that care more about releasing than about solving user problems. This is not how you produce great teams and great engineers.

The decisions fundamental to great engineers and teams are not only large but small as well. It is easy to see how answering the right high-level questions early can excise many expensive decision sub-trees from consideration. However, great teams make many day-to-day choices which add up to efficiency, whereas disempowered teams suffer constant friction. We must recognize that the fundamentals of customer-focused decision-making reach all the way down to the choices we make even about moment-to-moment tasks. The process must become habit. Deviations should make us uncomfortable.

As we've discussed, we're in the business of posing the right questions. This means that some waste is inevitable as we must write prototypes to explore options. In innovation, there is no way to map out the path we will take from the start, but by exploring the landscape early, we can make our largest leaps more efficiently. In the extreme, it is sometimes said of Lean (which we will discuss in later chapters), that in its ideal form we receive a direct customer order and react with a product infinitely fast. This is an unattainable target, but this ideal is often at odds with many company's existing software development processes.

While great engineers pose the right questions as early as possible, they also recognize that the future is uncertain. When projects swerve from their course, committed work can be wasted. Thus, the great engineer commits decisions and work as late as possible. This is set-based development, as we've discussed previously. Given our current position in time, we must consider the set of all possible technical outcomes that we could produce given our budget — along with an understanding of risks for those outcomes — which determines the possible decisions we might take. Nothing outside our constraints is possible. As a great engineer, we should even inject a bit of extra work on our architecture — which could be construed as necessary waste — to keep our option space wider. In a world of certainty, this would be inefficient. In our uncertain world, however, it gives us flexibility. It lessens the need to throw away work and rewrite poorly targeted systems.

Even so, the great engineer understands that this can be abused. There are windows of opportunity for technical choices. If we delay too long, those possible outcomes are lost. The great engineer understands that making decisions late is not an excuse for vacillation, but instead a reaction to the threat of uncertainty. We ask the right questions, gather data, and then make decisions when necessary to remain within our constraints while delivering maximal value.

Further, one of the key skills of decision-making is the ability to gather and amplify knowledge while reducing noise. Great engineers must be humble to recognize that. Answers come not just from ourselves, but from the team, the customer, from anyone — there is no one we should consider too unlikely. Thus, great engineers must possess the emotional intelligence necessary to engage the full capabilities of everyone around them.

Don't get us wrong. Being a great engineer does require many technical skills beyond foundations only. If the team lacks expertise, they will learn many practical lessons of poor architecture the hard way. Engineers need to be aware of the hot topics in their field. If an engineer can't write correct, maintainable code, then they aren't going to be a great engineer. But these are the skills we already test for. Where we fail is determining whether our engineers can see the pole star that defines the value of their work. Work with no purpose makes all other skills meaningless. We must train our people and test for their capacity to answer larger questions.

Great engineers should also recognize the afflictions that we have mentioned in this book, as well as the many others that can arise. Even if an engineer understands that customer value is their goal, if they themselves get caught up in twisted reflections, they might not be able to seek value efficiently. Similarly, engineers who get caught up in death marches can enter long periods of lower quality and

Deep Management

inferior creative output due to the many causes we've already outlined.

Most importantly, a great engineer knows that every process is subject to improvement.

What should be clear through all of this, is that most of the skills of a great engineer are not esoteric learnings that only a few can master. Recognizing value is a talent that can be learned through practice. Moreover, we cannot simply read a list of rules and become instant master decision-makers. We will stumble as we learn the art, but with time we will improve and see the tangles that tripped us up in the past. In other words, given its value, there is no excuse for any engineer to not learn to be great. It is a realization equal to that of the power of automation. It multiplies our productivity. Fewer lines written will produce greater positive outcomes.

So, what are some immediate steps an engineer can take to grow?

To start, we should recognize that everyone has an opinion, including ourselves. Opinions are hypotheses about how the world works, and not worth much. For a hypothesis to be valuable, we must show that the model represented by the hypothesis is effective, which means that it must be a statement that can be validated either true or false over some domain of experience.

Without data, however, hypotheses cannot be validated. Hypotheses in engineering are grounded in the dirty realities of day-to-day production. Thus, we realize that we have nothing without great data, and to have an ample supply of great data, we need to ensure that we have the infrastructure that can generate what we need. Great engineers prioritize telemetry as one of the first steps to be accomplished; it's arguable that the most grotesque of prototypes can proceed before telemetry, but even that can be questioned, as the better the data that we have for validating our prototypes, the better our subsequent steps will be.

Not all data is equal, however. Some projects collapse under a hurricane of data. Engineers are often trained in information theory, so it comes naturally for them to understand that there is signal and noise in any sampling. Part of the sign of a good engineer is that they can filter the data rather than get lost in the morass. This also means that engineers must understand common errors in analysis, such as overfitting, coincidences in high-dimensional sets, and so on, as we discussed previously in the chapters *Twisted Reflections* and *The Specific Dangers of KPIs*. We must learn to see what the data supports, rather than what we expect it to show.

In fact, a challenge for some bright individuals is that they are too skilled at argumentation, and thus sometimes skip the need for validation. They win by eloquence and quick-thinking but fail at uncovering the truth. This can lead to bad habits that hamper their ability to deliver a great multiplier of value. We must watch out for people who call others out on the spot for answers: such people claim that if the other person can't respond immediately, then they don't know what they're talking about. This is a great way to propagate bullshit.[161] Truth tends to be considered. We must learn to place less emphasis on validating our own beliefs. The smarter the engineer, the more they must struggle to remove themselves from the equation.

Truly great engineers realize that the mind projects onto the outside world what it wishes reality to be, and filters perception to match. We've discussed this previously, but it is well established in research that the human mind is more comfortable when its own precepts are validated, and that it often ignores cues that do not match its generalizations.[162] It is precisely the exceptions, however, where the scaling value of a great engineer is to be found. Unrelenting humility and constant direct absorption of events as they occur is necessary to see and thus find the path with the fewest dead ends. The struggle to clarify our filter of reality is lifelong — habit makes it easier, but it is precisely when we believe we see clearly that we will begin to lose our sight.

While many engineers don't think about decision-making in this detail on a day-to-day basis, it comes naturally as it aligns well with habits good engineers develop otherwise. Every engineer knows early in their career that they can't optimize if they don't know where the time is being spent. The 80/20 rule is an aphorism that they are intimately aware of — that most of the pain is caused by a small set of problems. Moreover, they can all recall anecdotes where they optimized a system that they were sure was an issue, only to find out later it was irrelevant. And yet we see projects where no one can say precisely how much time is spent compiling, building, in meetings, doing email, or completing features that final users rarely touch — or alternatively, which poorly maintained features are used extensively by users, generating frustration. The impact of all but the largest changes are often not tracked.

If engineers have data on their systems early, then they can also understand what value their systems succeed or fail to deliver from the start. They can find out 5% into development that customers don't care about feature X, Y, and Z, and thus cut most of the work. Meanwhile, by saving that time, they can then discover what features the customers do value and deliver those instead.

All of this allows the great engineer to exercise their most important skill: not rapid execution of individual tasks but uncovering who they are building systems for and what that individual needs. Moreover, if in the end the data shows that there is no user, the great engineer cuts that system regardless of investment or personal stake (we emphasize later in Part IV that the choice to cut should ideally come from the team, not top management, as we discuss in the chapter *Cutting Our Projects*).

All great engineers are entrepreneurs. Great engineers act as if they were owners of the company, directly affected by its successes and failures. Organizations throw away enormous value by treating their staff as mercenaries, there only to execute on the plans of leadership.

The best engineers are defined more by what they did not do, than by what they did. Doing everything takes enormous time — no wonder it takes close to a decade to deliver a new game IP! But engaging in a process that focuses time and energy precisely on those tasks most likely to deliver value shortens the path to a delightful product. Knowing which decision-tree branches to prune is the heart of efficiency.

This is the final and greatest lesson for an engineer.

To an outside observer, however, all the code generated by a hundred average engineers seems unbeatable. The native PC, web, and mobile versions, the version that runs on your watch — all this seems overwhelming value. The noise here is enormous: all the managers that need to maintain the backlogs, the leads to guide teams and careers, the support staff, the communication technologies so that the team in Hyderabad can keep abreast of the latest VR interface. This is all distraction. It feels like industry, but it is waste.

13

Never Tolerate Waste

Often enough in the games industry, storied companies release incomplete products into the market and then bomb. We aren't referring to the occasional failure that's to be expected of a risk-taking enterprise. Sometimes no one predicts a failure, whether inside or outside the organization. Here, we explore a different case. Developers sometimes plunge forward with a launch that from an outside view seems indefensible. The developers ignore clear danger signals.

As we'll discuss, this is less the fault of the specific people involved and more that of the culture they exist within. Their native view blinds them to threats and pre-rationally censors any decision other than the one to move forward at any cost.

This situation parallels similar cases from other industries. Later in this chapter, we'll examine Diane Vaughan's evaluation of organizational behavior around the Challenger shuttle launch disaster,[163] which provides a framework for understanding how conditions can give rise to these outcomes.

It is critical to remember that had we been immersed in the same environment as these game developers, we too might have replicated the same errors. Only after we realize that we can fall prey to these blind spots, do we become capable of escaping these traps.

Bethesda's Fallout 76

On November 14, 2018, Bethesda launched *Fallout 76* to immediate critical disdain. On Metacritic, it settled down to an aggregate score of 51.[164] For comparison, the other Bethesda *Fallout* games scored in the high 80s.[165]

The product as delivered suffered from a missing heart in terms of design; for fans, it didn't feel like the *Fallout* game they wanted. If *Fallout 76* ever had a Razor, it was not one tested sufficiently with actual customers. Key expectations for the brand were missing, and the additions unique to the offering were not considered replacements. For example, they made the choice to have no human NPCs; in previous iterations, encounters with these characters gave life to the world. The thought was that as a multiplayer game, the actual human players would supply something more engaging, and while there was some of that, it wasn't enough. Game mechanics felt off to players as well — for example the V.A.T.S.[166] system not only functioned differently, but many considered it broken.

While Bethesda games are known for technical flaws, the disconnects, falls through the world, and monsters stuck in static non-animating poses all seemed too much, especially when placed next to lacking content — *Skyrim* and *Fallout 4* had both suffered from technical issues, but players tolerated the glitches due to those games' richer initial content offering.

Deep Management

Had the product at launch instead been an alpha to open an initial conversation with fans, the offering would have made more sense. Then, responsive changes to feedback could have resulted in graduated releases through betas until it entered into the mainstream market, which might have resulted in a *Fallout* iteration that surpassed its predecessors. Instead, Bethesda marketed and delivered the game as a final product at full price.

How did this come to pass? While Bethesda's games aren't cheap to make and aren't released yearly, their studios also operate with leaner budgets than many AAA developers. Moreover, they have amassed enviable windfalls on their previous products. *Fallout* is among the most valuable IPs in the games industry. Shipping in such a state seems a bizarre choice. From the outside perspective, there were clear warning signs. And yet from the native view, the interpretation of these signals filtered by team culture might have made the launch in November seem the only option.

While many potential root causes might already be apparent to the reader, the model discussed in this chapter should further illuminate *Fallout 76*'s outcome.

Bioware's Anthem

Similarly, how did Bioware not realize that *Anthem* was far from ready?[167] On release, it too faced critical headwinds, launching with an initial Metacritic score of 63,[168] and settling down later to a 55 aggregate score for the PS4 and 58 for the PC as of April 8, 2019.

After its release and day-one patch, multiple major patches followed, some of which wrought substantial changes. Massive last-minute patches for a GaaS strongly indicate a premature release. And as expected for a game showing warning signs, new bugs were introduced with these patches.

It didn't take reviewers long to realize that there were gaps in the release offering, as well as critical faults. Frequent and long loading times interrupted play, although early fixes improved this somewhat. *Anthem*'s game loop forced players out of the open world, whether the players wanted to go back to Fort Tarsis or not. See our chapter *Consider the Hideout* for the challenges that choice poses. Many reported that there was not enough end-game content at launch, with only three strongholds (or dungeons). Given experience with *Star Wars: The Old Republic,* this seemed particularly surprising.[169] Perhaps most importantly, however, as a Bioware game, *Anthem* brought high expectations for narrative quality; most reviewers found the story flat.

Six months before *Anthem*'s launch, when commitments were being made, the native view within the project must have suggested a real chance. As the date neared, despite the stakes, proceeding with launch must have seemed the only option. At least from the inside view.

The Odd Behaviors of Organizations

As we delve further into organizational behavior, the mystery of how these mistakes come to pass becomes clearer. When we are inside the machine, our understanding of the world is defined by the machine's rules. Developers are caught up in a paradigm without realizing it. The actions they can select from have been filtered without their conscious awareness. Danger signals become normalized. Only after developers step outside their culture can a broader horizon be seen. And only once they have that outside view, can they realize that the paradigm not only can be broken, but that it must be.

Some will note that since these are GaaS games, there might be a strategy to release in a broken state, capture money, and then tailor the games to their audience after the fact. Many GaaS products have released in states that didn't immediately garner acclaim, but then later rebounded — Ubisoft's *Rainbow Six: Siege*, for instance. To us, this seems an unacceptable threat to valuable brands, some of which can be worth hundreds of millions, even over a billion at times[170]; however, we'll have to see how the arcs of these products pan out in the future. It could be that an attempt is being made to change the default assumptions players bring to shipped products. Even so, given the risk to their respective IPs — in *Anthem*'s case, the potential value as this was its first foray into the consumer market — it seems unlikely that this was the logic.

If, however, these products had been released in a polished state but with a smaller immediate offering, this would have been more credible as an argument. Games such as *Apex Legends, Overwatch,* and *Fortnite* all launched with few maps, but offered compelling, rock-solid immediate propositions. Perhaps there is an ongoing evolution in terms of what it means to be a AAA game, but if that is true, it must involve an engaging core that grows, versus an immediately uneven experience.

The sociologist Diane Vaughan studied this type of launch-failure blindness in a different context. She wrote *The Challenger Launch Decision* about the shuttle disaster, which tells a revisionist history of the root causes for why that tragedy occurred. She shifted the blame away from middle management and located it instead in organizational dysfunction, establishing how internal work culture produced the outcome. A similar analysis can explain these failures for games as well.

Vaughan showed that from the inside view of those within the work group for the space shuttle's solid rocket booster, it was far from obvious that they were in a state of imminent peril. They had normalized operating with deviations from design as acceptable flight risks, which in terms of standards at NASA was acceptable not aberrant behavior. Some voices raised concerns, but even those dissenting opinions were absorbed by the mental framework in which the team operated.

After we have discussed her work in more detail, it will become clear how game developers can misinterpret critical signals in the run-up to their launches. From the native view, these signals arrive amid development noise, often within deep crunches. For individuals, even those at the top, not only are there tremendous pressures to not buck assumptions, but those assumptions might seem axiomatic. We can see how wires become crossed. Moreover, even veteran companies often have no training in recognizing these kinds of organizational threats.

Hindsight bias, after all, is an outside view. We look at failures knowing already how they turned out. Thus, due to the eventual outcome, we highlight signals that might not have been obvious at the time. We also suppress other signals, because we know they did not cause problems. We should be careful to see things as they were.

By understanding how these cultural factors warp our inside view, we can understand not only that we must step outside our paradigm, but how to do so. Only then can we deliver sharper, more predictable offerings to our customers.

The Challenger Disaster

On Jan 28, 1986, at 11:39am, the Space Shuttle Challenger launched and then broke apart 73 seconds into its flight. The failure of a joint in the right solid rocket booster caused the explosion. It is believed that unusually cold weather in Florida at the time hardened the O-rings, which aggravated long-standing issues. This was a particularly noteworthy flight as it was meant to demonstrate the safety of the shuttle program: already two politicians had flown, and now the civilian school teacher Christa McAuliffe would teach a lesson live from space to children on the ground.

Immediately after the disaster, then President Ronald Reagan created a commission to investigate the incident. This produced the Rogers Commission Report, which ascribed blame primarily to middle management. They supposedly had violated decision-making norms at NASA. Under political and scheduling pressure, these managers overrode the warnings of the engineers the night before, who had been concerned about the effects of low temperatures. The report also pointed to a history of problems with the O-rings and the joint dating back to the 1970s, which had never been rectified.[171] Many outside also ascribed the failures to groupthink, in line with Janis's work analyzing the Bay of Pigs Invasion.[172]

Given the Rogers Commission Report, records from the House Committee on Science and Technology hearings, and NASA's unusually robust decision histories, Vaughan decided there was a unique opportunity to study organizational misbehavior around the Challenger disaster. She began with the assumption that the Rogers Commission Report basically had it right. Early on, however, she realized that the story didn't make sense, especially the view that middle management had been engaged in coldly amoral decision-making, balancing politics and scheduling delays versus safety. After all, a delay of a few more hours to the afternoon launch window would have allowed cold temperatures to subside. Relative to even a small risk of launch failure, such a delay could pose no threat. Delays happened all the time. The previous shuttle flight had been pushed into the new year as it was, which had moved the Challenger launch already. As Vaughan dug deeper, she realized that the behaviors of middle management were far from deviant — they were explicitly rule-following.

What Vaughan discovered instead was a pattern of organizational behavior that allows us to see more clearly how these omissions in judgment arise, despite everything being so obvious in hindsight. The main identified root cause was normalization of deviance, a concept she developed for this case. Normalization of deviance occurs when deviant behaviors that potentially signal eventual critical failures are gradually normalized because those failures have not yet occurred.

Vaughan's conclusions shifted the focus to the way organizations frame behavior. The culture itself caused deviations to be normalized, ironically through the exercise of accepted norms. From the inside view of staff within NASA and Thiokol (the contractor for the solid rocket boosters), danger signals weren't recognized as long-term issues. They appeared sporadically and each time after investigation were considered resolved or shown to be within acceptable limits, even though the signals became more deviant from initial standards over time.

Both NASA and Thiokol executed patterns of reasoning that existed as an internal scientific paradigm within NASA. At every point, at least from within, the choices seemed reasonable. NASA operates at the limits of technology after all. Space flight is dangerous. Thus, NASA always had the notion of acceptable flight risks. There were procedures that governed how to evaluate threats and how information regarding them flowed through the organization. Working within this paradigm, the NASA/Thiokol work group established a pattern where a problem would be first identified and evaluated; then each time they would decide to approve flight with some fixes, rather than ground the shuttle program for a redesign. Only after the outcome was known did the aberrations in decision-making become clear.

Normalization of Deviance

As we noted last section, normalization of deviance describes how a cultural entity gradually accepts some previously deviant behaviors as normal, because the deviations have not yet caused a catastrophe. This can occur despite lacking enough experience for the problem to have likely arisen yet, so there is no established relationship between safety and normalization. It is akin to the false confidence we experience when we infer conclusions from small sample sets.

For the Challenger disaster, Vaughan posited three key root causes for the normalization of deviance that occurred with the Challenger's O-rings and SRB joints: work group culture, the culture of production, and structural secrecy.

There can be other causes for normalization of deviance, but these three are general sources of error.

Work Group Culture

All work groups develop their own flavor of the global organizational culture. Every culture is a set of norms. As put by Vaughan:[173]

> Norms — cultural beliefs and conventions originating in the environment create unreflective, routine, taken-for-granted scripts that become part of individual worldview. Invisible and unacknowledged rules for behavior, they penetrate the organization as categories of structure, thought, and action that shape choice in some directions rather than others.

This is key. These taken-for-granted rules generate the gut calls we make. They are the default mode of reality.

As we discussed in our chapter *Principles*, it isn't bad necessarily that work-group culture differs from global culture. Individual groups might have principles unique to their problem space. Principles should, however, conform to the overarching culture, acting as refinements not departures. When work groups deviate too much from global norms, it becomes harder for different teams to understand each other. Moreover, work groups can more easily become trapped in fraudulent perspectives. Unacceptable choices are then made, as the decisions appear in bounds according to work group standards.

After the work group is initially created, its first cultural framing decisions can seem trivial at the time. The early team might be small and the immediate stakes low, so a judgment call to take a shortcut seems safe, except it can gradually grow into a norm. Early on, we might decide to "temporarily" use a prototype as the foundation for our AAA game. As we build more atop this "temporary" core, it becomes easier to decide to continue using it, despite the instabilities and bugs that begin to mount. The cost to switch rises as well, and management glowers whenever we suggest a rework. One day we ship the final game with this prototype as foundation, with all that entails for maintenance and scaling problems. It is by no means inevitable that an initial choice cascades in this way, nor that we will be unable to rework it later; however, if that decision becomes a seed, we will find it increasingly hard to change our direction. Sometimes, only if an outsider joins our project and forces a break will we overcome our cultural inertia.

Robert Emerson noted the importance of this first choice in his research.[174] Our initial decisions set a normative standard. This can happen even when we don't intend for such a decision to be taken as instructive. We establish the precedent regardless. In turn, this creates patterns of reasoning that become our default.[175]

Vaughan showed that early in the development of the shuttle program, a critical pattern stabilized for the Thiokol and NASA work group. In the 1970s, long before the first launch of any of the shuttles, testing revealed that joint rotation exceeded design specifications. How much and what this meant depended on which location's testing setup was used. This rotation could cause the O-rings to fail to seal over some span of time during the initial launch. Here, the first key choice occurred. From it arose the pattern of decision-making that delayed a redesign on the rocket boosters. In the end, it justified the go that allowed the Challenger to launch on Jan 28, 1986. The pattern proceeded as follows: given a problem followed by an engineering investigation, should the team proceed with what they have, potentially applying fixes, or should they ground the shuttle and redesign the booster rockets. The first decision was to go. This pattern reoccurred over and over, yielding the same call, at least for matching cases. Distinct danger signs around the joints kept arising: increasing erosion of O-rings, holes in the putty, blow-by past the primary ring, burning on the secondary O-ring, and so on. No event by itself was a catastrophe. Each case was normalized as being within acceptable ranges or thought to have been fixed by a workaround. Each choice to proceed without redesign was validated when the problem failed to immediately reoccur. In the last year before the tragedy, O-ring erosion and blow-by became normalized, especially after they added a new process to guarantee better seating in the joint. The fix for that problem was expected to cause increased erosion, although it was still believed to be within safe limits. So, when they started to see higher erosion frequency over 1985, it was explained in advance. They even knew that cold weather could harden the O-rings and had evidence of increased erosion correlated with this but didn't investigate it since the cold weather snap of January 1985 in Florida was supposed to have been a rare event. No one expected it to reoccur the next year, repeating the same scenario, but now with the greater erosion due to the changes to improve seating in the joint. Every step conformed to established norms for the work group. Each choice expanded on the decision history. To overthrow those choices would mean that their process had been wrong from the start. From within the group, this seemed impossible.[176]

The Culture of Production

The accepted norms of an industry define its culture of production. As an organization and as a work group within that space, we inherit this culture, even though we can override it as well. Doing so, however, is never easy.

In AAA game development, there are many expected norms: those that govern crunch; whether shipping within pre-specified windows matters or not; when and how we interface with customers; what final-stage production phases should look like; and so on. Some of these beliefs arose for practical reasons, which might or might not still apply. Others arose from faults in our cognition, or as habits taken from social norms in other venues. Industries change over time and these norms can lag best practices.

GaaS games, for example, require that our products be functional earlier, as we must remember to allocate enough time to learn how to operate our service, fix our glitches, and serve new functionality stably and swiftly to customers. The hard crunches that typify many non-service offerings are also at odds with GaaS releases. In GaaS, launch is only the beginning. Oftentimes, a successful GaaS product grows a larger staff after it launches, in order to meet its customers' demands. Exhausting the team just to ship is a good way to engender poor service later, which often presages eventual failure for a service-based game. Even if we insulate a live team from the hard development crunch, should the project need more resources post-launch than expected, our development staff will be burnt out and unable to support the game for months.

To consider another cultural norm, while having a well-orchestrated marketing campaign greatly increases sales for a specific release, the brands themselves often have values close to a billion dollars. For predictable products like EA's *FIFA*, there is little risk to a yearly production schedule. *FIFA* releases are iterations. Because many publishers have become acclimated to this pattern, they attempt to map the same approaches onto far most risky propositions. This becomes a set of norms. For innovative products, especially games exploring new spaces, it can be better to foster the long-term value of the brand over a perfectly orchestrated marketing campaign. If we favor the long term, we at least generate value eventually. If we lock ourselves to a specific window, we will deliver on time, but wreck an IP and endanger our corporate brand. It's true that when there are many releases to compete with, we can become concerned about delays creating scheduling conflicts, but like software development itself, we should adopt more agile patterns of publishing. For public companies, we face additional stresses from shareholders, but we need to manage expectations rather than capitulate to demands for growth that will in time sabotage us. We should react to opportunities as they arise, rather than attempt to prognosticate futures that are only somewhat more predictable than the weather.

Much of the intent of this book is to point out where the culture of production in AAA game development no longer supports the goal of delivering customer value. We need to step outside our assumptions, look at other industries and cultures, and determine what principles give rise to success.

The Challenger work group similarly inherited norms from the aerospace industry. The NASA side of the team also inherited principles from Wernher Von Braun, who had brought his views for how scientific engineering should proceed. As NASA started to face scarcity for resources and competition with other government agencies, that too became part of the culture of production that surrounded the Thiokol and NASA work group. This defined their pre-rational framing of the world, which established what decisions were possible and desirable.[177]

Just as we discussed in our chapters *The Hero Complex* and *Creativity*, anything that unconsciously filters our decisions poses a threat.

Structural Secrecy

By structural secrecy, we mean the filtering or concealment of information that arises in response to scale. The larger the organization, the more information it generates. While Big Data approaches have altered the chemistry of this reaction, the problem remains. How we compress, highlight, and conceal information molds our decisions, so we must consciously evaluate our procedures.

There are two forms of structural secrecy we should consider. The first is systematic censorship.[178] Since we produce too much information, we curate the stream, potentially using distinct patterns targeted to particular audiences. Necessarily, this causes some information to be lost; however, we strive to engineer these filters such that salient information passes with critical cues highlighted, while noise for that specific audience is suppressed. In the second form of secrecy, the information is not curated, but is sent *en masse*. In this case, so much information is sent that the user can't consume it. This sometimes happens with large documents that lack a quick and targeted abstract. The receivers ignore the data dump due to time constraints. Here, information is hidden in plain sight. This is the firehose method of secrecy.

In the case of the Challenger disaster, Vaughan discussed patterns of communication that were taken for granted, but that concealed information. As an example of the first form of secrecy, when information was passed up the chain, there was a policy that only changes and exceptions were mentioned. This was done to reduce the stream to consumable chunks. This meant, however, that if a concern was raised in a previously noted area, but that concern was resolved according to standard procedures, then nothing would be reported. Thus, at the highest levels of administration on the day of the Challenger disaster, many did not realize Thiokol had suggested no-go for the flight but then switched back to a go, or that there were concerns about the cold temperature's impact on the O-rings. As Vaughan discussed, there were numerous cases where data filtering hid danger signals — not with any intention of concealment, but to make the information reports readable.

There isn't an easy resolution for structural secrecy. Each of us can only absorb so much information. This means that important cues can be lost. Due to its critical impacts on our understanding of the world and our decision-making, it is worth our time to evaluate our communication graph. Do we send information to the right people and in the right quantity? What aren't we sending?

One of the core principles for our decision-making system is also full transparency. While we need to filter our information streams, we should allow access to the complete data set. It is important that our databases also be easy to access and use, as difficulty can itself impose a form of structural secrecy.

Never Tolerate Waste

Deviance isn't necessarily bad. It's just behavior that falls outside the standard. In fact, for innovative industries, deviance is required! All new ideas break norms. The greatest of them break paradigms, and usher in new eras.

In truth, we are concerned not with normalization of deviance, but with normalization of waste. Next chapter, we'll define waste in more detail, but for now, waste is behavior that leads to sub-par outcomes for our customer. Waste should never be normalized, although we might need to tolerate it for a time.

As an example, imagine we have an automated testing system that runs every submit through a battery of tests across both PC and console systems. Our system is stable and sound, which is critical as we've entered a stage in our project where new features are pouring into the build. A harried engineer develops a new feature; the test associated with it doesn't meet our standard of quality. It is unstable and gives a false negative 10% of the time. The developer is behind on their tasks, so no one badgers them to fix it. This state persists — after all, tasks keep pouring in, and it's such a minor problem. Eventually, everyone comes to accept that this test is periodically wrong. Then another test for an already existing feature starts to give false negatives 10% of the time. The owner looks at it and puts a solution in; for a time, everyone thinks it's fixed, but then it returns. This gets ignored as the owner is now also busy — there's a demo due next month! It's harder to make the argument now that the test should be a priority, since the first failing test remains unresolved. So, we decide to ignore this one as well. Over time, more tests become undependable and the failure rate stacks up. At a certain point, no one bothers to check test successes when they submit. Actual failures still trip tests, but with all the noise, no one notices for hours. Failures compound as people submit over broken builds. Eventually, the mainline is frequently busted, so we try to pull it only when required. When we merge our feature with the current head of the mainline and discover a new glitch, we blame it on the existing codebase rather than consider if our code is interacting poorly. We thus inject another fault. We reach a point where the mainline is never functional. We still need to release builds, so when necessary we trigger an emergency push and stabilize what we have. We never resolve the problem, however, as we have accrued excessive technical debt. To face the situation and fix it, we would have to acknowledge that our past decisions were in error. Since the work required is now large, there might be repercussions if we own up to it. The best leaders accept responsibility regardless, but for many, this is a hard choice to make.

Unlike deviance, waste is never defined relative to normal behavior. Waste is defined relative to customer value only. Deviance can be good or bad, depending on our norms. Waste is always bad relative to specific customers. Something might be waste for one customer and a desirable feature for another, however.

Thus, we must never tolerate waste. We can't always resolve problems immediately, but we must recognize that they are problems. Waste can never be normalized as inevitable. It must be tracked, and if it lives too long, we must deal with it before it becomes a *de facto* part of our environment.

When we join a team to help them out with their problems, establishing any normalization of waste should be a priority. To do that, we must first ensure that they have a solid Razor. Since waste is defined relative to a customer, if a project doesn't understand who their customer is, we can't know whether something is waste. We should then check for decision histories and telemetry, since waste is hard to quantify if we lack data. After those steps are taken, we need to get out onto the floor and search out the team's accepted wastes.

We must also coach the team to recognize waste for themselves, as we won't have enough bandwidth to suss out all the problems.

14

Historical Foundations

Our philosophy arises from a long tradition, some of which originates from post-war 1940s Japan. It required decades, however, for these traces to spread all the way to software engineering. While Agile and Lean approaches are prevalent today, it is still the case that old assumptions remain the norm in many companies.

The fundamental schism between the old and the new is that between predictive and exploratory development.

In predictive development, we presume that early on we know what the customers' problem will be and the form of the solution required; the challenge is then building a schedule and executing on it. When we start with this framing, we prioritize planning to favor construction costs, rather than integrate our features and validate them early. This assumes that we begin with the solution, know the parts, understand how they fit together, and that our processes of assembling everything are mostly flawless.

This is an insidious problem. Many teams claim they prove out their games from the start, but when we examine their actual practices, we often find critical and risky elements have been pushed back to the end. We assume that we have the solution even though we haven't exposed it to our customers. We test how much we can get away with, often to our detriment.

If our assumptions about our predictive capabilities were true, this would be fine. This is a tempting paradigm as we can commit more features upfront, giving us the appearance of a stronger product. We're doing so, of course, by pretending that large amounts of necessary work and exploration do not exist. In the end, we reap what we sow.

This view still prevails even where Agile practices such as Scrum dominate. We believe we have the right answer, and we resist evidence that suggests we are mistaken. After all, we're experienced developers, we know what we're supposed to build. And time pressure is upon us. We are afraid that if we are wrong, we're doomed from the start anyway.

For one project I was on, there were two kinds of levels, each associated with a different kind of gameplay. We had been testing the first type for a long time: these were small levels of around a few square kilometers in playable area. We had built and tested these for team-based player-versus-player combat. The other type of level was much larger — around two hundred square kilometers of playable area. Here the mode was player-versus-environment (by which I mean against computer-controlled game objects). Other human players were in the area as well, but in small numbers. The feel of combat against NPCs was completely different than that against players. There were key differences in how the player might interact with these worlds and with the elements of gameplay offered. Even the core navigation and controls had different implications — in PVP, all games were tactical with fixed environments, but in this

Deep Management

PVE mode it was more about exploitation of the world and traveling. Plus, the size of the levels posed challenges to resource budgets and how objects should be constructed. These larger levels defined most of the technical requirements for the game as they produced the most stress; the smaller levels placed more pressure on moment-to-moment movement precision, but otherwise were simpler. At one point, we even considered loading the smaller levels entirely into memory, whereas this was impossible with the larger ones! As usual with games, this project was also under heavy time pressure. Thus, the decision was taken that these large levels would be built up incrementally, without ever having an example taken to final quality and then exposed to an actual customer. The assumption was that we could predict all the challenges these larger levels would encounter *a priori*. We instead focused on the smaller levels to polish an aspect of navigation visible to top management and hoped that everything would work out.

It is hard for people to see that their assumptions can be wrong; this is doubly true when wrong assumptions mean that our state of progress is worse than we have communicated.

In exploratory development, on the other hand, we realize that we might not even know the proper question. Our goal here is to start the best experiments immediately. To validate these tests, we need customers in our product as soon as possible. That makes us nervous, but we need to get over our ego.[179] We also mustn't pen ourselves in too early. Once we've figured out the right thing to build, we build across the board as fast as we can. Whereas in predictive development, we are fragile to being wrong, in exploratory development we are resilient, as we commit as late as possible and build only what we need.

In keeping with a theme of this book, though, we will note that the late decision-making of exploratory development can be a twisted reflection. Some technical answers we need to know early on. Software architectures can be radically different, and while we should do our best to mitigate this, sometimes we're stuck. We need to push back decisions that aren't critical now and prioritize any questions concerning the rest. Sometimes leadership teams will try to exploit late decision-making to keep the maximal set of potential features far longer than wise, often to dangle bait for marketing and business teams. This can result in situations where a game could either be completely linear and story-based or heavily multiplayer and systemic, all at the same time. The specific type of product we build will generate many questions that we will need to answer, so we need to focus and get to our core issues immediately. Doing otherwise leads to chaos. The key is to recognize that late decision-making is good, which is true, and balance it with the principle that critical decisions need to be tested empirically early.

The Agile Umbrella

In the 1980s and 90s, there was a recognition in software development that we were doing something wrong. Initially, we thought the problem was that we weren't using "mature" development processes — our concept of mature was that of manufacturing from the 80s and earlier, not realizing that manufacturing had already moved on. These methods established work to be done upfront and tried to make employees fungible by strict requirements definitions. The thought was any engineer could then do the task. This was all well-intentioned to address scale for software development. Unfortunately, many of these projects failed along numerous dimensions — quality issues, cost overruns, scheduling problems, and so on.

Gradually, many practitioners realized something was wrong. People independently discovered practices that worked and started to adopt them as methodologies, even though these practices were at odds with the older manufacturing paradigm. Ken Schwaber started using a method in the early 90s, which eventually became Scrum. Around the same time, Jeff Sutherland, John Scumniotales, and Jeff

McKenna used a similar approach; the name Scrum came from this system and was brought over by Sutherland. In 1995, Sutherland and Schwaber published the paper that made Scrum public. Meanwhile, Kent Beck began refining the methodology that became Extreme Programming in 1996 and published the book on it in 1999.[180] Jim Highsmith created the Adaptive Software Method,[181] based off previous work with Sam Beyer on the Rapid Application Development approach. Alistair Cockburn created a family of lightweight methodologies called Crystal with levels of color for industry requirements such as safety and security.[182] These methodologies piecemeal began to upend assumptions about what worked and what didn't.

Gradually, cross-talk between software developers and other manufacturing and engineering disciplines exposed that software had been stuck in the past. These lightweight approaches that developed incrementally in the 90s were related to ideas that had become prevalent already elsewhere. We'll discuss the Toyota Way and Lean in more detail later, but these models had been the foundation of Toyota overtaking the American Big Three in terms of cost and quality. By the mid-1990s, research had already begun to answer why some of these methods worked, through studies in operations research, complex systems theory, and related fields. These methodologies were based on concurrent engineering (also known as simultaneous engineering) — where the stages of production were all done at the same time instead of sequentially. This approach was done so that once customer demand was established (preferably by an actual order that arrived), a solution could then be developed and delivered with the least time to market. This directly related to the priority these Agile methods placed on working software from the start, rather than building up layers of software that only worked together at the end.

In games, this is akin to getting a subset of the game up, fun, and operational. We then test the true boundaries of our proposed system (or more likely, showing where our game is broken and needs fixing). The older model was to build the entire game as functional pieces that only existed in integrated forms at the end (thus finding out where our game is broken and needs fixing at the last minute).

In service-oriented games like Bungie's *Destiny*, Bethesda's *Fallout 76*, and Ubisoft's *Rainbow Six: Siege*, this tension arises in terms of the question of how early developers and customers should be consistently playing on somewhat realistic server environments (spoiler: as soon as humanly possible). Some of these games try to cut short the pre-launch service operation period to compress schedules and avoid risk of negative press from early builds. It's usually visible in the final product when the developers attempt to do so.

Over the course of the 1990s, through many conferences and workshops, the proponents of these changes found each other and decided their common ideas required framing. This led to the generation of four key values and twelve principles of Agile, which were expressed in the Agile manifesto, published in 2001.

Each of Agile's values flipped previous assumptions:

1) Individuals are more important than conformance to processes
2) Working software is more important than documentation
3) Customer collaboration is more important than contracts
4) Be responsive to change over a plan

In putting individuals first, Agile presumed that the people on the floor have the most immediate access to what the best choice would be. Processes can be useful in that they encode protections against mistakes we have made in the past, but they also can be poorly targeted or invalid. This isn't a negation of the value of process — after all, we advocate processes in this book and members of the Agile family are themselves processes — it is a statement that the judgment of an individual can override the methodology, or for that matter correct it. We do not serve the system; the system serves us.

Working software meanwhile validates our decisions immediately, whereas documentation is usually out of date. If we have working software, we can take it to the user and determine value. If our algorithms are flawed, we get exposed to it early. This is a principle related to concurrent engineering. Don't build software in layers that work only at the end. Build it all together and test it as it grows.

Customer collaboration reflects the notion that we cannot define contracts upfront that specify what we need. If we interact directly with the customer (especially with working software), we will find out whether we are headed in the right direction or not. This is a repudiation of predictive development. It also helps promote trust between the development team and the customer.

Being responsive to change over a plan recognizes that software development is a series of experiments, and that plans often generate waste if they are based on poor assumptions.

Altogether, these values make Agile an exploratory development approach. Agile embraces that we don't know what the full problem is from the start. What is important is that we establish the best means of seeking it out and solving it. And the best means of seeking out the problem and the solution is to iterate with actual customers, preferably without bringing our own assumptions.

These values were justified not on theory but based on projects that had employed them and produced better outcomes. The products so produced might have had fewer bells and whistles, but the software was more valuable to users and available earlier. Again, this is the key takeaway: less is more, if it is the right core of features. Fewer lines of code doing the right thing are superior to many lines doing many things. Direct experimental interaction with users guides projects closer to theoretical golden paths.

The Agile Manifesto[183] then outlined these twelve core principles:

1) Customer satisfaction by early and continuous delivery of valuable software
2) Welcome changing requirements, even in late development
3) Working software is delivered frequently (weeks rather than months)
4) Close, daily cooperation between business people and developers
5) Projects are built around motivated individuals, who should be trusted
6) Face-to-face conversation is the best form of communication (co-location)
7) Working software is the primary measure of progress
8) Sustainable development, able to maintain a constant pace
9) Continuous attention to technical excellence and good design
10) Simplicity—the art of maximizing the amount of work not done—is essential
11) Best architectures, requirements, and designs emerge from self-organizing teams
12) Regularly, the team reflects on how to become more effective, and adjusts accordingly

Within Agile, there are many methodologies — Scrum, Kanban, Extreme, Lean Software Development, and so on. This book isn't about these specific approaches. We've worked with many of them, and the mainstream ones all have their place. We will mention Extreme shortly as there is an aspect of its formulation that provides a wise lesson. Later, in the Lean section we'll discuss Lean Software Development.

It is within these methodologies that we can find a rebirth of reliance on process, which creates some controversies. It is almost a cliché that teams implementing Scrum argue that whatever the team is doing, it is not legitimate Scrum. For hardcore adherents, deviation from the standards can nullify entirely the value of the whole proposition. There are some points of violation that are problematic for sure (changing stories post commitment being one of the most egregious). However, in keeping with Agile goals, we mostly want a system that works, as long as our alterations haven't fundamentally violated the principles that underlie our approach. This is, in fact, one of Agile's key values! Individuals over processes. Part of Agile is understanding that what works is what is best — experiment can overthrow assumptions. This is equally true of the methods we espouse in this book. We should, however, watch out for normalization of deviance.[184]

For clarification, when Agile asserts that working software is more important than documentation, this is not the same documentation we've mentioned in terms of our decision and principle history. That system exists for a different purpose. In Agile, working software is a demonstration of what is true at a point in time; documentation reflects more what we thought was true, would like to be true, or was true at some point in the past, all of which might have nothing to do with what the actual software does now.

The purpose of our decision history is instead to record our choices and their foundations when we made them. We are trying to immunize ourselves against distortion of history, which is critical to maintaining a culture where the truth is not dominated by narrative.

Working software serves a similar purpose, as it is an artifact that is irrefutably true and that does something that is empirically testable. In fact, we recommend that these versions of working software be kept someplace secure in addition to our decision and principle histories, although generally a different storage system should be used.[185] It's common enough that our people will argue about the state of our software in the past, viewing it either harshly or nostalgically. Especially if we have undergone pivots, there are risks of regression in terms of fun and value. Usable artifacts can shorten these disputes.

Working software in this case often implies more than the binaries. With services, it often involves environmental set-up as well. A working software artifact should include everything necessary to deploy it via automation, although it's possible that it will take longer than a current deploy, as it might require time to configure machines to previous states, whereas our current systems might have machines ready to go.

Extreme Programming

We won't discuss the details of Extreme Programming here, but there is a key approach to its philosophy that should be highlighted. Kent Beck started iterating on Extreme on the 3C project for Chrysler, starting in 1996, and published his book on the topic in 1999: *Extreme Programming Explained.* His method is most associated with practices such as continuous integration, paired programming, rapid releases, test-driven development, and listening. Many subsequent methodologies incorporated Extreme ideas into their own approaches.

The details, however, aren't what we want to point out. What is most interesting about Extreme is this: Kent Beck created his methodology almost entirely by taking accepted software engineering practices and asking why not do this more.

Peer reviews are considered valuable for code submits, so why not do peer reviews continuously while writing the code instead of at the end — hence paired programming.

If it is good to submit your chunk of code into the mainline as soon as it is ready, why not always work in the mainline and submit daily? Hence continuous integration.

If It is better to get features into users' hands as early as possible, why not rapidly (or continually) release?

There are similarities here to the Theory of Constraints (discussed later in this chapter). We take a practice that works and see what it would look like if we pushed it as far as it will go. The result can be terrible — for example, some documentation is good, but voluminous documentation is unmaintainable (and runs against Agile values). Pushing all the way to the limit can go too far — a gallon of coffee a day might be too much. Even if we overshoot, by pushing as far out as we can go, we often clear out unknowns rapidly. Then we can step back and establish a position that's more reasonable.

Extreme is a perfect example of how we can flush out our blind spots. Construct bold experiments, especially early on. As we noted in Part II: *Distortions of Reality*, we humans often fall into mental traps. If we are jolted out of our safe space, we will recognize that some of the crazy solutions are the only sane options when viewed from the outside. A project might struggle in development for years because a large pivot seemed too risky — perhaps our customers' needs required we change architectures or change the game mode. But then we make the change as risky as it is, and the project ships and succeeds. Meanwhile, the project would otherwise still be in development or have been canceled. Which path was riskier — the bold or the timid one?

So, we should remember, Kent Beck made a huge impact merely by asking this question: "What if we did more of this good thing until it breaks?" Anyone can do that. We just need to recognize that it's an option.

Lean

The Toyota Way and Lean influenced the philosophy of both manufacturing and software development more than any other trend in the last thirty years. We often associate Lean with eliminating waste, but this can be confusing to people new to the approach. They fail to understand what waste is and get stuck on issues of low-level waste — for example, frictions in development on the floor. Those are indeed wastes, but when we're failing to get to customer value early, we are missing the far more significant ones. When we work without a purpose, the value of our work is multiplied by zero.

Even though we don't know the destination at the start, knowing that we are here to augment customer value is enough to allow us to produce effective work.

To break through this confusion, in modern parlance it has become more common to talk about optimizing customer value instead of eliminating waste. This doesn't change Lean, as the message was there from the start. Waste subtracts from value, as the effort could have been directed towards faster concurrent engineering solutions to meet demand or otherwise add value for a customer by precise targeting. Focusing on the positive aspect of delivering value makes Lean easier to explain to newcomers, without altering the fundamental message.

While we prioritize eliminating waste, it is critical to note that the process begins by seeking a profound understanding of the customer. Waste is defined relative to this customer, as features are waste or value depending on the customers' needs. For a canonical story of this aspect from the history of Toyota, we can consider Ichiro Suzuki (one of Toyota's most famed engineers) and how he had his team establish the customer problems to be solved for the first Lexus LX.[186] When Suzuki and his team first started the project, they did so with mistaken understandings of what their American consumers would want out of a luxury vehicle — they saw the world through the cultural lenses of Japan. They came to California, however — seen as a core market for their product — and began with in-depth customer interviews before they commenced any design. This established that functionality was a far less important factor than they'd imagined. Prestige was primary. They followed up by then having their engineers drive around the United States, in so doing recognizing the many practical differences about how US drivers experienced their vehicles versus Japanese drivers. This led to Suzuki defining the "no-compromise objectives" for the Lexus, which were extremely challenging but necessary goals. It is characteristic of the Toyota Way that there is a primary voice who creatively owns the product from the outset. It is also characteristic that this voice must explain the reasoning behind these goals so that the team is fully engaged in a process of ownership.[187] Even though the goals seemed impossible, the team embraced their necessity. Lexus went on to become one of the premier luxury car brands in the world, renowned both for quality and dependability.

Originally, Lean came from the Toyota Production System (now branded as the Toyota Way). This was a managerial and technical approach developed at Toyota between 1948 and 1975. The problem faced by Toyota at the time was that after the war, they wanted to produce vehicles as cheaply as possible, but that required mass production; the Japanese car market could not absorb the number of units that such an approach required. They needed to be able to generate many different types of vehicles in smaller quantities. Moreover, there was a premium on inventory, since holding unsold vehicles increased cost.

Taiichi Ohno is most associated with bringing together the various threads of philosophy both from practices at large and internally developed at Toyota in earlier days, going perhaps as far back to when Sakichi Toyoda built mechanized looms. Originally, the approach was called "just-in-time production." This formed a loop where customer demand for cars would arrive and concurrent engineering practices would respond with delivery as fast as possible. To enable this loop, Toyota was forced to build a system of continuous self-improvement rising from the floor. Thus, through what were fortuitous circumstance in retrospect, the pressures placed upon Toyota forced them to generate a methodology that not only solved their local challenges but generated levels of quality and efficiency far beyond that of American car manufacturers. At a time when the quality of American cars had been in decline, Toyota took a dominating lead in the 1980s.

Stripped to its core, there are two root principles of the Toyota Way:

1) Just-in-time manufacturing
2) Jidoka aka autonomation

It is out of these two core principles that the other characteristics of Lean arose.

The common approach to car manufacturing at the time, at least as practiced by the big three US automakers, was to operate factories as a series of queues focused on throughput to satisfy enormous demand, especially in the United States. An assumption of the model was that any shutdown on an assembly line was unacceptable. To avoid shutdowns, two practices were common. First, parts were ordered in large quantities and stockpiled so that the assembly lines would never be stopped due to starvation of inputs. Another perceived benefit of this was that the cost per part would be lower when ordered in large lots due to amortization. Second, a final-stage quality-control process occurred at the end of the pipeline to address any faults that might have occurred in assembly, rather than stopping assembly lines immediately at the point where the fault occurred to correct it. While this kept the assembly line operating without bubbles, this also meant that some portion of the products were faulty and that whatever caused the fault might not be addressed until much later. Oftentimes, the final-stage quality-control process did not catch all defects.

Just-in-time manufacturing in the Toyota Way means that "one should make only what is needed, when it is needed, and only in the amount that is needed.[188]" From our earlier discussion, it should be apparent how this addressed the local problems experienced by Toyota in Japan from the 1940s onwards.[189]

Beyond that, though, it addressed the two key problems we just mentioned. As the Big Three pushed harder for throughput, they aggravated core problems and quality declined. Ordering massive quantities of parts all at once and doing quality control at the end meant that defects in parts were discovered late if they were discovered at all. This made total quality harder to achieve.

For the first problem, suppose that a part for a car has a defect, but that the issues aren't apparent until the part is installed, or the car is fully assembled. Because one aspect of the motivation of the Big Three system was to reduce the cost per part, parts were ordered in massive lots up front. This meant that one could receive large quantities of defective components. This resulted in two possible unpleasant decisions. First choice: eat the loss and return or throw away the rejects, accepting the subsequent bubble in throughput, and hope the next lot is corrected. Second choice: accept the defect and try to resolve the issue in final quality control. Resolving issues in the final stage generally meant either patching or ignoring the fault if it was common, of if it was rare, taking the car apart and replacing it with a non-defective component or outright junking that specific vehicle. Fixing the car at the end was expensive, as many layers had been installed over the defect at that point — moreover, taking the car apart to fix an issue could break something else. Patching or ignoring the fault reduced quality. Junking obviously was expensive.

Second, the final quality-control pass was not as thorough at detecting faults as the assembly-line workers were when the part was initially installed. Anything could be wrong at the end, but at the point of installation, the fault could have been known. However, according to their process, the worker could not stop the line to address the problem when it occurred, as this would slow throughput. The assumption was that it would be caught later.

These two issues meant decreased quality in US cars. In fact, as the pressure mounted to increase throughput, it meant a continuing decline.

Just-in-time manufacturing, on the other hand, meant that we only order the parts that we need. If we discover a defect, there is no inventory to be junked. We go to the vendor and correct the problem immediately.

Moreover, if a worker detects a fault, it is their duty to stop the line. This is Jidoka or autonomation — automation with a human touch. The workers have access to a cord that they could pull to stop the line; there was no need to get a manager first. When this occurred, the floor manager would go to the point of stoppage along with the engineers, and they would determine how to resolve the issue and get the line moving again without the fault (for the short-term, this might involve getting rid of the part). Afterward, the engineers were required to find the root cause of the fault and get it fixed, so that this problem would not occur again. The results would then be documented for future analysis. In terms of the Toyota Way, this is called "building quality in." Fix errors at their point of inception. Don't assume they'll be resolved later.

Workers were also tasked with raising issues about the production flow itself. For example, a worker might notice that the positions of tools in a workspace meant that they needed to reach unnecessarily. Tools would be moved to reduce motion. Perhaps some tools did not have designated locations — all tools would be assigned to optimal positions, and workers would return them after use to their slot, so that no search was required. Perhaps when parts were delivered to the line, the worker needed to stop to put them in place — this would be noted and a solution found, oftentimes by the workers themselves.

The hiccups generated by bubbles and stoppages were themselves subjected to analysis. Removing the direct cause of the stoppage would address the issue, naturally. However, recognizing that issues arise, engineers and workers also provided solutions for shortening the length of these bubbles when a stoppage occurred. For example, knowing that parts were ordered only as needed, sometimes parts for a car model would run out — the assembly lines were retooled to make it as fast as possible to reset them to build a different vehicle until the necessary parts arrived. This also addressed the issue that the company didn't want to overbuild product and store it as inventory. Or if a worker pulled a Kanban cord to stop the line, how could they accelerate the resolution process and get the line moving again without impacting quality?

Sometimes, engineers would deliberately stress the systems to expose problems. For example, a factory might have two assembly lines, but a manager might decide on a slower day to shut down one line and run the other at higher speed to expose weaknesses. Fixing the issues that arise from such a test means that the line is more likely to remain stable and high quality on higher production days when we place both under pressure. Or alternatively, if one line broke down, the other line was better prepared to take the burden. This is akin to the common modern practice of chaos testing (also known as chaos engineering). Netflix's Chaos Monkey tool would be an example.[190] Here, deliberate faults are forced in live production systems to validate and strengthen resilience.

Fundamentally, the Toyota Way and Lean seek out weakness and address it.

Both methods also place great value on their staff. Toyota engages their people as owners, and they strive to retain them — for life when possible. Toyota invests in its personnel with training and continued-learning initiatives. This is common to Lean as well. This also means that engineers must be humble when working with staff on the floor. In some companies, engineers hold themselves as superior to assembly-line workers. At Toyota, the engineers need to be able to hear the solutions from the floor, rather than assume the floor has nothing to offer. As a side benefit, this also improves the engineers' capacity to hear the real problems of their customers.

At this point, it's worth noting a specific technique that was used to ensure the highest quality solutions to problems. This is known as the Five Whys. It is easy given a problem to just consider the immediate issue. To cite a terrible but common enough mistake by new programmers, consider a program that crashes on a null-pointer exception. The general worst fix for this is to check if the pointer is null before running the code that uses it. For car manufacturing, perhaps the case is a misaligned axle, so we stop at the fact that the axle is misaligned, correct that, and move on. The question missed in both cases is why that condition occurred. Why was the pointer null? Was that to be expected? If not, what caused that? If the axle was misaligned, why was it misaligned? Was it a fault from earlier in the process? Did a preceding step jitter it? Is it a defect in the part? The problem is that the most immediate solution often only covers the fault, which remains and will either reoccur later or degrade the general quality of the product.

One might consider the quality of rendering in video games as an example. Sometimes inexperienced engineers think aliasing problems can be resolved at the end through a final anti-aliasing pass (a common example of aliasing in games would be jagged edges for objects, but moiré patterns in screen doors, stairs, brick patterns, and the like would also be cases, among others). While a final AA pass is recommended, it hardly addresses the root problem, nor will it generate an acceptable result. Rendering is a layered process, and aliasing arises from sampling incorrectly at earlier stages (sometimes unavoidably so), which causes damage either by losing information or by injecting information that shouldn't be there. Once the damage is done, post-processing can mitigate the error somewhat, but we no longer have the correct data. The proper answer is to determine why the aliasing occurred in the first place.

Thus, the practice of the Five Whys. Given a symptom, we establish the first set of causes, which represent the first Why — note, there can be more than one cause. We then ask what generated these causes. Why was the pointer null? Why was the axis misaligned? That is the second Why. Then you ask why that occurred. We do this until we have reached the fifth layer. In truth, sometimes once we've dug to the third or fourth, the Whys become less valuable. We might argue what is special about five. Maybe six is better? Practitioners assert that five is almost always enough. In the end, go as deep as necessary, but ask why until the results cease to valuable. Then address the root problem.

Waste

Waste is the term most commonly mentioned when someone first hears about Lean. Waste is deviance from optimal resource allocation in advancing customer value.

Thus, anything that reduces value, involves work that doesn't increase customer value, or doesn't increase it as much as it could is then waste. Not all waste is equal, however. There are two types:

Type A: Waste that doesn't increase value but is required — this could be to satisfy regulatory requirements or for HR purposes, such as employee reviews. This waste cannot be removed, but it can be reduced. For example, employee surveys throughout the year might reduce the expected length of review meetings that happen sporadically, thus being a case where automation offsets human effort (and perhaps the more frequent check-ins so engendered will result in earlier notification of dissatisfaction).

Type B: Waste that is unnecessary. Typically, the primary target of reduction efforts.

Originally, the Toyota Way defined the following seven types of waste:[191]
1) Transport — unnecessary movement of components for processing
2) Inventory — any product waiting to be used for processing
3) Motion — unnecessary movement of workers for processing
4) Waiting — idle workers and machines, waiting for inputs to process
5) Overproduction — producing more products than are in demand
6) Over-processing — doing more work that isn't necessary for the product to have value for the customer
7) Defects — work arising from discarded defective parts or fixing defects

Later, the Toyota Way adding an eight form of waste — underutilized skills. The Toyota Way places a great deal of value on human capabilities. This is the case where our people are not used to their maximal effect.[192]

Lean Software Development

After some time spent in manufacturing, Mary Poppendieck returned to software development and founds its processes antiquated. She and her husband then developed and wrote *Lean Software Development: An Agile Toolkit*, aiming to bring Lean principles across disciplines.

Early on in the book, Mary Poppendieck describes how she was brought onto a project that needed to be in place within five months for reasons of legal compliance, where the first five months of the project had been creating thick documentation that the clients wouldn't sign for fear of what might or might not be in it, only to have the documentation invalidated in the weeks just before her arrival — essentially reducing progress on the project to zero with an unmovable compliance deadline. This project resolved on time and met legal obligations, but the history of what happened shows how unstable these older approaches were. Older methods assumed that changes were so expensive that they couldn't be allowed as the project went on, and therefore everything needed to be defined up front. As we've discussed in this book, this is a fragile approach.

A better approach is inspired from Lean, where we make our systems more flexible to change and focus first on discovering the customer's problem. Lean Software Development is a translation of Lean processes from physical products to the software development space. Classical Lean approaches tend to focus on manufacturing problems, where recipes drive the reproducible production of outputs. Software development is more about the creation of the recipe, and thus has some different priorities. As we will discuss later for games, though, the final phase of AAA development tends to resemble the product manufacturing phase, so we shift from a software development focus to a production mentality at the end. As Lean Software Development also belongs to Agile, many of its core tools are in common with other methodologies. At the same time, other tools came in with Lean Software Development and then migrated to the rest of the family later.

The key principles of Lean Software Development[193] are akin to the principles of Lean:

1) Eliminate waste
2) Amplify learning
3) Decide as late as possible
4) Deliver as fast as possible
5) Empower the team
6) Build integrity in
7) See the whole

Eliminate Waste:

We will discuss the categorization of waste provided by the Poppendiecks more in its own list shortly, but this principle is equivalent to the notion of waste in Lean. It has become more common to talk about optimizing customer value rather than eliminating waste, but again it is just for clarification. The point of all Lean approaches is to deliver more value relentlessly.

Amplify Learning:

Again, a common principle for Lean. If we are faced with a failure, that is an opportunity to improve ourselves. If someone learns from an experiment, that knowledge should be made available, not hoarded. Our entire company should share the same frontier of understanding as much as possible. It should never be the case that solving a problem is the end of the story. Doing otherwise is a lost opportunity to generate more value.

Decide as Late as Possible:

When we make decisions too early, we often waste effort on the wrong features. If we do not need to decide today, put it off until tomorrow when we'll know more. This is part of set-based development. As we've mentioned earlier, however, not making decisions when they need to be made is a twisted reflection. Also, using late decision-making to continue offering temptations to internal marketing and business teams also runs counter to fixating on customer value.

Deliver as Fast as Possible:

This is the core principle of concurrent engineering. Once we have established what we want to deliver, get it to the customer fast. Work on our delivery pipelines to foster this. This is also central to working software. Get useful features to users as fast as possible, rather than delivering all in one final clump.

Empower the Team:

Value comes from the floor, but it can only arise if we empower the team. If we treat our team members as owners, they will behave as such. If we engage in micromanaging and top-down control structures, we will induce waste. Our teams should focus on the outcome for our customer, not race through task queues.

Build Integrity In:

This is a classic Lean concern. Build integrity throughout our systems, not just on the surface at the end. When we build an internal system, make the system sound. When our pipeline has issues, rectify them. Do not accept a high normal of deviance. In doing this, we will improve our capacity to deliver on all our principles, while also bringing higher quality to our customer. Again, this can be taken too far. Systems can also be overbuilt, which is an example of the overproduction waste.

See the Whole:

It is common in some cultures to worry about dusting the cabinets while the house burns down. All of us must see the bigger picture. We must seek quality in our work, but at the same time, sometimes that effort could be better spent elsewhere. Further improvements of the toolset for our content generators can be excessive, especially when that time could be better spent. Everyone should strive to see the whole, not just the top managers. Again, our team should see themselves as owners. We need to develop the capacity to both zoom in on a specific problem and then step back to see holistically.

Types of Waste:

Lean Software Development enumerated eight forms of waste:[194]

1) Partially done work
2) Extra processes
3) Extra features
4) Task switching
5) Waiting
6) Motion

7) Defects
8) Management activities

Partially Done Work:

This is a symptom of not getting to customer value early enough and not propagating that value to the developers. This is work we start but then later cut. Typically, in a rush to get a project out, speculative work begins. Sometimes this is not easy to avoid, but when making such a choice, we should always ask if we can schedule key questions earlier that would either justify the work or invalidate it. Other times we should ask whether this work can begin later without jeopardizing our production constraints. Sometimes people try to avoid the appearance of partially done work by shoe-horning an incorrect system into an alternative role, instead of cutting the work and doing the correct system. Misapplied systems are equally a waste to the degree that they do not fit the solution. Adaptation can re-purpose a system to a degree, in which case the degree of misalignment represents the total amount of waste. Oftentimes, such systems also result in defects.

Extra Processes:

This is self-explanatory. As part of our software-development practices, we might engage in redundant or otherwise non-value adding processes. This could be forms of documentation that are never used. It could be approvals by managers that aren't relevant anymore. It's not unusual that over the course of time, there is a build-up of such activities, which we must continuously challenge.

Extra Features:

This is one of the most classic forms of waste. Sometimes we don't know what the customer wants and so we build things they don't need. Such products become packed with modes that go unused and are distractions to users. In turn, this causes unnecessary maintenance and defects, even ignoring the work it took to develop the features in the first place. It is characteristic of Lean philosophy that we often find that the users desire different features than we expected and far fewer of them. Users frequently don't care about purity, but do care about usability, responsiveness to inputs, and loading speeds.

Task Switching:

The issue of task switching is well known across most disciplines. Multi-tasking results in substantial lost time as we need to put ourselves back into the problem-solving mindset after each switch. It is well documented that the more complex the task, the more time is lost to an interruption. Doing two tasks sequentially gets the tasks done faster than trying to do them at the same time. We discussed this previously in our chapter on *Creativity*.

Waiting:

This is a classic scheduling concern. Any time spent waiting for inputs to arrive so that work can begin is an obvious waste. We can mitigate this by switching to secondary work, but we must remember that if we allow this, that work should be allowed to proceed until completion, or we risk task-switching as above. If we can make sure the correct questions are answered early and the associated decisions made, we can schedule our resources more smoothly. Another form of waiting is micro-waiting, which is related to the wastes of Motion below. If I need to wait to connect to a service before I can run a tool, that is waste. If submissions take too long to run validation, that can be waste (we typically aim for ten minutes for a submission to allow appropriate validation). Slow build times are also a waste.

Motion:

This is a classic Lean concern. Unnecessary activities are waste. In manufacturing, this was often motion of the assembly-line worker. This can be true of the software developer as well. Forcing a user to click through numerous menus or use multiple hot keys to reach where they need to go in an application would be a prime example. Moreover, if a developer must get up and travel across the floor to get information, that too can be a form of motion-related waste.

Defects:

Defects are a reduction in customer value, but they also produce waste in many ways. Most directly, we need to fix them. If we don't fix them, defects generally cause a cloud of uncertainty about the quality of our product and can increase our normal of deviance. Also, some defects directly impact our developers, causing crashes or making autotests undependable.

Management Activities:

As mentioned with Lean, these are typically type A wastes. Of course, some might be type B, in which case we should cut them. For those that are necessary, we should ask whether we are allocating excessive work given the benefits of the activities. As much as possible we should make management thin, while still meeting our requirements.

The Lean Software Development Loop

The book *Lean Software Development* covers many tools to implement its process, which we won't be covering here as they go outside the scope of this book. We will, however, cover a high-level view of how the lean software development loop proceeds. It is akin to the experience one might have of Scrum at many companies. It has a few distinguishing characteristics, however, although by now many of these have been incorporated into the practices of teams that are using Agile in general.

To start, Lean Software Development focuses on the connection of the developers and the customer. It's assumed that the customer doesn't fully know what they need yet. As with Agile, Lean Software Development rejects the notion of a contractual software completion date and focuses on value delivered. A key here is that the developers and the customer must be directly in communication from the start. If possible, developers should even be moved to customer sites to build these relationships. When not possible, tools such as Slack are recommended.

The first steps are often meant to assure the customer that this approach is a useful one to them. So, the initial goal is to produce actual working software the customer can use which solves some aspect of their problem. This could be a simple spanning application, for example, which takes an easy case and runs it through a prototype version. The customer can then look at this and determine whether this is the right or wrong approach.

To accomplish this, the development team works in iterations that give the customer features and provides feedback to the team. After an iteration, the team can respond to this feedback and course correct. This process will continue throughout development.

To support the principle of deciding late, Lean Software Development uses the concept of set-based development, which we've mentioned earlier. When a customer problem is posed, developers don't go to meetings to hash out solutions, but instead provide the set of constraints for their domain. They might present these constraints in meetings, but it is key that the solution not be determined at that point. This is a matter of efficiency — as the Poppendiecks point out, meetings that seek solutions can sometimes end up going in circles. Once the sets of constraints are known, the solution can only be in the intersection. We keep the known constraints around and only make the decision to pick a solution once it becomes necessary to do so. As the Poppendiecks discuss, this is an art.

As part of late decision-making, we will sometimes engage in practices that result in local waste to allow us to delay choices. We might explore multiple solutions at the same time, for example, to evaluate how well they fit our need. Alternatively, we might engineer our architecture such that the details of implementation for modules are opaque to the rest of the solution.

Throughout this process, value-stream mappings (see below) will often be created to find and eliminate waste in our processes.

Aside from a focus on waste, there are several keys to successful Lean Software Development: small chunks of work that are pulled when necessary; short queues of pending work; continuous communication between developers and customers; feedback and learning; and keeping options open until — but no longer then — the decision-making window closes. For the most part this is standard Agile practice, but it is distinguished by emphasis on waste, just-in-time production with short queues, and option-based thinking with set-based development.

Value Stream Mapping

Value-stream mapping is a common technique in organizations employing Lean practices to differentiate the tasks that are adding customer value from the tasks that are not. In classic manufacturing, these are broken up into information flows and material flows.

Similar mappings are done for software, except the material flow isn't quite the same as we aren't dealing with physical products.

The value-stream map is a flat graph with directed edges. The top portion of the graph is for information flows. The bottom portion is for the material flows. These two subgraphs are often disjoint, but we sometimes see them connected on the left, where the final information-flow node connects into the originating material-flow node. It is common for value-stream mappings to displayed as a large poster on the floor, or as one of the periodic screens on the dashboard displays throughout our workspace.

Information flow represents control over what is built. This could be, for example, customer orders arriving in the system, being routed, and then directed back to continuous planning. By convention, information flow starts with the customer on the right of the graph and proceeds left through any stages until the order arrives at planning. For a game that is live in production, it could be that customers have begun to demand a new level in a new environment, so we are responding to that demand. For a game in progress, typically these controls come in gradually as we refine our understanding of the customer through continuous delivery of improved working software.

Material flows contain the actions that result in customer value. Here every activity in the value-stream mapping goes left-to-right in order of application (or in whatever direction one likes if it is consistent). For example, building the art for a level might involve a paper sketch, then a design block-out, then bronze, silver, and gold art passes once we are already in the production phase. Each of these activities proceeds in order of their completion, connected by arrows left to right. Meanwhile, there are other tasks that do not deliver value to the customer. For example, one might be working with an IP holder and have conformance meetings that ensure contractual requirements are met. The arrows for these activities should be placed orthogonal to those that generate value to emphasize that they are waste.

Lead-time measurement marks the critical path from start to finish of the material flows. In the case we've mentioned, the time to concept a level through the time to deliver a gold version to production would constitute the lead time. Low lead times are desirable, to the degree that they are possible without causing other problems. It can be interesting to consider how much of our lead time is producing value. For example, at one time a value-stream mapping for the lifetime of a cola can was done.[195] From the mine to the arrival of the can to the consumer, an average period of 319 days was established. Only three hours of that time was spent adding value. Since the needs for aluminum cans don't change that much, this can be okay, but it isn't for many industries. Almost a year in games can result in radical changes in customer demand. This isn't the same as saying that most of the cost of a can is waste, this is instead time. There will be in impact to waste, though, as this time involve lots of motion and storage.

Then given a value-stream mapping, we can note tasks that represent either type A or type B waste and locate areas where the lead time is unnecessarily long due to avoidable dependencies in the critical path chart. We can thus target our efforts for improvement and deliver more value to the customer.

Theory of Constraints

Our focus isn't on Theory of Constraints in this book, so we'll be discussing it briefly; however, it has relevance for its influence on modern software approaches. Originally, the Theory of Constraints was presented in the 1984 business novel *The Goal* by Eliyahu Goldratt, later followed up with *Critical Chain* in the 1990s. Many will note that the ideas Goldratt presented existed in some form before, but this was the point where it was structured and then popularized for management theory.

At its core, the Theory of Constraints aims to improve the desired outcome of the company, which is typically some form of revenue flow. Theory of Constraints assumes that the system being used to achieve this goal is bottlenecked by a small number of constraints — it is essentially stating that a chain is no stronger than its weakest link. Theory of Constraints then outlines a process to address the problem.

Theory of Constraints Loop:

Step 1: Identify the system constraints
Step 2: Pick a constraint to target and decide how to exploit it
Step 3: Subordinate everything else to the above decision
Step 4: Alleviate the constraint
Step 5: If the previous steps have resulted in other constraints being broken, return to step 1, but do not allow inertia itself to become a constraint[196]

These steps are specifically engineered to address politics, which differs from many of the other approaches in this book (we address some aspects of politics ourselves later). Theory of Constraints emphasizes how to select the right problem and then pursue agreement on both the issue and its solution, dealing with negative obstacles, and then bringing the solution into place, overcoming layers of resistance to change. Partially because of the author's background and audience, the challenge here is not posed at its root as a technical concern, but as a people problem.

It has been noted that Theory of Constraints relates to the notion of linear programming. It assumes that pushing a constraint all the way to its limit ends up with the optimal result (in linear programming it can be shown that there is one optimum and it must exist on the boundary). This isn't true in general as it's trivial to provide constraint examples where the winning point is not on the edge. As an exploratory technique, however, this is powerful —

we've mentioned a similar notion in our discussion of Kent Beck's approach to Extreme Programming. People get trapped in cycles of failure because they are unwilling to make the bold push to drive something out of the local pit and see how the consumer would react to that — this method mandates that we make the bold move. If one's push aligns with customer value, then such a move can free oneself to cut out all the nonessential features, thus allowing a redirection of effort that achieves the grand objective. Alternatively, if the bold push overshoots a maximum, it is still often the case that such exploration exposes a better solution.

Theory of Constraints is thus useful in that it focuses people's effort in keeping with the 80/20 rule — usually a small set of issues cause most of the pain. It emboldens us to make grand steps. Nonetheless, as explicit in the model, after making a bold move we need to consider whether we broke the system or not and then adjust to get the best result.

It is also worth noting that Theory of Constraints was associated with the development of the Current Reality Tree and the Future Reality Tree as models for making decisions. These models are related to the Five Whys we discussed earlier in the section on Lean. The Current Reality Tree is a way to summarize and map symptoms to ultimate root causes that is easily understood by people who aren't on the floor. At the top of the tree, we list symptoms — this could be that the builds we wish to demo are often broken. Then for each direct cause of that symptom, we add a parent to the symptom in the Current Reality Tree (there can be more than one parent if there is more than one cause). This parent could itself be a symptom of something deeper, so it too can have a parent. The tree is as deep as necessary to reach root causes that are considered worth pursuing. This frames affairs as they exist at the point of construction. This is essentially identical to The Five Whys — it is just a graphical description intended for executives.

Once we have done this, we consider resolutions for root causes of problems in the Current Reality Tree. This constructs the Future

Reality Tree. One of the core concerns of this construction is determining if we create "negative branches." These are outcomes that arise from changes to the Current Reality Tree which result in violations of constraints. In this way, we can consider whether a change is wise or not before embarking on it.

A key point here is that Theory of Constraints has built up a suite of tools, many of which align with the goals of our decision-making system. Also, we should bear in mind that simplifying a problem and tackling its primary issue with all our focus can be an effective way to move the needle of quality and create a controlled leap forward. Unlike many of the models we have discussed here, Theory of Constraints was not created as a customer-centered approach. It is assumed that the motivation comes from ourselves — so our goal might be to make more money. It might be that making money is best served by delivering value, but it could be arrived at other ways. It's an older method, which was more typical then; now we have flipped the relationship so that our goal is foremost customer value.

DevOps and SRE

The adoption of Agile and Lean processes in software development ratcheted up pressure between developers and operations for services (especially anything XaaS — or something as a service). Developers wanted to release software to the customer as frequently and often as possible in small increments. New features were their mandate. Operations staff, meanwhile, remained classically tasked with maintaining the health of a service — change is a root cause of instability, so they were motivated to push back. Moreover, operations and development teams were often siloed into separate groups, sometimes not even co-located in the same city or even country at times; they often didn't even speak the same "language," both in terms of how they thought and in terms of the programming languages they used when working — operations personnel more typically worked in scripting languages whereas software developers used production languages like C++, Java, etc. Thus, developers and operations personnel lacked a common understanding. This separation of groups and goals created tensions and inefficiencies, resulting in fewer releases to customers with more bugs than necessary — along with emergency late nights on releases and frustrating pager calls at all hours.

There was another larger lost opportunity. Operations personnel were often not trained in software engineering, which meant that many of the core automation practices ingrained in development were not equivalently hardwired into operations personnel. As operations demands scaled, staff required similar scaling, which wasn't viable long term. Software engineers, meanwhile, lacked an understanding of the demands and needs of operations, which aggravated their interactions. Software developers were often unfamiliar with how their development artifacts were deployed into live production environments.

Google recognized this problem around 2003 and created Site Reliability Engineers,[197] which were one of the first exemplars of this trend. The term itself has now entered wider usage in the industry as a role definition at many companies. The key idea is that operations would now be run by software engineers instead of dedicated operations personnel. The software engineering department would swallow operations. This was meant to bring an automation mentality which would resolve scaling issues. At the same time, some operations personnel were trained in software engineering, so that they could bring their specialized knowledge into the SRE group as well. Thus, the result was a composition of people from different backgrounds who were all expected to be engineers. These SREs were then required to spend at least 50% of their time working to automate and improve operations systems, rather than addressing tickets. Google's problem was serious — they needed to scale to levels never seen before. Sub-linear scaling was now a requirement.

Deep Management

Meanwhile, other companies throughout the 00's realized that the division between software engineers and operations personnel was a barrier. This broadening realization led to the adoption of the DevOps name and the first conferences dedicated to the topic in 2008. DevOps is not a specific implementation of a methodology, but an umbrella of many approaches.[198] It posits that our problem is the delivery of faster, high-quality increments of customer value. Ultimately, the ideal would be push-on-green, where a developer submits, the change runs through automated testing, and then proceeds to live production servers, with easy roll-back if required. Some companies such as Etsy, some projects at Google and Facebook, and many others have achieved this standard. We can easily note the traces of continuous delivery and Lean principles in this approach.

The goals of DevOps were agreed to be as follows:

1) Improved frequency of releases
2) Faster time to market
3) Lower failure rates on new releases
4) Shortened lead times between fixes
5) Faster mean time to recovery

Many of the solutions to these problems have already been mentioned in the context of Agile and Lean methodologies. After all, these approaches created much of the pressure that led to the need for DevOps in the first place. DevOps also placed an additional emphasis on automation, which was there in previous methods, but lacked the same centrality. This has led to other preferences, such as using declarative languages to define the target health states of environments.

Overuse of the term DevOps (and SRE as well) has weakened its value. People will note that many companies have such positions in name, but that practice isn't in line with principles. Nevertheless, the ideas that arose from these communities are key to future growth and will no doubt continue to shape service-oriented industries for years to come. Games have increasingly adopted DevOps as a solution to the challenges of GaaS (games as a service), where developers are trying to make GaaS less of a product that happens to be a service, and more of a service that is treated as a proper platform for delivering fast increments of customer value to players.

15

Common Tools for Modern Software Development

To close out Part III, it is worthwhile to discuss some common practices. These aren't new — some are quite old - but they've become trends.

The characteristics of modern development include greater emphasis on rapid iteration, fast delivery, predictability through automation, and greater opportunities for humans to focus on creative work. These methods are meant to foster anti-fragile[199] organizations. We embark not knowing exactly where we will end up, but with a toolbox that allows us to grow stronger in the face of challenges.[200]

The main trends are the following:

1) Communication & Collaboration
2) Continuous Integration & Delivery
3) Measurement
4) Automation
5) Infrastructure as Code
6) Declarative Languages

Communication and Collaboration

We want to spread information as rapidly as possible while reducing noise. This means direct communication with the consumer, and if possible, a collaborative relationship. We work with the customer to understand and solve their problems iteratively.

Improved communication is also necessary between developers. This has led to policies such as paired programming from Extreme, where developers work together from the start rather than review code at the point of submission. This isn't universal and there are negative aspects to paired programming, but what is clear is that getting feedback upfront and continuously is desirable, even if we use another format.[201]

Deciding late means building adaptability into systems, which isn't free. We need to continuously communicate to offset that expense by making improved decisions that eliminate bad paths early.

Communication tools such as Slack, Facebook@Work, Confluence, and Wikis all serve to support these goals. As we've mentioned elsewhere, it is preferable for collaboration tools to be asynchronous by default, by which we mean that the receiver of the message isn't interrupted and can address it when they finish their task — there shouldn't be pop-up notifications for example. It's important that our employees understand that they aren't expected to immediately answer, as it's been shown that even if communication is asynchronous, if our employees compulsively monitor it, it has the same impact as a synchronous method.[202] Our employees should only engage with these tools after a natural pause in work, and we should have no expectations of a quick response. It is reasonable to expect a response within 24 hours, if the employee isn't out of office or has just returned. Synchronous communication interrupts our thinking, which research suggests can cost us as much as 40% of our productivity.[203] When we are actively collaborating, this is different. We can use video and voice chats to enable remote collaboration (even within the same building), although asynchronous tools also work for this if we keep the message window open.

Continuous Integration & Continuous Delivery

We've already discussed the motivation for continuous integration and delivery earlier in this book. Concurrent engineering practices are most directly expressed through a focus on delivering working software using these techniques.

Continuous integration means that whenever we write code, that code is exposed to the rest of the source as quickly as possible. This is typified by developers working only in the mainline, as with trunk-based development. Users should also submit their changes every day. To support this, it is necessary that there be continuous automated testing (preferably with a suite of fast tests on submits). If a problem arises in the mainline, it must be dealt with as a priority by the entire team. In this way, we avoid the costs and defects generated by integrations, and we see from the start if changes make sense or not. Moreover, other people are exposed to our changes and don't get caught by surprise later when their work intersects our own.

Continuous delivery is another step on top of continuous integration. Now, not only do our developers work in the mainline, but we deliver small increments of change to our customer. The ideal would be that every submission that passes tests goes out immediately. For many reasons, developers can't always achieve this, but the faster the rollout the better. This supports feedback and makes it easier to debug issues, as there will be fewer potential causes.

Measurement

We've already emphasized this as part of our decision-making system, but since it is core to modern development as well, we'll mention it again. Theory doesn't matter, only results. And the only way that we can validate our model is through measurements. When empirical results tell us an approach is better, we take it. We must, however, also consider low probability negative events that our measurements might not have exposed yet.

As we discussed in Part II, we need to maintain our awareness of the faults that we humans suffer from. We must consider partial knowledge and unknown unknowns, so that we do not forget there are aspects we measure and aspects we do not, and that this creates bias. We must also watch out for measurements tied to incentives.[204]

Nevertheless, our success or failure is measured by actual results in the real world, which we can only know through data.

Automation

Modern practices rely heavily on automation to produce increased reliability and confidence in our systems.

Human error is the most common cause of faults — sometimes catastrophically.[205] We want all our production deployments to be reproducible and idempotent.[206] No human should be required to set variables for an environment. If we can automatically specify and set up our environments and the contents of our deployment, then we can scale freely with reduced risk. Tools such as Ancible, Chef, Docker, Kubernetes, and so on, all solve various facets of this problem, but we must assemble them according to our requirements.

Push-button deployments are the ideal. Often, we often want cloud scaling to be automated as well in response to demand.

Second, we require automated testing to support our continuous integration and deployment pipelines. We want feedback from changes as rapidly as possible, and neither the scale nor speed of that can be attained by human testing. Moreover, humans are expensive.

Automation also takes the burden of rote tasks off us, which is why it's a core principle of most software engineers. The more we automate, the more we can focus on the creative and more challenging problems, thus heightening the value of our contributions.

Automation should not be done mindlessly. There is no point to automating a one-off task. What is sometimes said is that the second time we do a task we should automate it. That's a rule of thumb, but it represents the premise that if we expect to do something multiple times, once we've done it ourselves and understand the solution, it should be made into a recipe.

Infrastructure as Code

Infrastructure as Code relates to automation. Our production deployment products are already source-controlled and treated as a deployable artifact. We now want to treat the specifications of our environments as code as well. This is as opposed to older practices where operations teams set up environments according to their rule books, which were often stored separately and out of sync with software developers. This in turn led to some unpredictable behaviors, such as when people had misunderstandings about the nature or set up of the target environment. With infrastructure as code, if we change our environment variables, that change is in source control. It is also much easier to sync back to a point in time to see exactly how an older system worked. This is also critical for rollbacks, as if we roll-back the product but not the environment, we might end up with a combination of software and infrastructure that no one has ever seen or tested.

Declarative Approaches

While many imperative languages remain in place for good reasons, there is an increasing trend to favor declarative languages when possible. An imperative language specifies a set of actions that are taken on state. For example, given a machine, the language might install a piece of software. With imperative programming languages, a variable controlling the number of live servers might have 5 added to an integer in its memory space. The problem with reasoning about imperative languages is we don't always know what the state of the environment is. If a different version of the program was already installed, installing this other piece of software might result in an aberrant set-up. If the integer isn't what we expected it to be, adding 5 might result in a state we didn't expect. We harden our code against such problems, but it is easy to make a mistake in reasoning.

Declarative languages, on the other hand, specify how the world should be and then rely on an engine to bring that state into being. For example, rather than installing a piece of software, we require that the software be installed at a specific version. The engine will then check — if it finds the wrong version, it will uninstall it, and then install the correct one. Moreover, if it finds that there are missing dependencies, it will install those as well. If it can't reach a valid state, it will then emit an error. With the integer case, we might require that there be ten servers currently operating, rather than trying to add five servers to the five servers we believe are already up. Then, regardless of how many servers are operating, the engine will shut down or start servers as necessary to reach the target. With an imperative language, if there happened to be six, we might end up with eleven.

Deep Management

The main advantage to declarative languages is that they make it easier to reason about the state of our environments. For that to make sense, though, a good declarative engine must exist. Prolog, for example, as a programming language is founded on a unification engine. It is hard, however, to see how a game can be programmed effectively in a declarative way any time soon,[207] although the game might be deployed using declarative tools. Kubernetes, for example, is a good case of a declarative system. Ansible can be run in either declarative or imperative modes.

PART FOUR

Practice

16

Dealing with People

If we could remove people from the equation, optimizing the decision-making processes of a group would become a pure organizational engineering problem. We could then emulate machine learning and strive to organize ourselves to best expose and react to our reward signal.[208] In the ideal, we would asymptotically approach optimal game-theoretic and decision behavior.

But that's not going to happen.

As individuals, we have developed strategies for interacting with our families, friends, and neighbors, all born from the fabric of societal norms. These strategies, however, often operate at odds with the overarching goals of our organization. What is good for us, is sometimes wasteful for our company. In most of life, we negotiate as independent agents; within the organization, we negotiate as part of a cooperative whole. While we prefer to choose our hires based on alignment with our corporate intentions, talent is hard to find. Some will answer wait for the right fit, don't hire early. Even with that, people change or don't turn out the way we expected. Or the organization changes, and previously aligned employees become square pegs we are trying to fit into now round holes.

We've already discussed many of the cognitive defects that lead us astray. Each of us has our own framing of reality. This makes us blind to many possibilities and causes us to overemphasize others; even when our biases do not distort our vision, we place undue importance on the known possible choices, largely because we are ignorant of the alternatives. The choices we do not imagine are not part of our decision calculus. We are certain of what we see, believing that what we see is all there is.

This framing can be surprisingly damaging even when the right choice should be obvious. This is the frustration that might be before us whenever we step in to help a project that has lost its way. The leaders aren't dense or obtuse, they just can't see what we're showing them. They are not keyed to perceive our argument, so it doesn't pass their filters.

The lessons we are bringing the team have precedent, sometimes even decades of history behind them, but still teams resist. Arguments are raised: it's too theoretical (even though it's used elsewhere), it doesn't apply to our complex case (even though other companies are doing more complex work at greater scale), it's too expensive (even though the point is to reduce cost and increase quality). The team has worked in particular ways and they embrace their own methods as best — a cognitive glitch also known as the IKEA effect.[209] This is the frame we find when we join an existing team and are tasked to resolve its dysfunctions.

They have trained to become experts at areas we now devalue or outright call waste (such as politics). Now they will need to struggle to develop new masteries. Before, they might have copy-catted the latest hot game without considering whether the model makes sense for their audience.[210] They might never have pursued high-resolution customer value. Breaking established patterns means that the team must learn new strategies. Old dogs can be taught new tricks, but some old dogs don't want to learn.

At higher levels of the organization, the culture can often be more about turf than customer need, which can be a challenging battle. I've seen new directors come in and immediately create a department by taking employees out of an existing project. This sometimes takes the form of a new engine-development initiative, a build-team infrastructure group, a machine-learning team, or any other highly visible (and prestigious) aspect that can be extracted. They justify this by claiming the problem can't be handled by the project itself. And sometimes the project does face difficulties in offering a long-term vision; at times, it's even the right choice to pull this work out. However, doing so also severs any relationship between what that new department develops and any customer need. These directors aren't to blame in these cases, really. If fresh employees as individual agents enter a company where this is how the game is played, they are conforming and pursuing the existing incentives. That is to be expected. They advance or not in such a culture by cutting out a turf and hyping their own products. This is part of the framing we'll need to break. And if it's deep in organizational culture, it'll be a hard fight of compromises to get where we need to go — after all, we're asking people to give up power for the benefit of the organization, which is exactly a case where the Tragedy of the Commons bias arises.

It's also common at companies that a high-level figure gets substituted for ultimate customer need. This temptation arises because that figure has power to stymie or advance the project. Thus, project leadership can become fixated on handling these individuals. We hear it said sometimes from the team that such a person is the customer. But when the project ships, success or failure for the product is based on actual people buying it. This is a hard habit to break people of. Their anxiety pressures them to cater to this person's whims. Internal organizational politics becomes the motivation for features instead of customer need. The only way forward in this case is to trust that a sound proposal can be pushed through with minimal compromises, so we should focus on orienting our features towards the customer only.

In worst-case scenarios, we might be walking into an organization which is governed by an economy of favors between staff and external departments. If our projects are funded more because of *quid pro quo* between top managers rather than customer need, we will find a hard road ahead of us. If people owe their position to absolute loyalty to a manager who shields them from the predations of other powers, we will find it challenging to expose problems that might make their manager look bad. In such a situation, by focusing on customer value, we aren't even playing the same game as the other employees.

If we find that project leaders accept demands from executive-level management without question, largely because they fear they will be replaced otherwise, then here too we find ourselves in an untenable situation. This is the root cause of many games failing to deliver their promise at launch. Eventually, in such a culture, senior managers excise any staff able to see risk and support customer value, leaving only those willing to promise anything.

We can also find that narrative holds precedence over reality. When we start adding measurement, especially recording of decisions, we might find that people become nervous. Suddenly they cannot manipulate their image anymore.

Resolving the Challenge

As we look at our team, it is imperative that we understand where they are, first. We must try to establish why decisions were made and how people came to hold their positions. Without a record, we must understand that we are only being told stories; this can be a starting point to model how they operate, however, even if we can't be sure of what they did previously. People who are toxic we will have to remove, but everyone else can start at zero — no blame. Our purpose is to see who the actors on the field are. Look as well for the people who are quiet. When someone brags about their team or their accomplishments, we assume they are exaggerating by an order of magnitude, but when we meet people who are humble or quiet, we exaggerate what they say by an order of magnitude. There is often great value in these quiet voices.[211] Moreover, they are often frustrated by the status quo and through observation have insight. Not infrequently, someone in this category knows the best path forward, but their voice has been drowned out. Having said that, we shouldn't overemphasize their insight either. After all, there is a saying that the wise speaks little and the fool often. This can mean that the wise listen and so know many things. It can also mean they don't have anything intelligent to say, and so look smarter by saying nothing.

We start by testing the waters to determine how comfortable people will be with the changes we must make. The two top goals to address are value and measurement. The other principles we've listed are critical, but if we start from zero, we should establish these two principles first. Finding the customer and their problem and conditions gives us value, and with value we can determine waste. We cannot move forward until we know what waste looks like; otherwise, we're just flailing, which is probably what the team was doing before. We must find the Razor and make sure it is known on the team, and that all decisions arise from it. Then, as soon as possible, we establish measurement. For this, starting with the decision history should be paramount, but we should follow up with telemetry as soon as possible. The other principles we can bring in gradually. We need to shift people bit by bit until we've rebuilt the culture.

After this, we can overthrow the anti-patterns of management and production, using our definitions of waste and measurement to counter the stories and resistance that will be thrown at us. It's good to start ratcheting up transparency as we go. This can be rocky, so we should be careful not to push too fast. Root-cause analysis is a gradual habit to teach, but since the team will now know what waste is and since we have metrics to test ideas, we can validate the execution of the Five Whys, producing visible results.

Once our team has enough faith, we can begin tackling the anxieties that make them cater to internal power figures. We would like to break down the influence such figures have, but that is a problem for later. If the team begins to understand that they have a sound product, we can manage internal politics more easily.

Above all, we must make sure that we go out on the floor and see what our team is doing. Some teams have management that strategizes in off-site meetings. We mustn't do that. We must be visible to the team and our team must be visible to us. We must directly know what people do and how they interact. We must understand how communication flows and how our software is built. We need to drag pre-existing management down to the floor with us if they are not already engaging at that level. The floor produces value, the managers don't.

As we see our managers on the floor, consider whether we have appropriate representation. For example, if our managers didn't come from product development, but we're making a game, that is a huge error. Managers are never going to understand what is going on if they don't understand basic concepts. Usually, when things get hard, the relationship between these non-represented groups and management grows toxic. If there are gaps in knowledge, address them. This will redistribute power, which will make current managers nervous. There is no easy way to handle this, other than to be clear that leaders need to lead from the front.

In doing all of this, however, we must be humble, and we must be empathic. We can consider this as an opportunity to grow our capacity to extrapolate the needs of our customers by handling the needs of our staff. If we can understand the conditions that our employees and managers operate within daily, we will better be able to understand the conditions of our customers as well. If we can see how reward flows through our team, we can redirect it to how it should flow. See the world from the viewpoint of our staff; understand how they will perceive the change we are bringing.

When approaching these problems, it's also critical to pick our battles. Consider how the project should be organized in a perfect system. We're not talking about the golden path of production for a project here, but how a perfect system would seek out such a golden path as reasonably as possible. Then consider our deviations from that ideal. When we have to work with the actual state of our culture and team, knowing this will allow us to focus on the most valuable 20% of conformance, using the 80/20 rule.[212] The 80% will have to wait (but not forever, remember normalization of deviance from the chapter *Never Tolerate Waste*).

Theory of Constraints has a substantial literature on how one works through resistance to achieve alignment and optimize the constraint as much as possible. We should consult such resources to sharpen ourselves. Within Lean philosophy, technical architects often have no official power to dictate change but are required to align teams with their direction — this is partially born out of Japanese consensus culture, but it also accesses distributed expertise on the team. Again, Lean literature sometimes has discussions on reaching alignment.

Regardless, politics is always waste within a company. When we start, it might be necessary type A waste, but once we settle more, we should start addressing it. Politics is time spent that does not deliver customer value. It often leads to features that appease internal power figures. It degrades our products and services.

Types of People

Before confronting our problems, it is useful to recognize that there are two types of people with respect to change. Neither is better than the other, although at times we have a preference. The first type of person takes their environment as it is and focuses their energy to understand how to work within that system. The second type of person assumes that their environment should change and focuses on how to transform it.

When we impose change, we must remember that the first group will have developed hard-fought expertise in existing models. They might have mastered technologies, managerial approaches, or learned to curate a politicized image of their competence, all of which were previously the route to success. Perhaps they have built up a currency of favors they expect to spend later. When we arrive with our decision-making system, many of these previously valuable skills will be rendered less valuable or will even be considered waste. Once primary figures will now become secondary and need to support others.

Our system is going to be an uphill pitch to these people. Since our approach flips where the power resides, we will experience pushback from people whose specialty is managing influence. The larger the organization, the more of a struggle this will be. Bear in mind, many of the people in this threatened first class are well meaning — this is part of why it's challenging as they believe they are in the right — but if we can convince them that it is more effective to rely on the system, then we can employ them to spread our message. If they can be converted so that they see that the change benefits the work they produce, then we have succeeded.

We've focused on members of the first class who are threatened by our changes, but we should note there will also be members of the first class who welcome them. They might have come from other organizations or perhaps never quite fit in, as their views differed from the norm. Our new system might benefit them greatly, as they were already skilled at aspects of our approach. Finding and aligning with these individuals can be a big help in the transformation of a culture.

The second class of people, on the other hand, agrees that change should come, so they are easier to handle in that regard. The problem is that many of these people have wildly different takes on what change should look like! We might enlist them as allies to share our message only to find that they have a different agenda to push. The problem here is that since there is no already agreed upon historical path to take, we must work closely together with these agents to avoid confusing the message. An ill-conceived implementation can cause the team to turn against our approach, so it is important that we make sure the steps we take are ones that can build momentum. If we allow too much chaos, everything will fall apart.

The challenge here is that we are trying to help people understand that bringing the reward signal of customer value closer to the developer is the best approach. The problem is that in large companies, customers can be a theoretical subject; for mid- and high-level managers, their goals might be proxies such as leading a prestigious project that bolsters their image, allowing them greater impact in the future. People follow incentives, and the higher up we go in an organization, the more likely it is that we will encounter people primarily driven by advancement. This is inevitable in a game-theoretic sense unless our company has an immune system that detects and eliminates bad actors and promotes those with strong character.

Also, transparency, which is intrinsic to our method, can be nerve-wracking. To enact transparency is to expose to analysis everything that we do, and that makes many people anxious — rightly or wrongly. In fact, our staff might legitimately fear the twisted reflections and KPI warping that we've mentioned earlier — that the transparency we bring will be used to mold signals that will lead to a dystopian corporate culture. We need to reinforce that while everything is transparent, the systems for analysis are as well and are subject to change as needed. Systems such as the Sesame (or Zhima) Credit system in China seem threatening because we don't understand all the details of how they work and because we have no power over the implementation.[213] Even with understanding of the system and power over it, some employees will never be comfortable in the kind of culture we are trying to build, so it might be that for them the changes we are bringing are a message that they will be losing their job. We can find legitimate push-back to changes as some people find themselves personally threatened. Be mindful of the place we are putting our people in.

    This tension leads to another problem, and this can be a fatal one to our transformation. People who are threatened lock up. It is a basic consideration of behavior. In counseling on marriages, once one or both of the parties have reached a point of "flooding," where their response to their partner is one of cynicism, anger, etc., by default, than it is almost always the case that there is a break-up.[214] If we reach a point where we cause someone to flood in our attempt to move forward, it will take them a long time to cool off. Effectively, we might need to consider that person lost, and if that person is required to bring about change, then we have lost. Not uncommonly, once a person floods, that person will strive to find excuses to attack us — and if we get attacked, we might end up wasting all our effort addressing the attacks rather than effecting the change our organization needs. Sometimes this can force us to abort the initiative, and at times this might lead to us needing to seek a new place to work. Still, it is worth the risk.

    This is part of why humility and emotional intelligence are so critical to bringing about change. We need to read where people are and respond to and validate their concerns. The tension must be kept below flooding. We'll need to compromise; we just need to make sure that the compromises don't undermine our approach so that we fail. It is better to not proceed than to move forward with a Frankenstein's monster that will taint our future. If we can ease up on pressure and bring a lighter note to the final mood of our meetings, then we'll be more likely to succeed — chat about their favorite games, families, pets, and events in their life. We mustn't be false, however. All our engagements with our staff must be authentic.

    We should try to plant the seeds that underpin our method in listeners' minds and encourage them to come up with the approach of their own accord. This is by far the best form of emotional judo we might employ. If they believe it is their own idea, then they will back it all the more — and when they are off-track a bit, we can correct them. They will accept this more easily, because we are perfecting the idea they already came up with. For some of us, it is hard to step back because the visible merit will go to other people, but the truth is we should be indifferent to public acclaim or disdain so long as we are able to bring about the change that is necessary. After all, our approach erodes the power of narrative and image projection within the company, so we should not take this as undermining our capacity to make future improvements. If it does, then we have partially failed.

It is also vital that we not let ourselves fall into the trap of regarding the people we are interacting with as game pieces to move on a board. It is easy to see someone as an obstacle, path to success, or champion; it is easy to allow our own emotions to rule our perception of them. Just as other people can flood and lock us out, we too can flood and fail to see the possibilities they offer. When someone is opposing and attacking us — especially if those attacks take the form of negative ratings in reviews — it is easy to reflect that anger back. That person is not just their immediate sequence of actions, however, but all the conditions that have surrounded them and given rise to the person who is making our life challenging today. It is difficult to achieve, but if we can see everyone as people in and of themselves and not as opponents, it will be easier for us to see the places where we can meet.

We should remember, most employees believe in what they already doing. As we discussed in our chapter *Never Tolerate Waste*, all teams exist within a paradigm. This comes with a set of norms that the employees for the most part adhere to. We've been brought in, however, due to dysfunctions that are crippling the team. It is never easy to flip a culture. If we remember what we are doing, we will be better able to appreciate what they have done in the past and what they can do in the future.

17

Cutting Our Projects

If we take enough risks, eventually a project will fail. Without risk, there is no innovation. There are even business models based upon failing fast and repeatedly until a low probability tail event pays off, so that success comes as a surprise. This is how some mobile developers work, as well as certain types of option-based investors in the stock market. Thus, we accept that there is a point when projects fail. When that happens, we need to understand our responsibilities. While we want our employees to fight for success and to show grit, the employees are also best placed to understand when we have lost the capacity to solve our customer's problems. The team should own the decision to cut itself or not. This is part of the ownership mentality.

A project facing difficulties is different from a failing project. Projects in difficult straits are off-track, but we can see how concrete changes can resolve their issues without too much expense, or how if they wait a few months, a few experiments might prove out a new direction (or alternatively transit the project to a failing state). Meanwhile, failing projects are ones that depend on miracles. We rely on fortunes outside our control to resolve our problems. If we as a team recognize that we require a miracle, then we must recognize that our journey is at end. We know better than anyone in top management where we are. If the cost of proceeding outweighs the probability of success, then as owners, we should shut the project down ourselves.

If we as staff on the floor do not feel that we own our choices — including the most important one concerning our continued existence — then we should understand from that alone that we are at severe risk of project failure. Whenever management overrides or discounts the team's expert judgment and enforces an alternative decision, leadership guarantees a crisis in the team. Sometimes, such projects succeed, and the teams later see the wisdom of management, but more often the lack of ownership is itself a self-fulfilling prophecy for failure, regardless of the quality of management's decisions. Such teams are quick to prognosticate negative outcomes because such a result would be in line with their own expectations. If we catch this situation early, this problem can be solved — it only becomes a failure if we let it continue for too long. To resolve it, we must work with the team to prove out either their position or that of management's. It must be the team that owns this process, or we are merely replicating our original fault. If the issue persists too long, the team becomes invested in its own failure. It's often easier at that point to restart with a different team that believes in the goal or to drop the project.

Teams that own their project, on the other hand, know that the ultimate customer outcome is their responsibility. They have a mission. As we've discussed before, this unlocks their full capacity to solve customer problems. They can see solutions from the ground that we in higher management cannot. It does, though, create a problem that we must monitor and help them resolve. When people own their project, they invest themselves in it more, which makes recognizing failure doubly hard. While we want to maintain a positivist mentality on our teams, it is also necessary that they remain capable of taking an outside view. Since employees own the project, if it is failing, that suggests that they are in error. This is hard to accept, especially for gritty teams — the people who remain in the game industry are the ones who do not fold easily. After all, we know that the world is full of projects that failed because teams quit, and similarly full of projects that succeeded because teams stuck it out. That the successes can be distorted by survivor's bias isn't something we usually consider. We rarely know what the probability spectrum of success or failure is.[215]

We must work with our teams to ensure that while they fully commit themselves, they retain the ability to periodically step back and view the broader state of their project. This should be triggered by our decision-making system. This offers us a check to ensure that we're seeing the bigger picture, regardless. It also allows us to see whether we've lost our path and if it's possible to recover it.

Let us back up to address a sore point, however. Cut projects often frustrate us. Many of us have experienced cuts that come from top management. Oftentimes, we disagree with the cut or feel that it should have come sooner. When cuts must come from the top, we require the team to evidence grit up until the last minute, even if the team has long recognized that there is a fatal flaw. Where teams have total freedom to fix problems, this can be less demoralizing, but they can still encounter the case where a fatal flaw originates from a deep-seated issue regarding their approach to the customer. In both situations, the team must push on despite knowing that they cannot succeed.

Even if we've adopted mission command (covered in the chapter *Seeking Alignment*), if we fail to also grant ownership over the project's lifecycle, we have undermined our approach. The team must push even after they've recognized that a premise of their project has been demonstrated false. We deny the power to make one of the most critical decisions to the people with the clearest insight.

To quote Yoda from the film *Empire Strikes Back,* for the Jedi "Do. Or do not. There is no try." This is taken sometimes to mean that we must never acknowledge failure. Do until you succeed. That isn't how this kind of aphorism (fictional as it is) should be understood. Our team should either put in their full effort or they should not engage in the task at all, regardless of the possibility of failure – many great projects that we should "do" have high failure rates. Trying means we have accepted failure not as a possible outcome, but as the given outcome. For Luke at the start, it was always impossible to lift the X-Wing out of the swamp, before he even attempted the task, so although he "tried," he failed. His effort was wasted. A team that doesn't own its project is prevented from engaging with their full effort because they are denied control over their choices. If we fully own our project, even though success is only one possibility alongside failure, when we can establish a clear set of actions that can move us forward without unreasonable cost, then we should move forward. We do it. If, however, there is no good path forward, we need to have the power to choose to not engage. To "do not" is also the correct choice when that is for the best. To try when we should "do not" is equally as bad as trying when we should "do" it. That is what full ownership means.

When we know that we must proceed forward no matter what, we experience dissonance. We possess the deepest understanding, but still we must advance even though there is no recognizable plan to reach success. That harms the team long term. In fact, that is how we breed teams that cannot succeed when faced with hard challenges — they have been trained by us to only try, with its implicit acceptance of defeat. In this case, surrender to authority has already been burned into the team. We should own our own continued existence, not those above us.

When a cut from the top strikes a team that lacks ownership over its own existence, then the team feels that their effort is wasted. They begin to distrust leadership. They lose the will to resolve their own problems, because no matter how hard they try, everything can be taken away from them. This can also build internal team tensions, where cliques within the group manifest and blame each other. This in turn generates team churn, as members leave for better pastures.

Now, sometimes such a cut must come from above the team. Even where our team owns their project, they exist in a larger organization, and might not be aware of global strategy. Suppose, for example, that top management realizes that due to market challenges they must convert to a new business model. Continuing to fund projects under the old business model would be wasteful. If a company decides to exit the mobile market and focus on service-based games on higher-end platforms like PCs and consoles, then they might cut old projects to increase focus. Such a decision inevitably comes from above. If the leadership team of the company is transparent about the shift in strategy, the team might recognize this is coming and be ready, but regardless it comes from the top. This move will still cause negative impacts, but framed within the larger strategy, teams understand that it is outside their control. This can be okay if such moves are rare and the need for it is recognized.

The key that we should remember is that outside of the above case, the group with the greatest understanding of the project's solution for its customer is the team itself. High-level managers don't spend every day immersed in the customer's needs. The project is only one of many for them. Frequently, the managers' view of the project might only be in terms of future projections of costs and profits generated by finance departments that also don't interact with the customer — working instead often with generic models.[216]

Nonetheless, projects run awry at times, and teams sometimes lose their perspective. It can be as simple as the team violating the principles that underpin the decision-making system we have built in the company. Sometimes the team lacks critical skills as well as the character to recognize their own capability gap. Faced with threats to their ego, our staff might delude themselves — they deny obvious threats. The team's monthly burn rate might exceed any credible market for their game concept. Experiments could be run to validate decisions, but the team refuses to do so. Sometimes, the project loses all concept of customer value and pursues shiny inconsistent feature sets. All these disparate problems can arise and represent a case where a project is failing, but the team has lost their ability to see their state.

In such a case, as a last resort, management must intervene. It should not be the norm, however, if we wish to engender strong teams with a sense of ownership. Our culture should be such that when a team finds that an external figure is being brought in to evaluate their quality with respect to user value and whether they should be cut or not, then that team knows it has seriously missed expectations.

Again, the counterargument here is to always argue that we want teams to be "fully committed" without concern for the future. This isn't absurd. The concept of grit has some correlation with success — people who give up early mathematically get fewer chances at bat which implies lower success on average over a lifetime.[217] It is easy to take the view that a team should knuckle down and fight out a project no matter what they believe, leaving the responsibility for whether the project makes sense to higher powers. People can point to success stories such as *Shadows of Mordor* and *Fortnite*. *Fortnite* in particular is a hard game to argue with, as it went from failing after public launch to dominating the Battle Royale space. Its revenues transformed Epic Games as a company.

Here, though, we need to be careful of survivor's bias. For all the projects that succeed this way, there are less noted projects that continued shoveling money down the hole until they ran out of funds. This is the competing factor of sunk cost, where our attachment to the work that we've already put into a project conspires to drive us to invest more, even though we would cancel

Deep Management

the project if we were able to get our money back. That is an irrational call.

If Hammer & Chisel had stuck with building games and doubled down on *Fates Forever* (which lacked popularity at launch), they wouldn't have then pivoted to build Discord.[218] They have since taken the name of their product for their company. Their current valuation is around $2 billion USD.[219]

Where teams lack ownership, we lose the capacity to access their decentralized expertise. We regress again to the notion that specific high-level individuals are the sole agents able to make the call. We are just leaving money on the table for no reason in such a case.

18

Conway's Law

We've emphasized that our decisions define who we are; they are the aspect of ourselves over which we have control. As we've noted previously, cognitive glitches can force decisions outside of our awareness. One such case that often catches people by surprise is Conway's Law:

> Organizations which design systems ... are constrained to produce designs which are copies of the communication structures of these organizations.[220]

We are not actually forced to follow these boundaries — it is more that they are the default channel we take. But as the aphorism goes, if we keep heading in the same direction, we'll end up where we're going.[221] Making no choice is a choice even if it is one we are unaware of having made; once we understand how our communication structures frame our initial architectural conceptions, we can break away from them. As with anchoring, however, it is impossible to completely eradicate the impact of this starting point.

Our problem is that architecture should be the outcome of analysis of a problem. What we now discover is that our interface structure can be molded by these non-architectural concerns. Our project managers might be tasked with dividing up our fifty engineers into groups and then spacing them onto the floor of our office. Sometimes sub-groups are clustered due to specialty, but it's not unusual for some engineers to be treated as fungible workers and moved just to solve the puzzle. Often, this is done without consulting the architects. In this way, project managers by solving a puzzle of floor allocation can accidentally anchor layering choices in the architecture.

Melvin Conway was one of the first public voices that noted this behavior back in the 1960s. He found that large projects tended to be broken up along institutional boundaries. In 1967, he set up a quick test for this: he had one group of three individuals and one group of four individuals each build a compiler according to a common set of specifications. The first group produced a compiler with three phases, and the second with four.[222] Since then, similar effects have been noticed.

After hearing about this effect, it begins to make sense, and we tend to remember cases of it. We want to create architectures that are clean and solve problems, but people on the floor also want to work faster. All our lives when working in teams we've divided tasks according to human resources. At home, the eldest child might take out the garbage, the next clean the dishes, the youngest clean up the litter box and feed the pets. Thus, we have a tension that arises from our impulses to divide labor between groups and the architecture of a system intended to solve a problem.

The more distinct the characteristics of the group involved, the more likely it is that the team will erect a barrier, and the more solid

Deep Management

that barrier will be. Sometimes these choices make sense architecturally, and so we proceed with them. Other times, these barriers constitute anti-patterns,[223] where current team compositions introduce architectural barriers that reduce maintainability of code.

For example, a division can wall off specialized knowledge. If game engineers and rendering engineers don't have clear boundaries of responsibility, they might end up working with code that is outside their specialty. The software architecture itself usually introduces a barrier in this case already. Game and rendering logic are separated for threading and pipelining reasons. If that were not the case, though, game engineers would need to know more about how their changes could impact rendering and vice versa. Back-end engineers, meanwhile, might be working in a language such as Python, while the client engineers work in C++, sometimes with no knowledge of Python at all. Again, in this case, the software architecture prevents cross-over, as we are dealing with separate products. If there is a common communication protocol handled by a glue language, however, it should not leak into the implementations of either side.

On the other hand, we might imagine two game systems built by separate teams with fundamentally distinct logics about object lifetimes. Eventually, the teams will change, and new game engineers will need to maintain and use both models, which will lead to subtle errors — this would be a clear anti-pattern for maintainability. Object lifetimes should be consistent, or we will introduce faults.

Even outside of specialized knowledge, we often want to wall off our implementations for the same reason that many prefer to branch off from the mainline[224] (something no longer considered a modern practice). As with branching, this segregation of our implementations for the sole purpose of limiting communication has become an anti-pattern. We do this because we do not want to deal with interactions between our code and others. This leads to many problems: late-stage bugs due to unforeseen interaction issues after we integrate it, duplicate solutions for common problems, inconsistent design choices for architecture, and so on. By engaging in this practice, we risk both present quality and future maintainability. We should remember that the system that was segmented off for one engineer's convenience will generate problems for our current team on integration and in the future will be inherited by another engineering team whose composition bears no resemblance to the team that built the product.

Obviously, we don't mean there should be no barriers. The proper divisions should be for software architectural reasons to simplify our analysis of the correctness of the program. We should write our architecture for the ages, understanding that the next teams to work with it will not look like our current teams. Even in the microservices paradigm[225] where there is an attempt to own a service from inception to obsolescence, we cannot guarantee that the exact same engineers remain within the team or even the company.

For teams that are spread across the globe, this is a particularly critical point. Ubisoft, for example, operates its largest projects through ubiquitous collaborations that allow round-the-clock development. This would be the case with the *Assassin's Creed* series, or for that matter any of their titles at equivalent scale. A common approach they have taken is to effectively reverse Conway's Law. Rather than treat collaboration teams as pools of generic engineers, a collaboration team owns an aspect of the game. For example, Ubisoft Singapore owned the naval aspect of *Assassin's Creed: Black Flag*, and the rendering of water in *Assassin's Creed: Origins*. Thus, work was broken out based on lines of communication. This was an effective way to scale up which originated as a reaction to problems they'd had in earlier days.

Such an approach can, however, lead to complications. Work can be proposed without a direct link to customer value because it happens to be easily dividable along studio boundaries. Then these sub-teams often focus on building snazzy ovens, rather than remembering the customer wants pizzas. Moreover, with the increasing prevalence of GaaS, a feature that was architecturally separated for the ease of an external team gets absorbed back into the main team after launch, who then must maintain it for years — in the older non-service approach, the bulk of both sales and support tapered off after a few months so this didn't matter.

We will also note that without oversight, the above system can go awry as decentralized decision-makers veer off onto their own approaches to problems. In a company as large as Ubisoft, external teams can have conflicting default assumptions about how software should be written. Since these teams bounce from project to project, the core lead group must deal with these different approaches. Since these distinct norms can result in conflicting architectural choices, the external teams must be brought into standardization. If this is not done, maintenance will be arduous, especially over a service's lifetime. Resolving this requires proper oversight and reviews from the central leadership team as a necessary cost of engaging in worldwide collaboration. Sometimes this is hard to achieve as we often scale because we are stretched thin in the first place. We must remember that this scaling comes with a price that is unavoidable.

When we take all these points and bring them together, what we come to understand is that the job of our project's architects is not just to define the proper architecture and technology choices, but also to ensure that the teams are formed on proper lines. We must make sure that the actual code reflects the maintainability expectations we built into our designs. When we have off-site collaborations, especially worldwide ones, we must exert extra effort to ensure everything remains aligned. However, we must do so in a way that does not make our collaborators feel untrusted.

The system of this book is meant to normalize decision-making through a shared lens of analysis and data such that we hope that given the same sequence of observations, hypotheses, and experiments, that the same outcome occurs. What we have seen in this section is that if we are inattentive to the structure of our teams, we will find out that the outcomes will not be the same. Team formation is not a managerial decision only, but also an architectural preference.

This is one of the reasons why architects should not be direct members of a team. Architects need to have an independent vision of the software architecture.

19

Review of the Process

We've traveled a long way together, and in so doing we've covered the philosophies that characterize the good and the bad about product and service development. In so doing, we've fleshed out the foundation of our decision-making system. Part of what we've developed is a theory; we must remember, though, theory isn't an idea made from smoke but rather a model of the world. It provides an explanation of why things work as they do, which we can then test empirically. Our system requires this self-introspection to validate that we're heading in the correct direction.

Here, however, we want to take a step back and talk about the rest of the story, at least for AAA games. We're going to discuss common game-production gate processes and how our system interacts with them. There are two extremes along one variable for software in games: development and production.

Development is where we determine what a piece of software does. For many software companies, this is their primary challenge. Our decision system is built around optimizing the development process, as this is often the riskiest, in the sense that if we get this phase wrong, everything that follows will be madness. Development is characterized by establishing customer value, the conditions of the customer, iterating solutions, and then executing. Here we produce depth — or verticality as it's sometimes phrased — by which we mean that development fleshes out the concept of a section of the game (which in some cases — especially certain indie titles — can be the entirety of the game). This process is distinct from that of manufacturing, where the goal is to generate products according to a specification. In the development phase, our task is to find the recipe instead. One of the challenges of adapting Lean to software was adapting its principles, which applied to manufacturing, and mapping them to development.[226]

The final stage in the pre-launch game process is production, which is a manufacturing phase. As we'll discuss in more detail later, at this point in AAA game development we focus on executing the recipes we've previously specified to produce vast quantities of content — art set pieces, environments, objects, characters, dialogue, programmatic scripts for local behaviors, and so on. Our problem here tends to be that we have large numbers of people, many newly brought on to the project. All these new joiners must be aligned in short order to produce content that adheres to constraints. At this point, we wish to produce width; we must produce more content according to rules consistently and efficiently. Of course, we also need to improve our pipelines throughout this phase, just as Lean manufacturing teams seek to improve their assembly lines. This is a fact tools teams sometimes forget after pre-production. Even if their tools are functional, fully usable, and feature-complete, the pressures of production will surface many issues.

Deep Management

In some software development spaces, perhaps even in many, there is no equivalent to the production phase for games. The process of software development is one of prototype and then execution. We do rapid iterations that we throw away to answer core questions, and then we write production code. This software tends to be more a tool or a platform. In some games, this is also true.

If we create a purely procedural game, where the content is generated according to mathematical rules or perhaps via machine learning,[227] then the development phase makes up the entirety of that game's creation. We keep tweaking the rules and testing the outputs, but never go wide except for human testing. There is no phase where content developers need to produce game-ready assets *en masse* according to our recipes.

For the latest Battle Royale genre entries, while they aren't procedural, their development practices resemble more the previous case than a large AAA project. This occurs because they ship with little more than necessary for a vertical slice. They must still reach final levels of polish to ship, but they avoid the worst of the final heavyweight phase. *Fortnite* and *Apex Legends* both launched with a single map, went live as F2P games, and then proceeded from there. A common mistake, however, is to forget that such games require rapid content-release cycles post launch. Here, EA's *Apex Legends* stumbled, at least in its first months. Epic's *Fortnite*, meanwhile, did well in this regard, but only through heroic efforts by its staff.[228]

For most AAA games, however, a massive production phase is standard. Someday, much of this heavyweight phase might be automated, but we remain distant from that for most games. Because the nature of these vertical and horizontal phases differs, we should keep them separated sequentially. At the same time, since we employ concurrent engineering, we strive to stack phases on top of each other. There is a tension between these conflicting demands that we must balance, which unfortunately is an art. There is always some leakage and that is okay. When we can stack development issues over a production phase without posing risk, we may do so. This aligns with our concept of making decisions late. Nevertheless, if continued vertical development jeopardizes our "manufacturing" phase, then we are increasing our time to market. Changing the recipes when we have large amounts of content built means massive rework, which can be a tremendous waste given the size of staffing common to this late stage in AAA.

The arc of a game at a AAA studio should be one with an inception and a long and unpredictable dev-hell phase with very few staff (we'll go over these concepts next section), followed by a somewhat predictable pre-production phase with more but not too many staff, which generates our production tools and sets all of our recipes, followed finally by the full production or "manufacturing" phase, where we execute on our plans and recipes to ship within a specified target window, often with large numbers of newly on-boarded staff. In a few game companies, there can be as many as a thousand people helping to close a AAA product in its last six months of production. This means that depending on the phase of the game we are in, completely different skill sets are often required — because of this, many games founder when transitioning to the final stage.

We should note that many question the wisdom of throwing human resources into closing a project, including ourselves, as it both costs and doesn't efficiently solve the problem; for now, however, this is a description of how it has been working and how to best handle the challenges.[229] Top-level management places extreme pressure on producers to meet deadlines, so when corporate heads offer a mass of workers to "help" us meet a goal, it is hard to reject them without exposing ourselves to political fallout. After all, if we reject the help but miss the deadline, they will pillory us for not accepting assistance. It isn't understood that more employees late in the cycle equal slower production, or even that too many employees at any point is counter-productive. Overthrowing this paradigm is its own intriguing topic. We do not dispute that a better future would result if we could reduce the cost and automate more of this final manufacturing phase.

Deep Management

Games as a Service (GaaS) poses an additional challenge. GaaS often inspires some leaders to head in the wrong direction, not understanding what GaaS implies. The key difference for Games as a Service is that we are promising our users a continued production phase for years after the product's launch.[230] While it is seen as new by many from single-player spaces converting to GaaS, in reality, it's old — in more recent years typified by AAA games such as *World of Warcraft and Star Wars: The Old Republic,* and in older days by games such *Everquest, Asheron's Call, City of Heroes,* and the like.

The priority for GaaS is that the production phase must be less chaotic, which is where many in management make their mistake. Oftentimes, they believe GaaS allows us to delay critical content till later under the promise that we'll get to it post-launch. The opposite is the case, especially when this content can impact our budgets and thus vertical slices. For better or worse, many production phases for games are death marches, often because developers have triggered the production phase too early with too many unanswered questions. GaaS games continue production post launch so must be more ordered.

Moreover, GaaS games have more back-end infrastructure expectations than other games — even ones that have some degree of multiplayer. Therefore, GaaS games need to handle live testing phases before releasing. They also must interact with their customers as soon as possible to phrase their value proposition, which means that more slices of vertical quality content must exist earlier. This is desirable for all projects, but particularly so for GaaS. The general estimate is that the first customer-facing technical tests should start at least a year before launch, but in keeping with Agile and Lean principles and our own system, the earlier we engage this the better. Early production-quality (as opposed to prototype quality) should be in place a year in advance to keep everything somewhat under control.

The key point to remember about GaaS is that we are delivering a service for a product, not just the product itself. Some GaaS teams fixate on the server and client software artifacts, although they're usually smart enough to do load-testing before launch. They don't saturate the service throughout their development process, however. This results in the neglect of the release-engineering pipeline, which makes post-launch changes riskier. Of course, this isn't the only problem — many systems can be at risk, from data analytics to proper check-pointing and rollbacks, and even the patching system. Frequent releases and long-term operations are treated as an aside. The developers work as they always have, and then pass off the artifacts to some other team. This other team then runs the external tests at a periodic cadence, which while better than nothing, isn't as good as continuous operation amongst the team. This runs against DevOps practices, as we discussed in part III. Running our game properly should be a daily matter. Subjecting the service to tough conditions throughout development shakes out its issues before launch. This is akin to the Lean factory case we mentioned in Part III, where the manager shuts down one of two assembly lines on slow days to test and strengthen the other line. We must execute the live aspects of our game throughout development, or we will only learn how to operate it post-launch, where our mistakes harm our customers. In other industries, these practices have become standard, but the AAA games industry is still learning these lessons. The poor service quality and slow releases that ensue for game launches are thus predictable.

To return to the high level, the core to remember throughout all these processes, is that our sole purpose is to maximally expose the reward signal from the final paying customer to our developers, and then to gather decisions and actions from the team to increase that value. It's often said that given time-to-market, cost, and quality, we can only pick two. If we do things right, we can move everything together, at least compared to the status quo. It requires, however, that we change the way we work.

At every point in the process we discuss, we also want our team members to embrace the project as if they were owners. There is a huge difference between teams chasing tasks and teams engaged with customer value. In earlier phases, this is easier, as there is a small team empowered to guide the project. In later phases, especially in the production phase, many people join who did not have input on initial decisions. To engage them, we need to emphasize an onboarding process that transparently conveys where the project is and why the decisions were taken as they were. We should also try to hear their voices concerning problems they see for production itself. These late joiners are often experts in production phases as they move from project to project to help close, while our leadership team has been mired in dev hell and pre-production phases on this single project for years. We can fully engage their input on this topic here, even if we have limited capability to address certain issues. We should still embrace discussion on any topic if we contextualize that we aren't going back to earlier stages unless a profound issue has been discovered.

Without engagement, these new joiners will just do as they're told. They won't own the project. When our staff doesn't own the project, more responsibility defaults to management. As team sizes scale, eventually managers won't be able to handle the load, which means the game will go out of control and fail to reach its possible quality bar at the last minute. Years of excellent execution in decision-making can be lost in the last few months.

It should be noted, the smaller we can keep our team, the easier all of this is. Most of the afflictions that impair innovation are born from a transition away from tight creative teams of makers to teams of people handlers. Always ask if more people help — often they hinder. Fred Brook's Law that "More programmers added to a late project makes the project later"[231] has application to more than just engineers, even when we are in the production phase doing manufacturing, as opposed to development.

Inception

There is a state that exists before a project is officially started. This state can be long-lived, where an idea bounces around for a while, going through pitches and refinements.

Eventually, a decision is made to proceed, and a small group is created to put together a proposal. Before a Go can be given to start the project in earnest, this initial group needs to answer some core questions.

The outcome of the inception phase should be a belief that we have a starting seed and an initial customer understanding. We also need to believe that the proposed direction of the project makes sense in terms of global organizational goals — we shouldn't start a free-to-play game if that's not a space our company wants to be in.

Once we get a Go, we want to start earnest prototyping to prove out this seed and capture our customers.

The process we cover here is for AAA game development, but we'll note that even for other projects some of the gates make sense. While a small indie team might have one to five members for its entire life, perhaps with a few contractors at the end, it is still useful to understand where we are in our game-creation lifecycle, even if some of the phases are minimal for us. Inception for an indie is the point where it's easiest to run through many ideas and kill the ones early that we don't believe have legs to run.

The key artifact that we want out of the inception phase is a first cut of the Razor. We've discussed this previously, but as a reminder, the Razor is a clear and concise definition of the solution to the customer's problem that is so strong that it is also implicitly a negative definition of what the project is not. This is critical. The Razor is so named because it can prune decision branches early. We cannot expect to find the golden path but tromping about in a swamp is often a disaster. It is not the case that we try and force decisions early — we want to make them as late as possible. But when we need to make them, we want to do so efficiently and consistently, and we need to understand the range of decisions we might want to make, to understand whether they are potentially in our constraints or not. We must recognize that this first Razor is likely to change. It is an initial hypothesis that we will be testing as we proceed. Despite this, we should still exit inception with our best starting guess.

Even if we pivot away, forcing a focus on the Razor ensures that our team engages with customer need from the start. For the future health of the project and our company, the customer must always be the pole star.

To reach the exit point of inception in the best condition, there are steps we should take.

First, we should compile the motivations for why this project is desirable. To begin, we should ask ourselves why it is desirable for us in particular! Ideally, we as the initiators provide a core team that shepherds the project throughout its life (although it is common enough that it doesn't work out this way on long, difficult projects). We need to understand our own motivations for being there, as they might create conflict when we find that our individual needs aren't being meant. If this causes us to later swerve the project away from the customer to satisfy our own purposes, it can be disastrous. A transparent understanding about why we specifically are on the inception of this project can avert many complications down the road. Moreover, when we are working on a project that meets our own needs as well as those of our customers, we are far more likely to exhibit the grit that will be required to drive everything to completion.[232]

Second, we should ask why the project is desirable for the company. While we probably won't be asked to explain our personal motivations to leadership, we will need to explain why it matters to the organization during the Go meeting. Is this project a case of executing on existing competencies? Does the company believe this project represents a critical strategic move? If we find that our project doesn't align with the company's aspirations, then we shouldn't proceed. We will save a lot of money by stopping short.

If we continue against current organizational need, we must understand that we are signing on for all the politics involved with pitching the project uphill against the resistance of higher-level management. Politics is waste, after all. It will make our project harder, when it is already a challenge.

Having said that, sometimes a project is necessary even if top management does not recognize this yet; projects born against the grain can save companies later; we just need to be ready for all the frustration and waste that will be generated as we fight to justify our existence. Also, be humble enough to realize that not all our grand "disruptions" are indeed that. Be careful that we aren't trying to make a splash for our own advancement, rather than serving need.

As part of this step, we should enumerate our company's strengths and weaknesses, relative to competitors. Bear in mind that it is not required to be stronger, only comparatively stronger in the sense that while our competitors might be better than us at something, we might be able to execute cheaper or faster, providing a better value proposition to our customers. If our team lacks key expertise, it is worth considering whether this is a direction we can afford to pursue; I've seen projects speculate on the acquisition of staff that never arrive. This step is more critical to indies than to massive AAA developers, who can more easily ensure that every expertise is covered somehow. Find a way to focus on adding value and not reinventing the wheel.

Ideally at this point, our initial project idea is a solution for a customer problem that we already knew existed. What is the customer's problem and what is the set of circumstances that exist for the customer when they want their problem solved? This would give us a solid Razor immediately, which as we mentioned earlier is the key artifact for our Go meeting.

However, often when a project starts, the understanding of the customer is speculative. Before we allow the project to proceed too

Deep Management

far, we must understand whose problem we are solving. This is best handled by getting out and engaging actual users. Put the proposition before them. Note here the opportunity is to focus down on specifics. Don't just get their feelings about a generic concept but explore how they would want to engage in it. See their needs in high resolution, as we discussed in earlier chapters.

For example, a concept might be "piracy." That can mean many things. We can show detailed images of seventeenth- or eighteenth-century islands and cool-looking ships on the sea, but that doesn't lock us down much in terms of what the game is. What we need to extract is how our players would want to engage with our product. Do they want to focus on realistic sailing with wind, tacking, positioning, and so on? Do they primarily envisage their own story for their captain lived primarily through their sword with the ship as secondary? Ubisoft's *Assassin's Creed: Black Flag* is enormously different from a game like Wargaming's *World of Warships*, where ships not captains are central to the fantasy. Rare's *Sea of Thieves* is a different proposition from both of those games. And then there is Grapeshot Games' *Atlas*, which arises more from the survival genre. Do our players want to battle other players, or do they want to explore lands never seen by humanity? Do they want to ply the merchant trade routes? Or battle sea monsters? If they prefer ship combat, what type of combat? Is it slow, fast, do we need precise targeting, or it a long, strategic game? Do our players prefer to play as relaxation after work? Do they want *Dark Souls*-like difficulty levels? Or e-sports competitive multiplayer PVP? Or would they rather be space pirates?

We will not be entirely right in the models we construct of our customers at this point, but by getting to know them from the start, we will shave off expensive decision sub-trees. Consider the discussion of the asteroid base in the space-pirate game from Chapter Seven, and how it might play out to customers with different expectations. We need to continually test our customer model as development proceeds. By keeping this hypothesis central, we maintain greater integrity.

This is the time to exercise all our empathy and storytelling skills. We need to be able to predict how these real customers will react to ideas that we propose.

We must be careful as well to not dilute our customer focus by premature considerations of how to capture maximal audience sizes. There will be pressure from business and marketing to do so. This can blur our vision of who we are serving — saying that we are targeting 18-35-year-old male consumers (a stereotypical target for many AAA developers) gives us little to refine our Razor. There are core fans of *Overwatch* and *Stardew Valley* both in that subset. We should, however, remember to consider blocking. Customers might want to engage with our core proposition, but some secondary attribute repels them.

When we do try to capture more users, we must require that our core offering never be compromised. We can add more to broaden the funnel of possible players, but we should do so by adding layers, not by distorting the core. And we must be aware that too many features can itself cause quality degradation. Naturally, marketing sometimes has better connections to customers, so we can engage them to better reach our target; we just should not allow them to dominate us.[233]

We should also engage business teams in terms of whether the project makes sense for the organization in terms of its model. If customers have moved away from particular monetization schemes, we might find that our proposal is dead in the water from the start, at least in terms of how we've framed it. Any advice, though, will be speculative; in AAA, we are far from release at this point, and the industry moves fast.

After we've gathered all the inputs and iterated, we should have a model of our customer that we can use to create our proposed Razor. For the Go/No-Go meeting, we should have the supporting data on hand to justify the Razor, but for the slide deck we present to management, a single slide should be enough. We should bring the more detailed summaries so that if questions are asked, we can address them. If the Razor is supported by actual play tests by customers with an early prototype, that is even better. The Razor is only a couple sentences, so it needs to be tight. The key here is that we have burned all the excess fat out of our ideas.

There is always the temptation when preparing for a Go meeting to blur the proposal, so that management can read into our pitch concepts that we didn't include. This arises from anxiety — we aren't certain of our pitch, so we want to accommodate any idea a powerful figure throws out.

We should avoid this as it can sabotage the project. We must be clear first and foremost. If an idea comes up in the Go meeting, we note it. If it conflicts with the customer model, we are upfront and explain that based on our studies, it isn't a good match for our project. If we're not sure, we tell them that we'll get back to them. If we're excited by the idea, we shouldn't buy into it on the spot, but get back to them later. When out of the meeting, we should delve into these suggestions.

People are often afraid of pushing back, and in some cultures, this can be a legitimate fear, but the downstream cost of vacillation is enormous. Management needs to see that we understand our customer. They need to trust that we've done due diligence. Meanwhile, we need to show that we respect their input, which is why we need to note down suggestions, consider them carefully, and get back to them. However, we're heading down a dark road if appeasing internal figures becomes more important than solving customers' problems.

Beyond the Razor, there are other expectations of artifacts at this Go meeting that indicate that the critical problems have been resolved for this phase. Typically, this includes a rough but reasonably detailed list of the expected challenges for the project; a list of proposed resolutions and rough timelines; key technologies including tech to be built; and any other main initiating questions for the project that the team will need to answer. This should be a short pitch deck — I would suggest no more than ten or twenty slides. Too much detail is premature. You want a digest of these core issues with some flavor, but not too much. A lot of the time at the Go/No-Go meeting should revolve around the implications of the Razor. We are not going to this final meeting of the inception phase with enough support to justify pre-production, only enough to justify paying for a small team to flesh out these details in dev hell.

For an indie team, this could be a presentation to themselves, perhaps followed by a small party — such milestones can be useful where an indie project is a long slog. Even for a small team, it's useful to spend some time here to make sure the group is all on the same page and that we all find the deck convincing.

At the end of this phase, we should make sure that our slides and the first definition of the Razor are put into our long-term datastore and/or version-control system, and then made available to the entire team including the new joiners we are hoping to get in the next phase. Many items such as the risk list will become live artifacts that undergo continuous updates, but the key point here is that later joiners can see the evolution of the project even from this early point. This can give context, especially if the core team gets replaced.

If all goes well and everyone finds the presentation sound, then this marks the true inception of the project. We shouldn't have spent much money at this point, and the staffing should have been minimal. This is the seed, however, out of which everything else grows. Thus, even this small team should have been executing according to our decision-making system's pillars, so that good habits grow. After the Go, the team size will increase but not much — our next step is to prove out and solidify what we just accomplished.

Dev Hell Is the Best Hell

The dev-hell phase is almost never called that. It's a phase that has many names. Regardless, when we are at this point, it can be one of the most frustrating stages as the most experimental questions must be answered here. The team often has no clear idea of when the product will ship, or sometimes if it ever will. While the members tend to be more senior, their team is small, so they feel cut off from the rest of the studio. All of this can lead to the feeling that it is a tough and hellish phase, hence why across several industries it has been called dev hell. Regardless, it is one of the most critical phases to get right. When the team is small, project delays aren't that costly; when the uncertainties of dev hell bleed into later phases after team sizes are much larger, then the pressures build and cost mounts, which can sabotage otherwise high-potential offerings. Regardless of how tough it is, this is a phase we need to approach thoroughly.

Our goal at the start of dev hell is to determine what we are going to build. This is necessary, because the next phase — pre-production — is about how to build at scale, both tools and recipes. We need to show that our customers consider this product a delightful solution. We often aren't free to move our value proposition arbitrarily. The current market often sets an anchoring for the consumer — a $60 USD console/PC title has quality and length expectations that differ from a Free-to-play (F2P) mobile app. We need to then mix together our core concepts and all these expectations to find a combination that makes sense. At the final Go meeting when we are approved (and we will likely see many Go meetings where we are rejected), we should have a convincing game concept with all critical content types shown to be reasonable. In terms of Lean considerations, this is the point where we've determined the customer order. Note, we don't mean that we are bound by contractual specifications at this point — that wouldn't be agile. We always iterate with the customer. Instead, we mean that the form has been determined sufficiently to answer necessary architectural questions. After we exit this phase, and as time passes, the cost of a major pivot rises.

The dev-hell phase is best started through a series of prototypes. We must keep the team small, and we need to prove out our propositions, not deliver shippable software. We will throw away many things as we iterate. We shouldn't waste undo effort on them. Test fast and reject early. While these rejects won't show up in the final product, they are critical to grasping actual customer need. We must be upfront with our staff that exactly nothing of the code and art they are producing will reach the final game. Moreover, we should select staff for this phase who are skilled at this form of iteration.

Sometimes teams are tempted to keep prototype code to shorten later phases but let us note that this should not be done. It has one of two negative effects: either the code is written to sufficient quality that it is usable long-term, which slows the creative loop in dev hell, or bad code is carried into the future codebase and causes defects and maintainability issues down the road. In fact, both problems can happen, when it is written at higher quality and thus more slowly, but not at high enough quality, which is discovered later. Writing to higher quality too early is a form of overproduction.

Part of this prototyping involves creating isolated test cases that prove out components. Then some critical pieces might be integrated into a test world to see how they interact. Often, imagination is used to fill in the blanks. We're not referring to a vertical slice of the game here, which comes later in pre-production. This is an earlier validation.

If people on the team can project these results to realized states, this can be a productive way to proceed. Not everyone can do this, however. We can create a bunch of viable features that together make no sense. If we find this out after dev hell, this will create an expensive late-stage pivots.

A better approach might be for this prototype to be treated as if it were an indie project, but without final polish expectations. It's prototype software, but it's working software for a real version of the game. It is not, however, created to the realization level of the final project, but rather to test what we believe to be the core game loops.

Our point here is this: it used to take much less time to build a game front-to-back than it does now. We used to do it in less than a year around the 2000s. Game mechanics today aren't that much more complicated, although the higher polish expectations drive up development cost in fully realized products. Given the excellent game-building tools available now, which we lacked then, it's credible to create an "old-timey" version of our game to prove it out. Then for some specific areas where we believe we need higher levels of realization, we can build specific test worlds with isolated feature sets, knowing the risk in doing so.

There are additional motivations for wanting to create a low-realization version of the game. Many games today have weak core mechanics because the layering of expensive realization on top distracts from the game as a game. While we care ultimately only about the final experience for the customer, weak foundations make it hard to realize our full potential. If we have a version of the game that emphasizes the core mechanics without the realization, then the mechanics must stand on their own. We can then layer the immersion on top and create a far more robust and compelling product.

It's possible there are games for which this type of prototype doesn't make sense, but it's worked well for many cases. Moreover, no customer that we bring in early to play this version of the game will confuse it with a poor-quality rendition of a AAA product. In fact, our biggest risk might be they like it so much (given the nostalgia factor) that they want us to release it!

Some teams even maintain this prototype game version throughout the lifetime of the product. This is done to allow faster prototype iterations in later stages, as production-quality AAA engines sometimes have higher friction for iteration. That has pluses and minuses. On the positive side, it creates a playground distinct from the production code base, which frames our engineers' understanding of what type of code is proper in that space. This prevents prototype code from leaking into production, and production standards from slowing down prototypes. On the negative side, this dodges a real problem. When people claim that a production engine has too much friction, that means we should allocate more time to fixing that engine. The friction has become part of our normal of deviance. We shouldn't accept that.

We need to iterate until we've resolved all our main gameplay questions. This is a process of experimentation, where we repeatedly pose questions. From the point of view of information extracted, it is preferable that these questions be as likely true as they are false. Practically, we often test questions with far more skewed probabilities to validate specific risky propositions. It depends whether we're trying to explore as rapidly as possible, which entails bold questions that are more likely to be wrong, or if we think we know the answer, but want greater surety. We need to understand how people want to experience our game moment-to-moment, and how they want to play it long term. Sometimes there are optional features that we think could provide value, but that we choose to prove out in later phases — this is only allowed when these features are not required to be in the game, so can be cut. Regardless, they will need to conform to any recipes we have generated by the time they are revived.

As we proceed into later stages, our teams are going to require greater stability.

Remember, our goal here is to establish what our customer wants. We want to get their order correct. The later stages are concurrent engineering where we attempt to deliver that order as rapidly as possible, at the greatest level of quality that we can reach.

As soon as we start solidifying our customers' expectations, we also need to engage technologists to establish what type of tech we require. This should start early as we must answer these questions before we can be given a Go to exit dev hell. Early shippable solutions should be in place as well. For instance, if we are making an *Overwatch* style game, the current expectation would be that we require dedicated servers to support that value proposition. If we want to do something else, we first must prove it viable. Second, even if we stick with a standard solution, we should have a credible if early version of it in place before entering pre-production. Our technology state at the start of pre-production should be in the right ballpark, as pre-production staff need to work in a legitimate environment.

For technical reasons, we also must establish the nature of all content we wish to build, unless that content is entirely optional and thus cuttable. If we require one massive open world, we are going to need to know that. This is necessary so that we can answer the requisite technical questions and ensure the proper early architecture is in place.

If we in tech need to do prototypes to validate the technical aspects of questions, then these prototypes need to be finished before we get a Go. While some prototypes can happen later, the immediate next phase is about building shippable code that will enable us to "manufacture" all the content we require in the final production phase.

While many try to shortcut this, it should be required that our team in pre-production work against an early but essentially valid version of the architecture. Thus, we need to exit dev hell with this in place. If we are doing a multiplayer game with dedicated servers, it is unacceptable for game programmers to be writing their code against an engine that is currently single-player. They will make enormous mistakes in the next phase if we do that. Thus, even once we're done prototyping, we must continue onward to do architectural conversions on our base engine before getting a Go. Our newly on-boarded staff in pre-production need to start valid work from the start. In GaaS products this is even more imperative, as we want to operate our service properly well in advance of launch.

This often requires us to onboard extra engineers in the middle of dev hell to straighten this out.

The challenge is top management always wants the project tomorrow. As we'll reiterate many times, there is always pressure to jump early into later phases. We desire to be as adaptable and reactive as possible, so we want to move quickly as well; however, skipping steps in the long term will end up making us slow, expensive, low quality, or some combination of these three. We must move as fast as possible, but no faster. For small companies, the issue is often their runway before their funds are exhausted, so we must watch our scope to avoid getting trapped in a lose-lose choice. For large companies, there can be pressure from desirable market slots, stockholders who want revenue sources in empty quarters, or just the relentless demand for growth.

There is also sometimes the view that we must hold our teams to tight deadlines: there is even some truth to that — projects given more time tend to take as much time as allowed. Making schedules using that argument is a dangerous road to take, however, as it can trip up projects straight out of the gate, just as they start scaling. They often never fully recover from that. It is better to ingrain our decision system with its Lean principles into the team, so that they strive constantly against waste.

The problem is that if we leap into these later stages before resolving questions, we are passing debt down the chain. Worse, these later phases have higher burn rates and trigger our shipping-date clock. When we start pre-production, we should know within three months when we ought to ship (barring a pivot), and from the beginning of production we should know the actual ship date. If we start pre-production with too many major risks before us, then we can't effectively project a date until well into the phase. Some people will suggest pre-production is just a name, and if we do the correct work regardless, that is fine. Questions still need to be asked in a similar order, and if we staff up too early, we sabotage ourselves just the same.

The debt we pass down is particularly problematic as our creators will need to spend time fixing those problems while simultaneously handling the organizational issues arising from increased scale. This can get out of hand, creating cascading problems that result in death marches and inferior products. It's well established that we perform much worse when we are multitasking.[234] We shouldn't pass work down the chain; we should handle it when we find it. If it can't be handled immediately due to other tasks, and we feel it must be done, we should queue it up. But we can't afford to cheat and claim that we're farther along than we are, not in the long run.

Remember, newcomers to the project require guidance. Oftentimes, projects that are stretched thin do not reallocate their personnel to support onboarded staff. These new staff then drift and rather than adding to the project, they create problems. Their morale then crashes. If we're going to bring in new staff, we need to do so at the right time, and respect that managing them will drain resources. If we can't afford that given where we are now in our development, then we can't afford new staff yet.

As much as possible, dev hell should not be subject to the pressures of time slots for shipping, if progress is being made. Team size should be kept to its absolute minimum. It might be that we risk missing a business window by taking longer in dev hell, but we risk project failure if we exit too early. Sometimes dev hell does move fast if we legitimately understand the problem of our customer and its solution from the start. There is no minimum time required. If we can move fast, we should. But we must be sure that when we exit dev hell, we have answered our key questions. In this phase, there is nothing specific to slot into the schedule as we aren't far enough along.

This uncertainty in terms of delivery date means that we should be careful of fads. As this book is being written, Battle Royale is the fad *de jour*, popularized by *Player Unknown Battlegrounds* and made particularly successful with *Fortnite*. The most recent entry is *Apex Legends* by Respawn Entertainment. By the time we get through dev hell, pre-prod, and prod, this fad might be exhausted. If we are certain of our specific take on Battle Royale and of our customer need, it's possible that we can race quickly through phases to exploit an opportunity before it is lost. We should do this only where most of the answers are obvious. Typically, this means a copy-cat production. *Fortnite* after all, was a reaction to *Player Unknown Battlegrounds* as well as being a post-ship pivot, so it can make sense to pursue a hot trend. In *Fortnite*'s case, it was necessary. It's easy to forget now that the view of *Fortnite*'s success before its Battle Royale mode was a different narrative.

While we shouldn't have a deadline for the dev-hell phase, we do need to make sure that the team is progressing and that they don't loop in their decisions. Progress is unpredictable, but we should be constantly advancing. If we pivot, we should do so for sound reasons, and we should watch out for considering old paths again. If the team does get stuck in a loop, we might need to reset them. A reset in dev hell has vastly less impact than a reset in pre-production or production.

This also means that dev hell is the time to take the most ambitious leaps. We should always front-load risk before we have invested too much. If something takes longer than expected, it's fine as we haven't been cooked it into our business expectations yet.

Pivoting

We assume that not only can we be wrong, but early on we probably are. While we require an initial and believable Razor at the end of the inception phase, this is more to habituate ourselves to the kind of customer-centered mentality we require. We expect the Razor might need adjusting as we head through dev hell. After dev hell, it's better for there to be fewer changes, although it can happen. It is critical that we are capable of changing direction. We must be able to accommodate pivots.

A quick pivot definition for us would be this: a change in the project's hypothesis about our customers' needs and conditions. Alternatively, from Eric Ries's *The Lean Startup*, a pivot is defined as "a structured course correction designed to test a new fundamental hypothesis about the product, business model, and engine of growth." We prefer our definition as it places the customer in their proper primary place, with the other aspects mentioned by Ries subordinated to customer need. It is fair to say, though, that a pivot could be a switch from a buy-to-play model to a free-to-play one, or vice versa. Even in that case, it should be viewed through the lens of how this changes the experience for the customer. Such a change implies a shift in who our customer is, as the customer spaces of B2P and F2P games are not the same. When we find that a particular customer does not allow a viable business model, we view the pivot as a change to a different customer. If our customer represents a niche that is too narrow, we convert to a customer who exemplifies a broader support base.

For a successful project, our probability of being wrong should decrease over time, or our challenges multiply. This is especially true of AAA game development, where there is a final heavyweight production phase. If we find ourselves still unsure after numerous pivots, we should pull back and ask if the project is critically off course. As we mentioned in the chapter *Cutting Our Projects*, in most cases we should be the ones to terminate the project, not higher-level management. If we find that we are spiraling downward, we either need to establish an experiment that will break us out of our decline or accept that the project has become a zombie. Undead projects should be cut.

Pivots are always disruptive. Work will be made invalid, thus inducing waste. It is critical that we do our best to make sure pivots happen as early in the project as possible while our burn rate is low. At later stages, a forced pivot will often either mean that we run out of money or that we cannot properly meet the full customer need, as we cannot rewrite our software fast enough.

Sometimes we have no option. Every pivot is a "Persevere versus Pivot"[235] choice. We must consider the trap of sunk cost and try to arrive at our decision to continue or stop as if we were an outside decision-maker brought in with no history, solely to consider whether further investment is worthwhile. Usually, a late-stage pivot is unwise, and we'd rather capture what we almost have. Sometimes, it is better to take the risk and switch.

To pivot effectively, though, it is important that people understand not just who they are pivoting to, but who their previous customer was and why that customer is no longer a valuable or a matching proposition. To pivot well, it is necessary that we can see both our starting point and destination. People in leadership are often subject to great amounts of self-doubt and second-guessing by others — blind pivoting to the latest fad of the day is a huge temptation, especially when political factors within the company are fixated on the latest trends. Knowing who our customer was and why and knowing who our new proposed customer is and why (and hopefully having tested this proposition) forces people to face their justification for pivoting. Knowing that these reasons will be documented prevents them from ill-conceived shifts to appease transient interests.

Pre-Production

Once we finally get a Go out of dev hell, which can take a while, we know what we're going to build and why, but we don't yet know how. Next, we need to build tools and prove out our recipes for later "manufacturing." Before we are approved to enter pre-production, we should have proposals for our technical choices. This is necessary as at this point our ship date is going to become more real.

After the Go, one of our immediate steps either with top management or with our investors is to establish a rough release window. Pre-production can still be a bit unpredictable, but any gross risks should have been dealt with before the Go approval of the dev-hell gate.

We should have already prototyped everything that matters. Our software architecture should be an early non-prototype version of what we'll ship with. For some games, this is just the default state of the engine out of the box. If our game requires a different architecture from that of the default engine, it is necessary that we get an early non-prototype version up. For example, if we start with a single-player engine, but we're making a multiplayer game with dedicated servers, we need to have at least converted to an early stage of that, although perhaps there are some shortcuts.

If we are not at least in that state in terms of our software, it'll be hard to estimate a release window as serious architectural risks have not yet been mitigated.

Normally, in AAA a pre-production stage can take anywhere from six to nine months, depending on what needs to be built. GaaS projects often have longer pre-production phases to allow for more time to operate the service in advance of launch. If we require more time than nine months, that probably means we should have gotten started on work before getting a Go out of dev hell. The core reason to control this is that pre-production is the start of a higher burn rate. Thus, mistakes in estimation at this point are costly. Because they are costly, we'll often be pressured to engage in shortcuts that harm user value or damage us in the long term.

As we mentioned earlier, some projects might not require the later horizontal production phase. For these cases, pre-production is better termed the development phase. Because this phase then has larger scope than a standard pre-production it might require 1-3 months more time, but the timeline at this point should be no less predictable than for other AAA games, and perhaps more so. This development phase would then end with the launch of the product.

The goal of pre-production is to exit with several key milestones accomplished: the tools to build the game must exist in a usable state; the baseline features and rough optimization on the client and server must be done (up to the point where we can see that we will be able to reach final targets with work); the specifications and budgets for how to build content must exist such that the engine can render the content in real time; the release engineering pipeline needs to be solid; and we need to be able to work and deploy in realistic production-like environments as well as do proper deployments into live production. Our key problem to solve is that production for a AAA product is a horizontal process where a great deal of content is built simultaneously. It is, as we've said, a manufacturing stage where we create many things according to the recipes we have established in the pre-production phase. If we are running a service, we should expect that on entrance to this final phase we are able to operate in production environments although not yet at scale. It is imperative with a GaaS that we do not learn how to operate it only after we launch. We need to be working with our customers early, so if we are a service, we need it to be functional as soon as possible. Experience suggests that you should be working with external players over a year in advance of launch. On *Star Wars: The Old Republic*, the Electronic Arts corporate-wide alpha was almost two years in advance of shipping, with a trickle of external players arriving some months after. Ubisoft's *For Honor* and *Rainbow Six: Siege* both had closer to fifteen months between their first customer test and release.

We cannot fulfill our requirements for exiting pre-production without empirical proof. For example, since there are content budgets, we must create a vertical slice. This means a subsection of the game must be polished to final quality. The result needs to satisfy art, design, tech, and any other critical stakeholders. Creating a vertical slice usually is an iterative process, so when planning we should expect multiple attempts until we have reached a version that satisfies everyone. Attempting to skip this phase is akin to us attempting to manufacture thousands of cars on the assembly line while finishing the car's design. It will be expensive to fold changes back into already produced content.

Deep Management

Note that as with dev hell, there will be pressures from above to exit pre-production early. The temptation will be for us to say that we will fix issues later. In some cases, this makes sense; after all, we are engaging in concurrent engineering. It can be the case that world-building takes an enormous amount of resources but authoring a couple cinematics does not. Here we can argue that a delay makes sense, especially if it's a separate team. Just be careful. Sometimes it is believed that something is small and can be delayed, but we then discover we are wrong. Then, a huge last-minute critical path gets injected onto an unsuspecting team. Production has immense organizational pressures already, which will make it hard to deal with leftover issues.

Predictability is also more important at this point as we start to invest in marketing. It's not unusual for a first showing at E3[236] (the Electronic Entertainment Expo) to happen in the pre-production phase. This makes sense because we are certain we've already found the right customer. Demos for E3 are quite expensive, both in terms of outright dollar cost and in terms of lost productivity on the development team, which often does wasted work to support E3. If we have allowed debt from previous phases to creep into pre-production and then allow pre-production issues to creep into production, we'll be placed in the undesirable and expensive position of having to either go to more than two E3s, or not being ready in time and shipping a broken game.

Pre-production is also a point where we're going to need to watch our scaling. At the start of dev hell, we probably satisfied Amazon's "two-pizza rule," where two pizzas could feed the entire team. This remains true usually through the pure prototyping section. As we begin to deal with technical choices and architectural conversions to ready for a final Go, team size increases but should still be carefully controlled. Once we enter pre-production, however, everything changes. New people pour in, and we need to onboard them and make sure they're able to contribute. We need to help them understand where we are, enable them to be owners, but

295

simultaneously avoid flipping our project over by challenging the customer focus that we've established. It is imperative that we not shut them down when addressing their concerns. If they feel that they can offer their expertise on pre-production, then they can perceive themselves as owners. Part of this is making sure that enough of our older staff are involved in the management of newcomers to incorporate them, rather than letting a clique of old members form against the newcomers and their "crazy ideas."

Towards the end of pre-production, we will also need to prepare for the even larger scaling that will come with the next phase. We must ensure that we have enough management expertise in place and that all our systems are ready to go for production with a much larger and globally dispersed team.

Unlike dev hell, the pre-production gate should be a Go with high probability. We should do everything in our power to enable this. In dev hell, we went to gates with regular preparations and were tested on our progress. In our pre-production gate, we should make sure we've had appropriate audits to ensure that we aren't caught off-guard. We should expect that some areas are noted as weak which we will need to address, but otherwise, a No-Go at a pre-production gate means that we missed critical expectations. Such a miss can endanger our release window, which as we mentioned should have been known within three months.

We also at this point wish to address the issue of closers, specialists who are sometimes sent in by senior management as early as pre-production. A closer's job is to find the best value proposition out of our messy product and ship that — for this to be necessary, we must have been generating waste. If we had adhered to our decision-making system, the closer would have nothing to do. When we haven't, the closer will try to piece together something, and cut the rest. Since the organization rates closers by their capacity to deliver projects on time, the closer will often make choices that favor the schedule over the customer. This is precisely what we wish to avoid with our system. If we think lean throughout our project and not just at the end, closers become redundant.

Production

Production is where the project pushes to release with the least time to market. As we've said, this phase is more akin to manufacturing than standard software development. Content-oriented staffing can now scale horizontally as the recipes have been defined in the pre-production phase. Moreover, the project should be at its most predictable.

In the current mentality of AAA game production, predictability combined with a desire for a shorter time to market implies an increase in staffing. Sometimes lead teams forget this. They fail to prepare themselves for the avalanche of managerial problems they will now face. If they are handling remote teams across the world, it is also easy for the lead team to fail to account for how many personnel they will need to allocate to handle those teams, even when we have given the collaboration teams full ownership of a section of the game.

Unfortunately for predictability, this is also where the final quality of the project becomes visible. If we've done our job well in pre-production, well-chosen vertical slices will have de-risked our core propositions, but it is not always trivial to foresee all ends. This is again a reason why we must be hard-nosed about our obligations. Plenty of other problems will arise unexpectedly later.

This is also the point where our staff starts to suffer the most anxiety. People worry that the game isn't good enough. It's important to have a critical eye and be unrelenting in providing customer value; people's fear can cause them to add features that have not proved their value. Moreover, these features often come at the cost of focus on delivering quality in the features that we know work. We must hold to our decision-making system. Follow the path. Pose experiments and see how live users react to the product in its current form. Make sure proposed features are addressing root causes of issue for users, not just symptoms. If people lose their cool, redirect them back to the process.

Especially for a GaaS project, it is imperative that our developers aren't just building a local game and then delivering artifacts for a production deployment under the assumption they work. In the production phase, developers should be working in environments as close to production as possible, as long as doing so doesn't compromise their agility too much (and if it does, we should try to address that problem to allow them to work in more real environments). Obviously, they won't be running with load balancers, but the more they experience the game as the users will experience it, the more service-oriented the resulting project will be. Practice is the only thing that drives perfection. Patching the game products over at the last minute is a common recipe for failure in service-oriented projects. It's also imperative that our developers play the game from home even at times when we aren't open to users. This is a useful litmus test to shake out simple problems.

Especially if we are a service, it is imperative to review best practices in release engineering and deployment. We will not be covering this topic in this book, but the reader should consider the literature on continuous integration/continuous deployment, DevOps, SRE, and the other best practices by top companies in the industry.[237] Automation is the foundation of a system that allows no-stress progressive deployments and rollbacks. Humans are consistent random sources of error, so we should remove them whenever it makes sense. Remember that if we start today, the bar will be higher tomorrow. Quality of service is partially defined in terms of our ability to make rapid and safe changes to meet consumer demand.

Note that our telemetry systems require scaling tests alongside our other back-end services. I have seen projects launch and leave the developers blind when their systems could not handle the load of tracking data from the live service. We must stress our game telemetry systems as part of our load tests.

On the content side, our horizontal production teams are pushing out content according to our recipes as rapidly as possible. There are a lot of moving parts here, so make sure that the critical paths are observed. It creates a lot of stress when a single type of content ends up pushing far past everything else. Also, make sure there are no bubbles in the pipeline. No one likes to run dry on work knowing that a big surge will come later and overwhelm them at the end.

So far, I've described a smooth production phase. Usually it isn't. We must deliver customer value; however, even if we've done our job well, innovation is not predictable. We will sometimes have to make bold late-stage changes. Therefore, it's imperative that we do not inherit debt from earlier stages. Too many pre-existing problems will hamstring us when we need to move fast. Given too much noise, we might find that we can't solve the key problems.

We should note, though, that regardless of time pressure, once we have solved a surprise, we must stop and ask why we didn't see it coming.

Red Dead Redemption 2, for example, had late-stage challenges because they chose to add cinematic black bars on cutscenes to make them more filmic. Staff on the project all agreed this was an improvement but doing this required that all the cinematics be retouched, for the shots were now invalid. This was a huge scheduling hit for animators.[238] It was the right call to make, but such a case needs to be followed up as to why this happened in the first place. After all, it's been a common practice in games for over a decade. Every problem of sufficient impact must have a postmortem. If decisions have been documented, it might be discovered that there were reasons why this was done, and that those reasons were later invalidated, but it wasn't noted until too late that the decision required changing. It could also be that it was a decision that was completely missed, in which case we might ask who should have had the responsibility for that choice. It is not a matter of blame but making sure that next time we avoid the problem by putting in proper guardrails. Perhaps this is a case where for all cinematics, this should have been a default requirement, rather than a request. Better choice architecture[239] might have prevented it.

After all, we know that there will be unexpected problems, so failing to deal with the known cases is unacceptable. Be ready for the blows no one could predict.

As leaders and managers, we also need to make sure that our teams execute on our decision-making system. So many things can be going on in this final phase that it is easy to let this drop. We must make it an issue of character to follow through. If we are overloaded, make sure our system is the priority and let the other issues fall off. Decisions must be logged, and experiments must have clear testability. People can't overturn decisions without reviewing the original justification. Postmortems must be followed through on for all problems that arise. Above all, we must keep our people calm. Cortisol, the product of stress, over the long term is well established to weaken creativity and cognitive function. Our team must not become a dull knife.

In the end, once we are done and launch our product or service, we will know that we have done a good job if our launch and subsequent releases are non-events. This is an achievable goal. If we have practiced live, incorporated customers early on, and done enough load testing, then we will have capacity to handle the unexpected issues and keep our cool. When something goes wrong, we fix it, and make sure the core issue is resolved. If it was a human error, we automate it. Our production pipelines will then keep churning out content post-launch either for DLC or continuous rolling content updates in GaaS.

Agile Marketing

We've mentioned that we must hold the line with marketing and business teams, at least those who operate according to classic behavioral templates. This applies more to AAA publishers such as Electronic Arts, Activision, Ubisoft, Take Two Interactive, and the like. In such environments, the default that marketing and business teams operate within runs contrary to the needs of innovative development – we historically have optimized these groups for predictable iterative releases. Game products from this view become abstractions that we schedule into windows for optimal synergy with marketing campaigns. This resembles the pre-Lean model of vehicle production practiced by the Big Three before Toyota, and the software methodologies used before Agile. We assume the products will be ready on time, removing that threat from the equation, because iterative releases pose lower risk. Because we abstract our products, we focus instead on scheduling and marketing patterns, rather than subordinating our campaigns to our development teams' needs. This emphasis on the waterfall scheduling of product releases results in the consolidation of our marketing and business personnel into specialized departments that work on many games at once, since overarching control matters more in this paradigm. To be fair, most modern companies do embed a representative into projects to tailor the campaign for their specific flavor, but the general edifice and assumptions about release windows and scheduling remain. Since these publishers make most of their year-to-year revenue off iterative products like *Madden* and *Call of Duty*, the marketing and business teams become biased by the patterns of such releases, even though the future iterative games arise from our innovative releases.

Iterative games begin with a previously viable product. Some yearly releases involve only whatever additional features made it into the schedule in time. Since the product already had a core, we have that to fall back on. Technological shifts across console generations pose an additional threat, but here these games play it safe with other risks, so that we can ensure a solid delivery. When we can ensure a dependable release window and still maintain the known good core of the iterative product, there is tremendous value for a well-honed and scheduled marketing push. It can boost sales enormously.

Innovative products, on the other hand, must build the core, which can only be refined through experiment against customers. Similar games might exist for inspiration, but the more innovative the product, the less we will have to fall back on. Oftentimes, demands of the new core entail risky technological advancements as well, since existing engine technologies were shaped by previous releases, not current need. This means that we cannot predict these products with similar precision, although we can reduce the uncertainty by engaging in the practices espoused in this book. Standard practices for marketing campaigns and business requirements can result in undercooked products releasing just to hit a release window. This in turn sabotages our innovation from the start.

For sure, if we can deliver a solid innovative product in the targeted window, that will result in an enormous sales boost that will improve future releases, but all too often that isn't the outcome. We substitute what we would like to happen, for what will probably happen.

We might consider an analogy. Imagine that we own a house that we rent out. Our previous tenants leave, so we have an asset producing no income. A group of potential renters show up, but we obtain their history, and find that they traffic illegal drugs and wreck whatever property they inhabit (a friend of ours unknowingly rented their house to a white supremacist drug-trafficking gang in Canada, and only found out about it when the police raided the property on live television). If we rent to this high-risk group, our house will deliver a monthly income, but we also doom ourselves to high repair costs and perhaps the total loss of the asset. Alternatively, we can recognize the risk, accept the shortfall, and wait till safer renters arrive. Of course, well-timed marketing campaigns tempt us with heightened sales, not just steady rents, but if a premature release burns the product, the long-term impact can extend beyond the loss of an IP to the degradation of our brand as a company.

In the long term, genre-defining innovations and new IPs enable the gold mines of tomorrow. Unfortunately, the rigid processes that arose to efficiently support our iterative product cycles do not work as well for our most creative endeavors.

In our section *DevOps and SRE* from the chapter *Historical Foundations*, we discussed how operations and development teams also produced inferior outcomes due to siloing and conflicts between their incentives. At one time, this seemed inextricable from service development. Once we recognized the need, though, we came to recognize solutions.

In the same way, as we come to realize that we are undermining our most important releases, we can adopt new methods of handling releases for our teams. The old way was easier, so just as with DevOps, we must overcome frictions. For the DevOps case, increased automation solved many of their issues. For this new case, we will have to discover how we can create more adaptable means. For example, *Apex Legends* launched with a non-standard marketing campaign, primarily linking the release with full-day streams by key figures on Twitch. Here, we won't get into the ethics of this method – whether the signals of paid streaming were clear enough or not to the consumer, for instance. Rather, we use this as a case to suggest the approaches we should favor. We should seek out low lead times and adaptability.

The lean transformations that have run through engineering and operations must continue until they saturate every part of software development.

Closing Remarks

Only now will we reveal the ulterior motive behind this book: it is our hope to wake people up. We have lost touch with customer need and become trapped in a quest for predictable monetization platforms. At the strategic level, we have lost our purpose. Instead of building products to solve our customers' problems, we construct what our organization desires instead. That approach has no future. It is a creeping normalization of waste.

We can see this sea change in the games industry if we examine new job postings. Every project now has positions dedicated to managing, designing, and coding systems for monetization. These positions explicitly require an understanding or at least willingness to learn about behavioral psychology. Our customers' cognitive glitches provide the meat for the feast.

To be clear, the people who fill these roles often deeply love games. They want their work to support a better experience. They desire to make incredible products. And, in fact, there is a place for those whose role exposes us to the value that our customers place in our creations. In-built market expectations can artificially cap what our users would otherwise be delighted to pay us.

That isn't the model that current industry practice supports, however. We build our monetization systems on the backs of whales and dolphins,[240] terms which have no fixed definition, but represent respectively those who spend a great deal (often cited as over a $100) and those who spend less but still a fair amount. While some of these individuals spend this money without regret, both whales and dolphins exhibit addictive behaviors. When manipulative forms of monetization collide with stressed consumers subject to dysfunctional coping habits, the results can be self-destructive.[241] This is a case of a twisted proxy. At least in theory, we only wanted to capture the value our games properly offer our customers, but we hook the susceptible instead. If we don't think too hard about the ramifications of what we have done, this is all quite lucrative and desirable.

Even if the moral hazards do not concern us, backlash from our consumers should. As we shift away from a focus on delivering customer value to constructing exploitation engines, we erode and destroy the fundamental contract between our customers and ourselves: that we promise a fun escape from the real world without consequences.

It is not surprising that these changes in our business model have come to pass. Once, the game industry was niche; it is now enormous and still growing. In 2018, game revenues including mobile, PC, and consoles reached a new record of $134.9B USD, up 10.9%.[242] In comparison, for the film industry, global box-office receipts netted $41.7B USD.[243] With home entertainment added, revenues reached $136B USD.[244] Games are no longer small fry, and that's been true for years. PCs and consoles make up roughly half the current game revenue numbers, with mobile taking up the rest. Stock-market investors took note long ago. Most critically, these investors view the largest game publishers as growth stocks, which gives these organizations higher valuations than current fiscal fundamentals justify. This premium is based on the expectation that these game companies will enjoy rapid and unbroken year-to-year growth. This drives top-level game executives to chase the dragon.

Innovation is risky and unpredictable. While new IPs can be enormously valuable, it is safer in the short term to squeeze iterative franchises with established customer bases. There are well-established techniques that sales and marketing professionals can employ to extract more juice. That extraction can only go on for so long, however.

We must remember that IPs aren't valuable in and of themselves. We prize these properties only because they can bring an engaged player base to our product. IPs must be grown. An initial concept from a trusted developer can pull in some players at the start, but it is our delivery and the sustained relationship we maintain that boosts an IP to the premier heights of iconic properties. The opposite is also true. Prolonged extraction of resources without corresponding nurturance of our IP can render once lustrous assets into has-been subjects of derision.

Furthermore, while a short-term squeeze can extract year-to-year growth for a while, the prioritization of iteration over innovation stifles the development of new offerings, which constrains our future customer base and eventual revenues. Thus, the pressure to meet these perpetual revenue growth targets ironically hamstrings our future capacity to do so.

This is an old story. Companies form, fight their way up from humble beginnings, and eventually deliver a sound proposition, usually to a niche. They then push up the value chain and spread out to more consumers, until eventually the survivors overtake the previous market leaders. Then they fall prey to demands that they mine the market they have built. Along the way, leadership gets replaced. The principles that inspired these companies fall away — after all, they are now unassailable industry leaders! For a time, there are no alternatives, so the riches continue to flow. The new market leaders lose their agility. They believe they have a right to their consumers, so they build products for their own aggrandizement. Then the next generation rises and supplants them.

Not all companies fall prey to this. Many have retained their innovative core and customer focus. Some thrive for decades, even though they see their ups and downs. For the long-lived, these periodic shocks serve as reminders that they must remain centered. If a company has built a sound internal culture on principles that are more than just words, then that organization can endure the pressure of outside forces. It is only once they yield to temptation that they sign their eventual death warrant.

Nintendo should remind us that customer focus can still drive success. They have long been a beloved company, but in recent years, their stock with consumers has risen due to their repeated deliveries of great games without corrosive monetization. In the past, there were times when their future seemed in doubt — the GameCube, while it had a loyal following, lacked the sales of its competitors, and while the Wii catapulted Nintendo back to the top, the Wii-U raised many doubts. These shocks, however, made Nintendo stronger, by reminding them not to take their position for granted. They must continually earn the loyalty of their fans. Their leaders remain humble and dedicated to core values. This has allowed them to repay the faith their customers placed in them, which perpetuates the virtuous cycle at the heart of their success.

Other companies, however, suffer a continuous cycle of backlash.

Again, monetization itself isn't bad — it is how we orchestrate it that matters. For free-to-play games, post-launch monetization is the primary source of funding. Some spaces have proven unfriendly to buy-to-play products. This is akin to the battle Hipstamatic and Instagram fought. Hipstamatic arrived first and achieved app of the year on iTunes, but Instagram won the war. Hipstamatic was a paid app, whereas Instagram was free. Since they were in the social-media space, user numbers prevailed. Instagram's population boomed, while Hipstamatic's price gated its growth.[245]

Free-to-play games require some degree of manipulation; many users accept this happily as part of the *quid pro quo* for the free offering, so long as the methods remain within legitimate bounds. Riot Games' *League of Legends*, for example, has a well-received monetization system — this even though some skins can be quite expensive! It's a fine line, however, that can be easily crossed. Audiences panned Electronic Arts' mobile game *Dungeon Keeper* for imposing long delays on actions that could be circumvented only by paywalls.[246]

Even in buy-to-play games, it's not necessarily problematic. If we've gotten value from a product, we might be happy to throw more money to the developers as tips. Moreover, if they offer us something we desire, which is beyond reasonable expectations for the initial release, we might be happy to purchase that as well. If a customer plays a pirate captain in a Golden Age of Sail game, they might be interested in a unique bear costume to wear as they pillage the seas. If we as developers interact with our customers and discover this is something they might enjoy, this could be a reasonable addition. This type of back and forth builds loyalty from customers. We give them what they want.

To cloud the situation further, the root of fun for many games derives from the designers' deft manipulation of our cognitive glitches! Take the looter-shooter genre exemplified by *Destiny*, *Borderlands*, *Diablo*, and *Anthem*. When these games work, play provides a continuous feed of loot drops, each of which triggers a blip of dopamine — so long as there's a reasonable chance for an upgrade. A dry run is a bad session. Too many dry runs and players drop out. This is the basic pattern used by many lotteries. In truth, players engage with these products as they want to be manipulated; they just want it done well. It's a feature of human cognition. Similar lessons apply to storytelling as well, and for that matter to any engaging activity. Again though, taken too far, even without the involvement of money, this becomes abuse.

When we exceed appropriate limits, we endanger our relationship with our audience. And since IPs are valuable only in terms of the engagement of their customer base, this threatens our most critical assets.

At its root, what many organizations lack is a sense of gratitude. No matter what our business, we exist because we have developed a relationship with our customers that is founded on amazing services and excellent products. They buy our work because they believe in our IPs and brand. Moreover, we retain the ability to meet our customers' needs only because we have built and sustained excellent teams that listen. Our gratitude should remind us what we owe to both our customers and our staff. When we forget this, our organization courts disruption and eventual irrelevance — even if, in the short term, we garner substantial windfalls.

The truth is that we must love our customers. They pay our bills, after all! If we build a relationship with them, they will invite us into their lives. If we deliver an engine of exploitation into their home, they will reject us. Long-term success is built upon trust.

This is the foundation upon which our decision-making system is built. It is a philosophy meant to best solve our customers' problems in a sustainable fashion.

To build our relationship with our clients, we start with listening. If we can't hear our customers' needs and understand their story, we will start our journey in the wrong direction.

We must go beyond empathy alone, however. We must respect our limitations. We do not know the true state of the world. Even our actions have uncertain outcomes. And we ourselves are nowhere near as rational as we would like to believe. In the end, as Daniel Kahneman said, our understanding of the world is WYSIATI[247] (what you see is all there is). Worse, it's what we think we see. Our decision-making system guardrails us against our weaknesses and grants us the ability to react to opportunity. While many improvements and challenges are incremental, the true refiner's fire forges us through the arrival of black swans[248] — events no one could have predicted that offer either existential threats or market-changing rewards. If we have evolved ourselves well, we will have the capacity to not only survive these key moments, but to grow stronger because of them. We will become anti-fragile.[249]

We have put forward seven principles as the bones of our system: a fixation on customer value, humility, trust, boldness, measurement, transparency, and root-cause analysis. Through these, we can build an ethical, reactive organization that seeks out knowledge while understanding our limits as rational beings. Other principles will be necessary to express our unique characteristics.

The road we advocate isn't an easy one. The norms that define our pre-existing paradigms must be overthrown. Some members of our staff might choose to move on. Transfiguration is never easy. In the end, though, not only will we exit stronger, but we will be worthy of our customers.

About the Author

John Bible started as an astrophysicist, poet, and fiction writer, and ended up a principle programmer and architect in the AAA game industry. He left the doctoral program in Computer Science at MIT to join the famed game company Bioware, where he worked for over a decade on titles such as *Neverwinter Nights*, *Star Wars: Knights of the Old Republic*, *Dragon Age: Origins*, and *Star Wars: The Old Republic*. Ever in search of adventure, he then jumped ship to Singapore and climbed aboard the upcoming Ubisoft pirate game *Skull & Bones*. After four years, he's now returned to Austin, Texas.

End Notes

[1] The prisoner's dilemma is the simplest example of this, but the field is rich with cases of distortion. Worse, many such examples occur where perfect knowledge of the world exists and where the agents are perfectly rational. Imagine how much worse it in uncertain worlds with imperfect agents.

[2] We'll talk a fair bit about grit. Angela Duckworth popularized the term in her book *Grit* and related research. We need grit to succeed in challenging, but it also causes problems. The problems it generates are themselves gritty.

The heart of the matter is that while perseverance is requisite when the correct path is to endure, successful individuals and organizations also defend their time. Amos Tversky (whose work we will discuss) would notoriously leave his wife behind at movies if he didn't find the show compelling and return home to work or watch what he liked (from Michael Lewis's *The Undoing Project*). Warren Buffet's rule was to slash out from his schedule anything that didn't support his primary five life goals (from Duckworth in *Grit*). Sometimes, we must push to completion, especially if we've had problems with that. Other times, we must recognize that our current path is a dead end.

[3] Descriptive decision-making and its associated discipline in behavioral economics form one of the cores of modern management, although it isn't consistently practiced.

It explains why so many of our theoretical beliefs prove out fallacious when executed. It is the heart of Nassim Taleb's ludic fallacy, where we believe we can project our tidy experiments to the complexities of actual life.

We thus must be cautious when we execute the system of this book, lest we fall into this trap ourselves, where we assume that our understanding of human fallacies shields us from making similarly optimistic projections.

[4] I worked at Bioware and Ubisoft, with the last few years of my time at Bioware also as an employee of Electronic Arts after the buyout.

[5] We reference Diane Vaughan's *The Challenger Launch Decision* multiple times in this book. Her book provides an excellent view into how group behavior defines the game in which our staff operate, by defining the norms that constrain our behavior. While her focus was on NASA and a solid-rocket-booster work group, the conclusions offer insight into many organizational pathologies.

[6] We frame this akin to Clayton Christensen in his book *Competing Against Luck*. The Theory of Jobs has been foundational to our model for understanding of customer value, along with research on preference by such figures as Amos Tversky and Daniel Kahneman.

[7] This is the problem of probabilistic robotics for SLAM (Simultaneous Location and Mapping). A robot must determine both a map of the world and their own place within it, where their measurements are prone to error and their actions have uncertain results. See, for example, Sebastien Thrun's textbook *Probabilistic Robotics*.

It's an apt metaphor for decision-making, except our space is more abstract than the concrete geometry of a room.

[8] This can come about as a result of workgroup culture and normalization of deviance, as defined by Diane Vaughan in *The Challenger Launch Decision*. We discuss her work later in our chapter *Never Tolerate Waste*.

[9] Culture binds us together in terms of identity, but any such identity is meaningless if it doesn't also define how we make decisions.

[10] In line with the work that gave rise to Daniel Kahneman's book *Thinking Fast and Slow*.

[11] Adrian de Groot, Thought and Choice in Chess.

[12] Quote from Klein, G., Calderwood, R., & Clinton-Cirocco, A. (2010). Rapid decision making on the fire ground: The original study plus a postscript. Journal of Cognitive Engineering and Decision Making, 4(3), 186-209.

[13] Hoffman, Paul J. "The Paramorphic Representation of Clinical Judgment." *Psychological Bulletin* 57, no. 2 (1960): 116-31.

[14] Note, there is a separate modern case where deep-learning algorithms outperform radiologists. These deep-learning algorithms aren't given expert-generated rules, but instead training sets corresponding to actual benign or malignant diagnoses, which they then use to learn signals that differentiate classes.

This is one reason why a major modern research topic strives to extract the rule that the deep-learning algorithm discovered.

For example, this study: Ehteshami Bejnordi B, Veta M, Johannes van Diest P, et al. Diagnostic Assessment of Deep Learning Algorithms for Detection of Lymph Node Metastases in Women With Breast Cancer. JAMA. 2017;318(22):2199–2210. doi:10.1001/jama.2017.14585.

There have been numerous examples of this vein of research in recent years. Companies like NVidia and Intel actively research this area, as deep learning requires substantial computational requirements, especially fast general matrix multiplies, which dovetail well into those companies' core competencies.

[15] Human evaluation doesn't remotely work in this imperative fashion. As we'll discuss later in Chapter Six, diagnosticians are retrieving the most available equivalents to what they're seeing.

[16] Choice architecture models options for people to produce better outcomes. For example, we prefer the default choice, so if this choice is healthier or better for society, setting that as a choice will incline us in that direction. Richard Thaler is well known for this, including for his book *Nudge*.

[17] Kahneman, D., & Klein, G. (2009). Conditions for intuitive expertise: A failure to disagree. American Psychologist, 64(6), 515-526.

[18] The researcher Philip Tetlock considered similar issues for the case of forecasting, which is related to decision making. He and his co-author Dan Gardner wrote the book *Superforecasting: The Art and Science of Prediction* on this topic.

[19] Why this is interesting relates to hindsight bias. Even if our company refuses to engage in recording decisions, it is useful for us to do this ourselves. We rewrite our history in terms of the events that eventually happened and alter our recollection of perceived events. When we record our views at the time of choice, we can come to understand that we are not as prophetic as we imagine, which in turn allows us to see our current state more clearly.

[20] This was determined from earlier experiments by Amos Tversky and Daniel Kahneman. If people were given no specifics, they generally made choices according to the base probabilities they were given — for example, what percentage of people in a set were lawyers or engineers. When given specifics, however — even though Tversky and Kahneman engineered those specifics to have no signal — the base probabilities were forgotten.

[21] Another appearance of the availability bias, arising from early research in human cognitive biases. We substitute ease of recall for probability. Thus, highly memorable unlikely events seem more probable than mundane likely events.

[22] This is hindsight bias. It also shows up in reinterpretation of history. We ascribe motivations to people and assume actions to

match the events as we understand them after the fact. These framings of the past then become hard to uproot and challenge.

[23] I've found it disturbing how some tactics have entered corporate life. Ironically, we justify the tactics as positive tools, typically to improve morale. These tools are reminiscent of *1984*. Consider, for example the scene where O'Brien holds up four fingers but pressures Winston to say there are five. The scene reflected brainwashing techniques.

We've seen versions of this where managers pressure staff to agree that evident problems do not exist. Leadership subverts the meaning of common industry terms such as pre-production to conceal the reality of projects. This isn't done for nefarious ends, at least not always. Leadership believes this is positive behavior — high-morale projects achieve more, after all! But it is a twisted reflection, as we discuss in Part II.

[24] For decisions, we prefer an immutable store, but if we want to store our principles in a version control system, we might wish to have our decision history stored in same repository. The reason for preferring a store is that decisions are point-in-time. Our projects are sequences of decisions, not a frontier.

Principles on the other hand are the rules that generate our decisions, so that at any point in time there were a set of valid principles independent of what came before or after. We will need to be able to understand what our principles were in the past, which is why we want a version-control system.

Generally, we should use the commodity version control systems and data stores that we use for other purposes. Perforce, Subversion, Git, etc., are all common tools. SQL, Mongo, are all good data stores, although there would need to be a useful front-end, perhaps via the web or an app.

[25] This can be controversial. Google and Facebook, for example, are notoriously secretive and non-transparent to internal employees about many topics, fearing that leaks to competitors will lose them an advantage. At the same time, Facebook and Google have both had transparent internal conversations about controversial topics (which have leaked and generated bad press for them). Every company must evaluate where they draw the line.

[26] Someone who feels safe in their competence isn't concerned with being shown wrong, because they know their value. They feel secure. Someone who isn't secure fears to be wrong, because they fear they will lose their position.

This is one of the reasons why we must ensure a safe work environment for our employees. With security, they can acknowledge mistakes and learn from them.

Cultures that do not admit their mistakes do not grow.

[27] This is most directly an anecdote from Adam Alter's book *Irresistible*, but also from personal recollection and numerous articles.

[28] There are counter-narratives about Dong Nguyen's reasons. Originally, some believed there had been a takedown order over assets, but this was denied by involved parties. Another narrative was that trolls were harassing Nguyen, and he wanted no further part of it. This is undermined somewhat by Nguyen continuing to develop other products built to tweak cognitive glitches less.

[29] There are many interesting books on Bayesian reasoning for the interested reader.

Judea Pearl *Probabilistic Reasoning in Intelligent Systems* is a classic book on the topic. He's written more recently a popular version: *The Book of Why*. It's a significant topic in many fields, so there are many resources available.

[30] Jim Collin's *Good to Great* presents the idea of a Level 5 leader to capture this concept.

[31] For example, the New York Times article: "*A Genocide Incited on Facebook, With Posts From Myanmar's Military*" https://www.nytimes.com/2018/10/15/technology/myanmar-facebook-genocide.html

[32] For a thorough discussion of this topic, consider *The Logic of Political Survival* by Bruce Bueno de Mesquita, Alastair Smith, Randolph M. Siverson, and James D. Morrow. This book gathers the results of their research on what characterizes leaders who rule for long periods, whether autocratic or democratic, putting forth an explanation for seeming contradictions in behavior by those in power, all based on game theory and empirical results. There is also a popular version of the book, called *The Dictator's Handbook*, by the same authors.

[33] As an example of how his audience viewed gamesmanship as their foremost principle, this is a line cut from the blurb for this book: "It is a book to recommend to your friends in industry - even to your bosses - but not to your competitors."

[34] Quoted from the entrepreneur.com article "Jeff Bezos: 'I Predict One Day Amazon Will Fail.'"

[35] This is a variant of Parkinson's law of triviality (also known as bike-shedding). Here we fixate on a minor but easily solvable problem rather than addressing the bigger issue. A common metaphor is worrying about the dust on our cabinet shelves when our house is burning down.

[36] Despite the historical and continuing popularity of brainstorming in groups, it's long been known that generating ideas independently and then bringing them together results not only in more ideas, but more creative ideas.

For example, we might consider the article from the Harvard Business Review: "Why Group Brainstorming Is a Waste of Time" by Tomas Chamorro-Premuzic. Or the discussion of the topic in "How to Fly a Horse" by Kevin Ashton.

[37] Lavabit was a case of this. The company had previously gone along with requests concerning cases such as child pornography, but after Edward Snowden revealed he had used Lavabit, the company shut down rather than give the government the private SSL keys to its service (which would have affected all users of Lavabit). This choice matched their stated ethics — the final request was too large for them to accept. Subsequently, Lavabit's owner Ladar Levinson worked on a protocol called DIME, which would remove the moral hazard from the company altogether by removing the capability for the company to expose its users.

[38] The machine-learning community is a great place to look for advice on this problem. Too much specificity on training data leads to models that overfit and perform worse on test or actual data. Too much generality results in models that can't sufficiently cover the space in question properly. There is a great deal of advice on this topic in that field.

[39] Diane Vaughan's book *The Challenger Launch Decision* is partially an analysis of the work group culture surrounding the solid rocket boosters of the shuttle.

[40] From Clayton Christensen's book *Competing Against Luck*.

[41] In games, this is the netcode problem, but this is a problem as well in any distributed simulation. Events happen in real time, but other nodes in the cluster only become aware of them later. We might operate the simulation in the future so the events have time to propagate before becoming realized, but that has responsiveness concerns, and in any event, there can be unbounded delays in the network.

Typically, different genres of games handle this problem in one of several ways. Shooters tend to use some derivative of event-based simulation with roll-back, other games sometimes use turns with input lags, etc. The quality of the feel of the game often arises from the integrity of this simulation.

[42] We'll discuss what this is in more detail in Part III. Mostly, though, it means not sequencing work that comes together at the end but building up working software all at once such that it is always usable.

[43] Kickstarter, of course, is more a matter of continuous engagement to be successful. Early Access often really means selling a beta of the product. However, it is a principle that the earlier we can get users to show us what they value by giving us money, the more easily we can see at least a useful proxy for value.

[44] The most notorious proof of this is that humans don't always perceive value transitively. For example, if we prefer A > B and B > C, we should prefer A > C. Suppose A is coffee, B is tea, and C is hot chocolate. For some people coffee is better than tea, and tea is better than hot chocolate, but hot chocolate is better than coffee. This occurs because we value different aspects of these drinks, and so when comparing A and C, we compare different attributes. Amos Tversky did some of the earliest work on this in prisons in Michigan to establish that inmates frequently broke transitivity.

The Undoing Project by Michael Lewis has a good story of this.

[45] Many would say that all products including tax software exist to serve an emotional need, which is true, but there is in my view a distinction between the satisfaction of a tax software and a game that draws us into a fantasy.

[46] Philip E Tetlock's book *Superforecasting: The Art and Science of Prediction* covers this. Superforecasters often produce projections down to specific probabilistic percentages, such as 77%. Rounding them off even to the nearest 5% often makes their projections worse. It is possible that gradual refinement of our skill in judging value might work similarly. But that hasn't been studied to our knowledge. And it is possible that judging value for project years out is harder than judging probabilistic forecasts in the Goldilock's zone.

[47] For a substantial discussion on this, see Naomi Wolf's book *The Beauty Myth*.

[48] For another relevant quote from Steve Jobs on key aspects of the Razor:

"That's been one of my mantras -- focus and simplicity. Simple can be harder than complex: You have to work hard to get your thinking clean to make it simple. But it's worth it in the end because once you get there, you can move mountains."

The simpler the Razor is, the simpler it will be to execute.

[49] This is from their article "Availability: A Heuristic for Judging Frequency and Probability" in *Judgment under Uncertainty: Heuristics and Biases*.

[50] For a quick overview, Harvard Business Review's article: "*Know Your Customers Jobs to Be Done*."
https://hbr.org/2016/09/know-your-customers-jobs-to-be-done
Clayton Christensen's book *Competing Against Luck* considers this topic extensively.

[51] This is a frequently used case in many articles, but for example Clayton Chirstensen's book *Competing Against Luck*.

[52] Someday, we can imagine the games industry's versions of Ralph Ellison's *The Invisible Man*, James Baldwin's *Giovanni's Room*, or Virginia Woolf's *Orlando* – games played decades after their authorship.

[53] For example, the New York Times article: "*A Genocide Incited on Facebook, With Posts From Myanmar's Military*" at https://www.nytimes.com/2018/10/15/technology/myanmar-facebook-genocide.html

This is a broader problem with any social media application – it affects FB's WhatsApp as well. In rural areas in India (and many other countries), WhatsApp is a major source of viral news, often spread by aunties and uncles with little skepticism applied.

For example: from the BBC: "*How WhatsApp helped turn an Indian village into a lynch mob*" at https://www.bbc.com/news/world-asia-india-44856910

Technology giants delivered a platform to connect people, and now they are perceived as holding a responsibility to police it. For those from the media industry, this seems obvious. For those from tech, this is unexpected.

[54] "*Encouragement for risk-takers*" by Yuen Sin. Strait Times. https://www.straitstimes.com/singapore/encouragement-for-risk-takers

[55] In Diane Vaughan's book The Challenger Launch Decision, she points out that work group culture is always somewhat different from global culture. In the case she studied (and generally in her work), early decisions in the work group can shape the possible future choices of the team.

[56] This is common practice at companies like Pixar, Facebook, and Google.

[57] Quote from Steve Jobs's book Steve Jobs: His Own Words and Wisdom.

[58] For an overview, the interested reader might consult Sam Newman's book *Building Microservices: Designing Fine-Grained Systems*.

⁵⁹ *"Understanding Mission Command"* by Col. (Ret.) James D. Sharpe Jr. and Lt. Col. (Ret.) Thomas E. Creviston.

https://www.army.mil/article/106872/understanding_mission_command

Mission command definition can be found in Army Doctrine Publication 6-0: Mission Command, U.S. Army, Washington, D.C., 2012, p. 1.

⁶⁰ Moltke, Helmuth, Graf von, Militarische Werke. vol. 2, part 2., pp. 33–40.

⁶¹ This discussion also owes influence to Philip E Tetlock's book *Superforecasting: The Art and Science of Prediction*, which discusses this topic in terms of desirable characteristics for forecasters.

⁶² The interview process is a fascinating one itself, and one to spend great effort on getting right. There are many notorious fallacies that trip us up here, so we must be careful to offset biases. In sports, ideas like Moneyball became prevalent, but they also have their limits. The militaries of many countries have systemic protocols for evaluating possible officers. There are many resources to delve into. The main thing to avoid is having the interview process consist of whatever the interviewers happen to be interested in that day.

⁶³ This notion of known knowns, known unknowns, and unknown unknowns was popularized by Donald Rumsfeld, but is an old idea that traces back to ancient philosophers. We are often completely unaware of the third category and discount its importance. The unknown unknowns, however, are often the most interesting, especially as by default our search biases itself to the known unknowns.

[64] This concept of heat has some relation conceptually to simulated annealing from mathematical optimization, but we're not using that method exactly. Here, the aggressiveness of our questions is determined by our lack of understanding, while simulated annealing causes us to prefer to take possibly non-optimal solutions in early phases, under the assumption that this will help us explore faster. In truth, the space of questions is usually not continuous in a mathematical sense, so just because we poke questions out into the unknown does not mean we can safely assume that we have truly exposed what is hidden from us. It is, however, a good way to get lucky early on and find some far more optimal solutions.

[65] This isn't to disdain the importance of solidifying core game mechanics early on. We should do that as well. That work, however, is a matter of continuous refinement, not existential existence. If we don't know whether we walk, teleport, or if motion has meaning at all, then perhaps there are more primal questions. If we just want to get motion to feel good, that's probably not so critical.

[66] Bayesian analysis is a useful tool to practice here. Many people who aren't trained in analysis fail to realize that alternative explanations can be more likely than the one the test indicates if there are false positives. A test that checks for cancer doesn't mean we have it if the test comes back positive, depending on the accuracy of the test and the base probability rate. Judea Pearl's *Probabilistic Reasoning in Intelligent Systems: Networks of Plausible Inference* is a classic in the field, but he has written newer books such as *Causality: Models, Reasoning, and Inference* and *The Book of Why: The New Science of Cause and Effect* on the subject, the latter of which is meant for popular audiences.

[67] Ray Dalio makes similar observations in his book *Principles: Life and Work*, where he asserts that the job of a great manager is that an organizational engineer. He makes the point numerous times, that the purpose is to constantly refine our engine of productivity.

[68] This is result of the Nassim Taleb's ludic fallacy. This is the problem where we believe that our theoretical ideas will project to the messy world of real life.

[69] The automation bias, for example.

[70] The Tragedy of the Commons game concerns farmers where a shared common land can be used for grazing. Each farmer is supposed to use the common land in a controlled fashion, but there is no penalty for overgrazing. Thus, each individual farmer decides to overgraze independently. This happens because whether their neighbor overgrazes or not, it is locally beneficial to overgraze. This is an example of a Nash equilibrium.

Even though there is a long-term potential severe outcome, the fact that one's neighbor local best strategy is to overgraze inspires the farmer to follow suit.

[71] For a deeper modern discussion of game theory, the reader might check out *Algorithmic Game Theory*

[72] Another fun game is perfectly rational pirates. Here, there is a pirate captain and her crew. They have just captured a great chest of gold coins. There is also a strict hierarchy in the crew with the captain and the top and the rest of the crew enumerated in order. The captain needs to propose a split, but the crew can vote on it. If the crew rejects, the captain will walk the plank, and then the next highest-ranking member of the crew is made captain, and then needs

to propose a split which the crew will vote on. The solution to this is brutal to the crew, but after all, it's that or the plank!

[73] "Impact of Social Punishment on Cooperative Behavior in Complex Networks"

Zhen Wang, Cheng-Yi Xia, Sandro Meloni, Chang-Song Zhou & Yamir Moreno

Scientific Reports volume 3, Article number: 3055 (2013).

[74] See, for example: Proctor, Darby et al. "How fairly do chimpanzees play the ultimatum game?" Communicative & integrative biology vol. 6,3 (2013): e23819.

[75] This is kind of what Jim Collins does in his books, such as *Good to Great*.

[76] This is a view advocated by Daniel Kahneman and Amos Tversky, for example, and is also sometimes called reference-class forecasting.

[77] For confrontation analysis: N. Howard, "*Confrontation Analysis*", CCRP Publications, 1999. Available online at http://internationalc2institute.org/

[78] Original formal version of drama theory: N. Howard, *Paradoxes of Rationality*, MIT Press, 1971.

[79] On a similar note, although not related to decision theory of hypothesis testing, queueing theory is an oft-neglected branch of mathematics in game development. Here, we might want to know how many invitations we need to send out to optimally load our

online service tests at specific times. Frequently, games send out more invitations than necessary. In other cases, we pay testers to do early technical tests, but because of a failure of analysis, we often hire too many or too few.

[80] Sebastien Thrun's book *Probabilistic Robotics* is a good technical introduction to this field.

[81] In fact, we as humans seem to find this process fun. Many video games center around this. Firaxis Games's Civilization series begins with a hidden world, which we then explore and exploit, all with the intention of reaching one of several goals of our choice. The loop of discovery and action appeals fundamentally to human interest.

[82] Perhaps not, though. Many things are hard to compute, even for superintelligences — they might need to rely on greedy and/or approximate algorithms. Even quantum computers have limits.

[83] Thus, the concept of *Homo economicus,* that the free markets eventually distribute value optimally on average.

[84] Yuval Noah Harari summarizes the research on this theory in *Homo Sapiens.*

[85] Dorothy L Cheney, and Robert M. Seyfarth, Baboon Metaphysics: The Evolution of a Social Mind.

For a more speculative journey farther afield consider Peter Godfrey-Smith's book *Other Minds: The Octopus, the Sea, and the Deep Origins of Consciousness.*

[86] While these quirks are errors in our perception, film and games both exploit these to make rendering better than reality in some

sense, or to give the illusion that limited ranges of brightness extend beyond the limits of the display hardware. Even the fact that our eyes engage in rapid saccades (fast eye movements where we momentarily see nothing) has been used to enrich VR.

[87] The image is courtesy of Professor Edward H. Adelson, copyright 1995.

[88] Image from http://persci.mit.edu/gallery/checkershadow/proof

[89] "*Optical illusion: Dress color debate goes global*". BBC. https://www.bbc.com/news/uk-scotland-highlands-islands-31656935

[90] Michael Lewis wrote his book *The Undoing Project* on them, and covered both their personal histories and paired histories, as well as popularizing their work. Daniel Kahneman wrote his book *Thinking Fast and Slow* to expose the larger public to these topics.

[91] Taken from Kahnemen's book *Thinking Fast and Slow*.

[92] Anecdote from *The Undoing Project* by Michael Lewis, but it's a well-known case.

[93] This story is from Kahneman's *Thinking Fast and Slow*, but Michael Lewis covers it as well in *The Undoing Project*.

[94] Kahneman, Daniel; Frederick, Shane (2002). "Representativeness Revisited: Attribute Substitution in Intuitive Judgment". In Thomas Gilovich; Dale Griffin; Daniel Kahneman. Heuristics and Biases: The Psychology of Intuitive Judgment.

Cambridge: Cambridge University Press. pp. 49–81. ISBN 978-0-521-79679-8. OCLC 47364085.

[95] Sarah F. Brosnan, Frans B. M. de Waal, "Evolution of responses to (un)fairness," Science 17 Oct 2014: Vol. 346, Issue 6207, 1251776 DOI: 10.1126/science.1251776

[96] "*Banksy Painting Self-Destructs After Fetching $1.4 Million at Sotheby's*" by Scott Reyburn, The New York Times, https://www.nytimes.com/2018/10/06/arts/design/uk-banksy-painting-sothebys.html

[97] For example, this article: "*Unequal Pay, Unconscious Bias, And What To Do About It*," from Forbes.

https://www.forbes.com/sites/kimelsesser/2018/04/10/unequal-pay-unconscious-bias-and-what-to-do-about-it/#527543e600e6

This is not restricted to gender but can be keyed off any signal that trips our expectations.

[98] Consider this summary article from the Harvard Business School "*Airbnb Hosts Discriminate Against African-American Guests*" by Carmen Nobel.

https://hbswk.hbs.edu/item/airbnb-hosts-discriminate-against-african-american-guests

[99] As described in Daniel Kahneman's book *Thinking Fast and Slow*.

[100] Daniel Kahneman's *Thinking Fast and Slow*, which covers the earlier work establishing these results

[101] This is covered in Kahneman's *Thinking Fast and Slow*, and otherwise originates from a large spread of research.

[102] "When More Pain Is Preferred to Less: Adding a Better End" Daniel Kahneman, Barbara L. Fredrickson, Charles A. Schreiber and Donald A. Redelmeier Psychological Science Vol. 4, No. 6 (Nov. 1993), pp. 401-405

[103] This is one of the signs that a marriage will fail. Once one party has rewritten their recollection to a narrative they view cynically, the marriage is almost always over. From Daniel Goleman's book *Emotional Intelligence.*

[104] Moritz, S., Ahlf-Schumacher, J., Hottenrott, B., Peter, U., Franck, S., Schnell, T., & ... Jelinek, L. (2018). We cannot change the past, but we can change its meaning. A randomized controlled trial on the effects of self-help imagery rescripting on depression. Behaviour Research and Therapy, 10474-83. doi:10.1016/j.brat.2018.02.007.

[105] For further details of this event, the reader might check George Knight's book, *Millennial Fever and the End of the World*, or David Rowe's book *God's Strange Work: William Miller and the End of the World.*

[106] Richard Thaler and Cass Sunstein's book Nudge: Improving Decisions About Health, Wealth, and Happiness

[107] This is an example of choice architecture, which allows us to direct our organization with a lighter touch.

[108] Star Wars: Knights of the Old Republic by Bioware. Dragon Age: Origins and Inquisition and Anthem by Bioware under Electronic Arts. The Division by Ubisoft. Fallout 4 by Bethesda.

[109] This is something to be cautious of. We can make players nauseous by placing them in experiences that seem cool but violate their physical embodiment too much. Sometimes it's better to just do the boring thing, rather than take on these extra problems.

[110] Bioware is owned by Electronic Arts. With a GaaS game like *Anthem*, we can only refer to the state of the game at a point in time, as later releases might change the game to resolve these problems. It used to be that PC MMOs released in a bad state as a matter of course, and only achieved stability over time. This gradually became seen as unacceptable, with only minimal hiccups allowed. It remains to be seen how the maturity of GaaS games evolves.

[111] This is the first zen koan of Nyogen Senzaki's book *101 Zen Stories,* published 1919. A more common source would be its reprint in Paul Reps's book *Zen Flesh, Zen Bones*.

[112] The case here is parallel to that of Winston's in the Ministry of Love from *1984*. O'Brien shows Winston four fingers, and Winston is pressured to say that he sees five. In fact, the true intention of O'Brien is warp Winston into not only saying that he sees five but to believe that he sees five. This is the premise of the thumbs up in this case. Not only should we raise our thumb, but no matter what the actual state, we should believe it.

[113] From Walt Whitman's poem "Songs of Myself." Also popularized in the movie *Dead Poet's Society*.

[114] From Clayton Christensen's book *Competing Against Luck*.

[115] Rob Austin discusses this topic thoroughly in his book *Measuring and Managing Performance in Organizations*.

[116] This case is cited from Robert Austin's book Measuring and Managing Performance in Organizations.

[117] If I have control of an omnipotent entity operating according to rules I set, eventually that entity will find an exploit

Nick Bostrum's book *Superintelligence* has several chapters on this topic, and the inherent challenge of the problem for AIs.

While the results tend to be less catastrophic for people management, the same difficulties face us.

[118] Strathern, Marilyn. "Improving Ratings." Audit in the British University System European Review 5: 305–321.

[119] An anti-pattern is a pattern of behavior or architecture that is common and also dysfunctional. They are the opposite of design patterns, which are common and effective ways of organizing code or people. The most common reference to design patterns in software architecture would be: *Design Patterns: Elements of Reusable Object-Oriented Software* by Erich Gamma, Richard Helm, Ralph Johnson, John Vlissides, and Grady Booch.

[120] John Doerr's book *Measure What Matters*. The book covers the adoption of OKRs at Google.

[121] Strathern, Marilyn. "Improving Ratings." Audit in the British University System European Review 5: 305–321.

¹²² From the introduction to Robert Austin's book Measuring and Managing Performance in Organizations.

¹²³ For a broad discussion of work policies at Google, Laszlo Bock's book *Work Rules!* is a good source.

¹²⁴ For a recent discussion: Benjamin Snyder. "Super Bowl Stock Predictor Has a Streak Going". Wall Street Journal. January 5, 2017

¹²⁵ This is a widespread internet meme meant to demonstrate the problem of correlation versus causation. Many sources can be found, but for *example*: https://www.forbes.com/sites/erikaandersen/2012/03/23/true-fact-the-lack-of-pirates-is-causing-global-warming/#67ed49693a67

¹²⁶ This could be a bad sign for a company if their employees recognize similarities from their work and the novel, and thus decide to leave! Consider this quote:

"The chaplain had mastered, in a moment of divine intuition, the handy technique of protective rationalization, and he was exhilarated by his discovery. It was miraculous. It was almost no trick at all, he saw, to turn vice into virtue and slander into truth, impotence into abstinence, arrogance into humility, plunder into philanthropy, thievery into honor, blasphemy into wisdom, brutality into patriotism, and sadism into justice. Anybody could do it; it required no brains at all. It merely required no character."
Joseph Heller, Catch-22

¹²⁷ Siconolfi, Michael; Pacelle, Mitchell; Raghavan, Anita (1998-11-16). "All Bets Are Off: How the Salesmanship And Brainpower Failed At Long-Term Capital". Wall Street Journal.

[128] Porcelli, Anthony J and Mauricio R Delgado. "Stress and Decision Making: Effects on Valuation, Learning, and Risk-taking" Current opinion in behavioral sciences vol. 14 (2017): 33-39.

[129] Many such studies can be found on the web site Gamasutra, which surveyed developers to start to get to the bottom of this problem. But in other industries, such results have been well known for a long time.

Eric Byron's *blog* on Gamasutra has a somewhat recent analysis of surveys and research:

https://www.gamasutra.com/blogs/EricByron/20160729/278113/Crunch_does_it_help_and_how_do_you_know.php

[130] Jason Schreier's book Blood, Sweat, and Pixels.

[131] Communication and behavior become more hierarchical under stress, sometimes resulting in disaster.

[132] Bill Gates, for example, is an advocate of this, stating that he learned this from Warren Buffett. Keep time available and use it for free activities.

[133] Team Gaming for Team-building: Effects on Team Performance, AIS Transactions on Human-Computer Interaction (2018). DOI: 10.17705/1thci.00110.

[134] Extremes aren't always bad! See Theory of Constraints in Part III: Waste. The Compromise Effect is a well-known related bias — in this case, given two extremes, we believe the best solution must be

in the middle, which isn't necessarily true at all. Consider a flat earther and an astronomer discussing whether the Earth is flat or not.

[135] Aristotle's *Poetics*

[136] This anecdote is from Kevin Ashton's book "How to Fly a Horse: The Secret History of Creation, Invention, and Discovery" and his article "The Creativity Myth" on Medium.com, including quotations. His and other books are great resources for delving deeper into this topic, as our book isn't specifically about creativity.

[137] Again, see Kevin Ashton's "How to Fly a Horse: The Secret History of Creation, Invention, and Discovery."

[138] No book we have ever written did so. At best, a fifth of a first draft might survive in some form —we rewrite chapters as we go through drafts. The same has been true of games. Although we can learn how to move through these phases faster and more predictably, they are never pulled whole from the ether. We believe that such projects arrive whole, because we see the final result only

This is an interesting thing about Games as a Service (GaaS), where a product is released and then evolved, or the Early Access model, where a game is released in an alpha state to players and then brought to its final form with their input. In this later case, we might see how the process occurs, even though we often only start once it's 90% in. Even here, creators are often careful to conceal anything too rough.

[139] Malcolm Gladwell popularized this concept in *Blink*.

[140] Once upon a time, *Duke Nukem Forever* was a subject of ridicule for taking nearly ten years to build and going through

multiple engines in its lifetime. Not so many years later, at top AAA companies, many new IPs take almost a decade, multiple reboots, and sometimes engine rewrites or switches.

[141] A key skill in AAA game development nowadays is being able to order a million-dollar feature and then go to sleep that night as if nothing happened.

[142] That a twist or turn of the plot is considered interesting is the related concept of novelty. Even knowing the general form used by many film studios, a deviation from the current direction remains intriguing. Creative turns are the most pleasing, where a twist retranslates everything that happened in the film up to that point in a way that was always a possible explanation, even if we didn't recognize it.

[143] These are both complex cases. Some will note that there were versions of AirBNB and Uber in the past, but safety concerns brought laws that caused the shift to hotels, motels, and the like — laws these new companies aren't subject to, which increased their efficiency. Still, Uber isn't like the unregistered cabs that used exist in the United States and remain problematic in some countries. The review systems have enabled this change.

[144] At the time Steve Jobs realized this, his competitors thought his naivety would guarantee his failure. They instead fixated on the inferior components of the iPhone such as the microphone, without recognizing what the product holistically meant, especially in the Apple ecosystem.

[145] This was created by the German Gestalt psychologist Karl Duncker and published posthumously in 1945. This work was specifically focused on functional fixedness, where an assumed

function for an object is getting in the way of seeing a different use for that object.

[146] Duncker, K. (1945). "On problem solving". Psychological Monographs, 58:5 (Whole No. 270).

[147] I recommend this book to everyone I work with, regardless of discipline. Software architects have plenty of room to learn about the affordances their interfaces offer, not just would-be designers of doors. Fun side note, doors in video games are notorious and surprising causes of problems in games!

[148] Which is where the term Norman door came from.

[149] The idea of scientific revolutions existed before, but Kuhn refined it. Immanuel Kant discussed revolutions in thinking in the second Preface of his *Critique of Pure Reason*, for example. Of course, the general concept of paradigms was well known long before. It was Kuhn's specific treatment that characterized the unique properties of scientific paradigms.

[150] Some take this to imply that each paradigm is equally wrong, and perhaps from some epistemological standpoints, that is true. That, however, is more the statement that nothing can be known than a deep commentary on paradigm shifts and scientific understanding. Kuhn believed that these paradigm shifts built on top of each other, and while aspects of a previous paradigm might be completely overthrown, the new paradigm was over all an improvement according to every measure.

[151] Clayton Christensen originated this concept as an explanation for why so many powerful tech companies were unable to see the rise of technologies that supplanted their own. The term disruption is

often used incorrectly to signify any major change. As it turns out, many creative innovations are easily incorporated by established companies. A disruptive technology is specifically the case where the established company is incentivized to not address the disruption. Even if top management recognizes it is coming, the demands of shareholders and accommodating higher-margin customers prevents us from addressing it. This is related to a short-term Nash equilibrium, where the optional state is not to react, until eventually everything flips.

The Innovator's Dilemma by Clayton Christensen was his first popular business book on the topic.

[152] Kevin Ashton's book *How to Fly a Horse* discusses this.

[153] *Comments by Bill Gates and Warren Buffett* on the *Charlie Rose Show* Jan 27, 2017. *https://charlierose.com/videos/29774*

For an article covering this theme: "*What Warren Buffett taught Bill Gates about managing time by sharing his (nearly) blank calendar*" by Catherine Clifford on CNBC

https://www.cnbc.com/2018/09/07/warren-buffett-taught-bill-gates-about-time-management-by-sharing-his-blank-calendar.html

[154] Edwin Catmull's book *Creativity, Inc* covers this and other aspects of Pixar.

[155] For example, Mark Zuckerberg: "Someone who is exceptional in their role is not just a little better than someone who is pretty good. They are 100 times better." Responding to comments about FriendFeed acquisition.

Marc Andreesen: "The gap between what a highly productive person can do and what an average person can do is getting bigger and bigger. Five great programmers can completely outperform 1,000 mediocre programmers." From the book *Mavericks at Work* by William Taylor and Polly LaBarre.

[156] "Great People Are Overrated" by Bill Taylor. Harvard Business Review. June 20, 2011.

[157] *Lean Software Development: An Agile Toolkit* by Mary Poppendieck and Tom Poppendieck.

[158] This is a point Tim Ferriss makes multiple times in his podcasts, as well in his books such as *Tools of Titans*.

[159] In 1995, Steve Jobs recorded an interview related to this point — it was released as The Lost Interview is 2012:

"It turns out the same thing can happen in technology companies that get monopolies, like IBM or Xerox. If you were a product person at IBM or Xerox, so you make a better copier or computer. So what? When you have monopoly market share, the company's not any more successful.

So the people that can make the company more successful are sales and marketing people, and they end up running the companies. And the product people get driven out of the decision-making forums, and the companies forget what it means to make great products. The product sensibility and the product genius that brought them to that monopolistic position gets rotted out by people running these companies that have no conception of a good product versus a bad product.

They have no conception of the craftsmanship that's required to take a good idea and turn it into a good product. And they really have no feeling in their hearts, usually, about wanting to really help the customers."

[160] As an aside, this is sort of how machine-learning systems AlphaZero and AlphaGo work. They have neural networks that estimate the values of board states and possible moves.

[161] If there were rules for bullshiteering, this would be one of them.

[162] This would be a stereotypical example of cognitive dissonance. See our previous discussion in *Part II*.

[163] Diane Vaughan's book The Challenger Launch Decision.

[164] This was as of April 10, 2019 on Metacritic.

[165] These scores taken from Metacritic April 10, 2019.

[166] The V.A.T.S. system was part of the key feel of Fallout 3 & 4, where players could target individual body parts in slow time. In *Fallout 76*, it worked differently, partially due to multiplayer necessities.

[167] It's worth referencing Jason Schreier's article "How Bioware's Anthem Went Wrong," available from Kotaku. This article released in the final stages of the book, so we don't reference its contents, but it offers an inside view at least from the perspective of some employees. We should be careful to take assertions as truth, however, as the employees themselves are caught up within a paradigm themselves.

¹⁶⁸ Bioware's *Anthem* had a complicated release schedule, fully opening for some customers on Feb 15, available to others for ten hours in that same period, and available to others starting Feb 22, after the "day 1" patch. This was after various demos on all platforms, with some players in the beta.

¹⁶⁹ For clarity, we were on *Star Wars: The Old Republic* for 5 and a half years, including its launch. So, it's a familiar discussion.

¹⁷⁰ *Minecraft*, for example, was valued over two billion at sale. Mojang was sold for $2.5B, and its only asset of real value was the *Minecraft* property.

¹⁷¹ Diane Vaughan's book The Challenger Launch Decision.

¹⁷² Janis, I. L. (1972). Victims of Groupthink: A Psychological Study of Foreign-Policy Decisions and Fiascoes. Boston: Houghton Mifflin. ISBN 0-395-14002-1

¹⁷³ Diane Vaughan's book The Challenger Launch Decision.

¹⁷⁴ Robert M. Emerson, "Holistic Effects in Social Control Decision-Making," Law and Society Review 17 (1983): 425–55.

¹⁷⁵ Diane Vaughan's book The Challenger Launch Decision.

¹⁷⁶ Diane Vaughan's book The Challenger Launch Decision.

¹⁷⁷ Diane Vaughan's book The Challenger Launch Decision.

¹⁷⁸ Diane Vaughan's book The Challenger Launch Decision.

[179] Bringing in customers early can expose a product to some security risks as well. Thus, we need to prioritize security earlier. Or, alternatively, we present to our users a second product that gives us advice for the primary product. This might be an indie-style game with great simplifications. If we remember to get testing against our real product as soon as possible.

[180] Extreme Programming Explained: Embrace Change, by Kent Beck and Cynthia Andres, 1999.

[181] Published in 1999 as *Adaptive Software Development* by Jim Highsmith and Ken Orr.

[182] For example, Crystal Sapphire, Crystal Clear.

[183] Available many places, for example from the Agile Alliance online, or agilemanifesto.org. There is also a rich literature around the interpretation of Agile.

[184] *Business Object Design and Implementation,* in the OOPSLA workshop proceedings, 1995.

[185] At the time of this writing, Artifactory is a pretty good choice, but there are many options. We want something that efficiently can store large binary blobs cheaply, without differences, and probably not requiring frequent access. Whether the storage is high reliability or not depends on our specific needs.

[186] This story is taken from The Toyota Way: 14 Management Principles from the World's Greatest Manufacturer, by Jeffrey Liker.

[187] My preference is that there are two creative owners for projects, where each owner has distinct skill sets to provide greater

coverage. Doing so allows our greatest ideas to pass and our worst ideas to be filtered. To be fair, though, the transparency of the Toyota Way and the allowance for decentralized evaluation also provides a similar countermeasure to a leader going rogue with untenable directions.

[188] This can be found at https://www.toyota-global.com/company/vision_philosophy/toyota_production_system/just-in-time.html as the page for "*Just-in-Time — Philosophy of Complete Elimination of Waste*."

[189] It's interesting to note that this just-in-time approach was inspired by the solutions used in supermarkets, which had similar issues due to the limited shelf life of many food products. What is known as Kanban in the Toyota Way was known before as the "Supermarket method."

[190] See for example the Netflix techblog: https://medium.com/netflix-techblog/the-netflix-simian-army-16e57fbab116

[191] Easily found either in *The Toyota Way: 14 Management Principles from the World's Greatest Manufacturer,* by Jeffrey Liker, or direct from *Toyota itself*: https://www.toyota-global.com/company/vision_philosophy/toyota_production_system/

[192] The same might be said of machine intelligence capabilities as well, which will be doubly important once AIs take over.

[193] *Lean Software Development: An Agile Toolkit* by Mary Poppendieck and Tom Poppendieck.

[194] *Lean Software Development: An Agile Toolkit* by Mary Poppendieck and Tom Poppendieck.

[195] This is cited from the book *Lean Thinking* by James Womack and Daniel Jones.

[196] From *The Goal* and *Critical Chain* by Eliyahu Goldratt.

[197] *Site Reliability Engineering: How Google Runs Production Systems,* edited by Betsy Bayer offers a selection of essays by Googlers in the SRE group detailing how they work.

[198] The DevOps Handbook by Gene Kim and Jez Humble is a good overview of the processes and motivations of DevOps. The Phoenix Project by Gene Kim, Kevin Behr, George Spafford is the business novelization for the DevOps Handbook.

[199] Nassim Taleb's book *Anti-Fragile* is the source of this term. It is partially an outgrowth of older philosophies such as Stoicism (whose authors Taleb frequently cites). It goes a bit further than the resilience that characterizes Stoic ideas to consider the conditions that make challenges strengthen us. Late decision-making, empiricism, and an emphasis on the customer make many modern software practices resilient, but it is through amplified learning and empirical focus that they become anti-fragile, where failure can make our subsequent products stronger than a success would have.

[200] Strictly speaking, not all challenges are good. Good challenges are learning opportunities in a positive environment. Other problems can be shocks. Corrosive shocks are hostile environments where employees feel the need to constantly defend and shield themselves. Also, some shocks are just outright fatal, such as finding that a key foundational technology is irreparably insecure, or that the customer

is undermining the contract. Not all shocks are bad, though. Recoverable shocks are the ones that can make us stronger if they don't strain us past breaking.

[201] To be honest, we're not fond of paired programming as it exhausts us. We can't work as creatively with someone over our shoulder. However, a variant where we check in with each other periodically does work well. Here we still get lots of continuous feedback, but we can operate without the pressure. The loss is that the review then tends to be more about higher-level topics, so small flaws can be missed.

[202] This is the phenomena Linda Stone labeled *continuous partial attention*. https://lindastone.net/qa/continuous-partial-attention/

[203] Rubinstein, J. S., Meyer, D. E. & Evans, J. E. (2001). Executive Control of Cognitive Processes in Task Switching. Journal of Experimental Psychology: Human Perception and Performance, 27, 763-797.

[204] Robert Austin, Measuring and Managing Performance in Organizations.

[205] The Knight Capital case is one of the most well-known examples cited for this. They were a high-frequency trader that relied on a couple machines being partially human-deployed according to a checklist. One morning, a step for a subset of the machines was skipped, which resulted in those machines using an incorrect module. This caused them to take up a huge number of options they didn't want over the course of forty-five minutes. The result was a loss of $460 million USD that day, which brought about their fall.

²⁰⁶ By idempotent, we mean that if we execute the deployment twice, the result is the same as having done it once. This is important if a set-up gets accidentally triggered twice — otherwise, it can be fault-prone to handle that case. This relates as well to declarative approaches.

²⁰⁷ Technically, there are games programmed in Prolog, but it's not common.

²⁰⁸ Which is a reminder that the fastest way to generate innovations in a field is to steal ideas from another field and convert it to our own space. Rapid cross-pollination of ideas is optimal when the generation of new ideas is hard.

²⁰⁹ The IKEA effect occurs where we value more what we have built ourselves. It's also the related NIH (Not Invented Here) syndrome, where we reject external ideas.

²¹⁰ At the time I'm writing this book, Battle Royale modes are the current flavor. They've made some companies enormously rich as in the case of Fortnite, but it's become almost a joke amongst devs that no matter what the product — even if it's a party dance game — that top management will ask for a Battle Royale mode.

²¹¹ Not exactly related, but I'll mention here that Susan Cain's book *Quiet* is a great read.

²¹² The Pareto Principle, which shows up everywhere in its various forms. A small number of issues generate most problems. This is a scaling issue, so once we resolve the worst "20%," there will still be a next "20%" that is the new worst set of behaviors.

[213] Ohlberg, Mareike; Ahmed, Shazeda; Lan, Bertram (12 December 2017). "Central Planning, Local Experiments: The complex implementation of China's Social Credit System" (PDF). Merics China Monitor. Mercator Institute for China Studies: 12.

[214] Emotional Intelligence by Daniel Goldman.

[215] From psychological experiments, this situation where the reward probability is ambiguous produces tension. Even though the reward could be enormous, it could also be small. People tend to be willing to pay less for a shot at such a lottery, even though this can be irrational. More recently, it has been shown that tolerance to ambiguity will result in more prosocial behavior despite unknown benefits, although this appears to not be the case with non-social decisions such as monetary lotteries.

[216] I don't wish to suggest that these models have no value. The information they generate can suggest to high-level managers where they should focus their attention. The outputs of these models can be fed into the team as well, which should have access to the best information regardless. Nonetheless, for the finance department and the high-level manager, the project is only an abstraction. Models are often wrong.

[217] Angela Duckworth's research in general and her book *Grit* specifically focus on this topic.

[218] Lazarides, Tasos (September 14, 2015). "Ex-'Fates Forever' Developers Making 'Discord', a Voice Comm App For Multiplayer Mobile Games". TouchArcade.

[219] "Gaming chat startup Discord raises $150M, surpassing $2B valuation". *TechCrunch*.

[220] Fred Brooks cited this in his book *The Mythical Man Month* and gave it the name Conway's Law.

Conway originally tried to submit his paper on the topic "How Do Committees Invent?" to the Harvard Business Review, but it was rejected for not proving its thesis. It was later published in 1968 in Datamation. (Story from *Conway's blog*: http://www.melconway.com/Home/Conways_Law.html)

[221] This quotation is often attributed to Zen, Lao Tzu, or said to be a Chinese proverb, but as far as I know, it's something that originated in the 1980s in the United States. I've never found an authentic source for it. It's since become a common adage used by many. Now including myself! But it does make sense when dealing with the results of cognitive default behaviors.

[222] This is from Conway's paper "How Do Committees Invent?" in Datamation.

[223] Anti-patterns are common architectural choices that result in problematic results. By comparison, a design pattern is considered a good architectural choice when used properly — a Facade, for example, simplifies and conceals an interface which doesn't properly meet our needs, all without exposing unnecessary details. An anti-pattern might be the Inside-Out model, where details of implementation are exposed to the external parties in an attempt to foster configurability.

[224] Trunk-based development started to become the preferred approach in the late 90s with Agile, but it has continued to pick up steam with later developments of DevOps practices.

[225] This has been a powerful movement especially for companies like Amazon which are predominantly back-end services (with different expectations of round-trip times for service calls). The approach has allowed a more radical form of ownership where a team designs, create, and then operates the service over its lifetime. All while keeping team size to around ten staff at most. An interesting discussion of the topic would be Sam Newman's book *Building Microservices: Designing Fine-Grained Systems* from Safari.

[226] Mary and Tom Poppendieck discuss this is in their book *Lean Software Development: An Agile Toolkit*. Fundamentally, though, it was a process that was worked out by many Agile proponents as they found that systems for governing manufacturing did not mesh well with software development.

[227] This is a big topic nowadays, but also one that is overhyped despite its admirable gains. Through the many adaptions of generative adversarial networks and variational auto encoders, we've been able to create new examples of content that can fool human viewers. We've even been able to make creative variations — style transfer began in convolutional neural networks but expanded. We will no doubt see future advances. Many issues remain, however, and we're not sure how far our current models will take us. We can do things like remapping mouths on image streams to insert words in video clips for real people, but we don't yet have solid synthetic animation for generated content. The notion of creativity is a tricky one as well. Machine learning is a backwards learning approach, where we take results and try to project backwards to the generating rules. That can expose generators that we didn't imagine. But sometimes it's better to just operate in the forward direction.

Nevertheless, all major engine developers and technologists are involved with machine learning in content generation or game production to some degree. It's not an approach that will fade away.

We will note this is a personal research area of ours. It is our view that game production costs have become too high. AAA development has become risk averse due to cost, so that the indie game development scene tends to be the only place where interesting innovation goes on in story and game concepting. AAA avoids controversy — we could consider *Far Cry 5*, where Ubisoft deliberately kept the main villain from being either a critique of white separatism or messianic religions. Even mild risks such as Electronic Arts having a female lead in the single-player campaign of *Battlefield V* can be viewed as taking almost too much risk due to social media blowback in the post-Gamer Gate area.

[228] From the Polygon article: "*How Fortnite's success led to months of intense crunch at Epic Games*" by Colin Campbell. https://www.polygon.com/2019/4/23/18507750/fortnite-work-crunch-epic-games

[229] The core challenge in the era of the Xbox 360 and PS3 was the realization of the highest level of fidelity possible in AAA. Mind, some of the most successful products of that era broke with that truth through excellent gameplay and appealing colorful visuals, but that was the dominant view of most AAA studios and technologists.

The era of the Xbox One and the PS4 have been more controversial, but I would say that no longer are there such great leaps in fidelity to be found, at least comparably to the growth in the previous era. In rendering, people have settled to physically based rendering and handling that pipe more carefully to reduce aliasing and constrain art to physical domains Animation has peaked as well.

What has become clearer is that the cost of game development appears excessive. It isn't unsustainable exactly, as the largest titles make enormous profits. The studios that have survived retain the capability to deliver. But it seems far from efficient, and as we've mentioned, far from fostering risk-loving game development.

Indies, meanwhile, embrace new ideas, but are constrained by budgets to limited quality. They could represent a brewing disruption, although it's unclear that this has the full characteristics of a disruption (disruption is an oft misused term, see Clayton Christensen's book *The Innovator's Dilemma* and its sequels). Companies like Unity and Epic Games are providing toolsets tailored to indies that allow small groups to scale their content while retaining their freshness. While AAA dev will certainly retain a fidelity edge, it might be that these smaller groups get close enough in terms of enjoyable visuals that their richer creativity starts tearing out the base of AAA dev and eventually makes the costs unsustainable.

Whether the big AAA studios will able to transition or be supplanted remains to be seen. It depends on whether the conditions in AAA are such that adapting to these new modes aligns with fiscal goals or not.

[230] GaaS in a way goes all the way back to CompuServe services or the free text-based MUDs and MUSHs that prevailed back in the 1990s. But we often view the GaaS model now as more distinct. MMOs have existed since the late 90s but were subscription-based. GaaS games tend to be buy-to-play (B2P) with downloadable content (DLC) and monetization options, rather than per-month fees.

[231] From Fred Brook's classic book, *The Mythical Man Month*.

[232] While I think Angela Duckworth's book *Grit* covers only part of the story, it is true that grit can be critical to pulling through challenges and that we are far more likely to stick with goals whose purpose gives us meaning.

[233] Incidentally, there is a huge difference in terms of how these customer engagement meetings occur. Some focus meetings are really about showing users a concept and seeing how they react. This is often a passive form of engagement. They give a score 1-5 based on what they see. That can be interesting, especially in later phases of development, but it isn't what we need in inception or dev hell.

We need two-way communication with customers where we can engage them not just with our project but what they like about other projects. We'll also need to filter these customers carefully to get to the ones who we want to pursue. If we're leaning towards a chill, relaxing game, we don't want *Call of Duty* fans confusing our data.

[234] Consider "*You Can't Multi-task so Stop Trying*" by Paul Atchley, from the Harvard Business Review (2010). https://hbr.org/2010/12/you-cant-multi-task-so-stop-tr

[235] This is a Lean concept in general, but this phrasing is taken from Eric Ries' book *The Lean Startup*.

This is a touch of nuance I feel lacks from Angela Duckworth's book *Grit* and discussions on the subject. We need the capacity to persevere through hardship, but also the wisdom and courage to change when we must.

[236] There are many important game expos over the year including others such as the Tokyo Game Show, Gamescon, and PAX, but E3

is the biggest, and we usually use the E3 demo to cover the other cases, or only do small amounts of additional work.

[237] *The DevOps Handbook* by Jez Humble and Gene Kim and *Continuous Deployment* by Jez Humble, for example. For SRE, Site Reliability Engineering, edited by Betsy Beyer.

[238] These comments were from release interviews on *Red Dead Redemption 2*'s final march to ship.

[239] This could have been a case where nudges saved the day before the problem occurred. Many bad decisions happen because we have too many decisions to make, so that many decisions follow the default choice. If we make the default choice correct, we can alleviate a lot of pain.

[240] "*The Relationship between Monetization and Gamer Behavior*" by Mantin Lu, Gamasutra blog.

https://www.gamasutra.com/blogs/MantinLu/20160803/275790/The_Relationship_between_Monetization_and_Gamer_Behavior.php

[241] "*Free-to-play: About addicted Whales, at risk Dolphins and healthy Minnows. Monetarization design and Internet Gaming*" by Dreier, Wolfling, Duven, Giralt, Beutel and Muller Disorder.Addict Behav. 2017 Jan;64:328-333. doi: 10.1016/j.addbeh.2016.03.008. Epub 2016 Apr 13.

https://www.ncbi.nlm.nih.gov/pubmed/27178749

[242] Based on research by market analysts Newzoo, as reported in "*Global games market value rising to $134.9bn in 2018*" by James

Batchelor, https://www.gamesindustry.biz/articles/2018-12-18-global-games-market-value-rose-to-usd134-9bn-in-2018.

[243] McNary, Dave (3 January 2019). "2018 Worldwide Box Office Hits Record as Disney Dominates". Variety.

[244] Global Movie Production & Distribution Industry: Industry Market Research Report". IBISWorld. August 2018.

[245] "*How Instagram Beat Hipstamatic at Its Own Game*," by Rebecca Greenfield. The Atlantic.

https://www.theatlantic.com/technology/archive/2012/10/how-instagram-beat-hipstamatic-its-own-game/322743/

[246] "*'A Cancer That's Eroding The Market': Reactions To EA's Dungeon Keeper*," by Jason Schreier. Kotaku

https://kotaku.com/a-cancer-thats-eroding-the-market-reactions-to-eas-1515121353

[247] As described in Daniel Kahneman's book *Thinking Fast and Slow*.

[248] Black swans were a term invented by Nassim Taleb to explain certain types of events, largely pointing to our arrogance about our ability to forecast the future. It was presented in his book *Black Swan*.

[249] This term was the heart of Nassim Taleb's book *Anti-Fragile*. Here, he considers the question of how we should operate in a world where the most significant positive and negative events cannot be predicted.

www.ingramcontent.com/pod-product-compliance
Lightning Source LLC
Chambersburg PA
CBHW031817170526
45157CB00001B/91